£ 2

A SENSE OF
BELONGING

Also by Howard Cooper
as editor

Soul Searching: Studies in Judaism and Psychotherapy

A SENSE OF BELONGING

*Dilemmas of
British Jewish Identity*

Howard Cooper and Paul Morrison

WEIDENFELD AND NICOLSON · LONDON
in association with
CHANNEL FOUR TELEVISION COMPANY LIMITED

First published in 1991 by George Weidenfeld & Nicolson Ltd
91 Clapham High Street, London SW4 7TA

This book accompanies the television series *A Sense of Belonging,*
produced for Channel Four Television by APT Film and Television Ltd

All drawings by Marc Michaels

Grateful acknowledgement is made to the publishers of the following
works quoted:
Vaclav Havel, 'Letters from Prison', in *Granta 21* (Penguin, 1987)
Arthur Miller, *Timebends* (Methuen, 1987)
T. S. Eliot, *Four Quartets* (Faber & Faber, 1969)
Chaim Bermant, *Troubled Eden* (Vallentine, Mitchell, 1969)

British Library Cataloguing in Publication Data applied for

ISBN 0 297 81097 9

Printed in Great Britain by
Butler & Tanner Ltd, Frome and London

Contents

for our parents
our partners
our children

Acknowledgements

We are deeply indebted to the many Jews from around the country whom Paul interviewed for the film series: parts of their interviews also find their way into this book. They came from all walks of the Jewish and not-so-Jewish world, yet in their different ways share the curiosity about their Jewishness that gave us the energy to do the work. Their openness, and generosity of spirit, made the project possible. In addition there were many others in the Jewish world – academics, teachers, therapists, rabbis, activists – who shared their ideas with us and whose thoughts helped to shape ours.

We would like to thank Mehri Niknam for the use of the poem on page 172; Jeffrey Newman for the story on page 200; Eugene Heimler for interview material described in *Night of the Mist*; and Allegra Huston, our editor at Weidenfeld & Nicolson, for her skilled and caring management of this book. Sadly, Eugene Heimler, whose material is at the centre of the fourth film and the final section of the book, died as the book was going to press. May his memory be a blessing to those who knew him.

A personal note from Howard: Apart from the friends who have supported me while I have struggled with this book, I would like to thank two colleagues, David Black and Deryck Dyne, whose concern, insights and understanding have been invaluable. Above all, my thanks go to Sara and Rafi, whose love and thoughtfulness have sustained me and enabled me to write.

A personal note from Paul: I would like to thank my friends Irving Teitelbaum, for helping to get the whole thing off the ground, and Victor Seidler and Louise London for sharing, in different ways, my journey of return. Many other friends have stood by me and had faith in what I was doing at times when I began to doubt it. Thanks to Bob Towler, Gwynn Pritchard and Susanna Yager at Channel Four for their commitment to this project, and Andy Porter and Tony Dowmunt, my partners at APT, for their encouragement and support, and for their curiosity which helped me believe that Jewish issues are of interest to non-Jewish people. I am ever grateful to my parents, who started my journey off in a warm Jewish community; I learned from them respect for the past and values of justice and freedom which I later understood to be deeply Jewish. My wife Barbara has been there every step of the way, with patience and insight. My greatest thanks are to her, and to my children Corey and Jacob. Their love makes all the effort worthwhile.

Line illustrations are by Marc Michaels, who wishes to acknowledge his debt to Escher, V. Finlay and M. Tinkleman, whose work and style proved an inspiration to him.

Introduction

It was four years ago. I was on the cusp of my own journey back to Judaism, and to a deepened sense of my Jewishness. I had become aware of my own ingrained reticence in owning my Jewishness or talking about my Jewish passions and interests when I was among non-Jewish people. I was aware of the messages I had imbibed growing up after the war. 'Don't be too Jewish in public.' 'Be careful about how you express your Jewishness in front of other people.' As though our good behaviour could save us from becoming victims of anti-Semitism.

I was encouraged to hide my Jewishness, and at the same time to be intensely proud of it. The number of Jewish Nobel-prizewinners was pointed out to me. Jewish genius, creativity, sensitivity. And also, strongly, the depth of Jewish suffering, which induced in me an intense loyalty, but a loyalty shrouded in pain and depression. Anti-Semitism encountered at school reinforced the double message.

I looked at my own back catalogue of documentaries made over twenty years. It is an honourable list. I had dealt with many important social issues – racism, unemployment, education. I had explored many themes of identity and empowerment in films about disability, masculinity and psychotherapy. There was much that could be said to be Jewish in my identification with the underdog, in my focus on the psychological scars of marginalisation, in my concern with healing and with self-discovery, even latterly with a sense of the divine. But not one of the films I had made was *explicitly* Jewish in theme or subject-matter. I wore my Jewishness in my films invisibly, as I had learned to do in my life.

Films, television and journalism in this country are peppered with successful and accomplished Jewish writers, directors and producers, even editors and programme controllers. Yet in the whole of the output I recognised little that reflected the lives and concerns of the Jewish people I knew. While there were numbers of programmes on the Holocaust and Israel, there was virtually nothing to be seen about British Jews themselves. I had heard the rationalisations from senior Jewish television executives.

I

'These programmes won't appeal to the broad mass.' 'I can't be seen to be unfairly advantaging Jews at the expense of other minorities.' Jewish broadcasters and journalists are skilled and sensitive in representing and exploring the stories of other minorities. Yet we, who had the opportunity in career terms to reflect our own concerns as Jews, had conspired in rendering ourselves invisible.

Unlike other minorities, there has been no Jewish campaign for better representation in the media. It is as though the Jewish public has taken it for granted that its own face is not there. And yet the excitement among Jews at the occasional exception to the rule is tangible. 'Did you see that film last night about the Jewish accountant? What did you think of his accent?'

I was not alone as a Jewish director without a Jewish output. Nor was I alone in my journey of return. I discovered adult education classes filled with others hungry for Jewish knowledge. Close Jewish friends were making parallel journeys into their personal histories. I perceived a new self-confidence among young people. Many young men wore their *kippah* on the streets. Young women on every campus were forming Jewish women's groups, re-appraising the old models for Jewish womanhood and creating new ones. The Jewish world I had grown up in was changing – not out of recognition, for the old patterns die hard. The changes seemed worthy of exploration.

While on my own journey I had met Howard Cooper, a rabbi and psychotherapist who, excitingly, was trying to bridge the two worlds which were at the core of my own exploration: the twentieth-century secular study of psychology which starts with Freud and Jung and ends with holistic health; and the stories and texts of the Jewish myth, from Abraham to Rabbi Nachman, the Hassidic master. The two worlds shared a common fascination with the human soul, and much beyond that: a recognition of the way creativity and destructiveness are intertwined, and a concern to find ways of transmuting the latter into the former; and a struggle with the ambiguity and complexity of personal choice, and thence with the mystery of that which lies beyond choice.

I asked Howard to become consultant to the film series, and later to be the main writer of this book. My own direction has been from the secular to the religious. Howard's, to put it crudely, has been the opposite. He had found that the language of Judaism, for all its richness and subtlety, wasn't adequate to deal with the incomprehensibility of his own life, nor the pain he met in the Jewish community he worked with. He needed to look outside the Jewish world to find the answers that he needed.

A further assumption that Howard and I share, which follows from our personal histories, is that, as much as we need one another as Jews, we need the non-Jewish world also. This is tough to own up to when the main lesson of the century seems to have been, 'If no one else is prepared to help us, we have to help ourselves.' But, true as this statement has been for particular times and places, it is not a truth for all time, and it is not a code to live by. We are all interdependent now, more so than ever as we need to find common solutions to the ecological disasters that threaten our planet. But also on the small level, the everyday level: people we share the bus with, people we work with, go to school with, the friends we make. As a people we are bruised and sensitive, understandably so, and it isn't always easy to reach out. This book and the films are for a non-Jewish audience no less than a Jewish one.

We began with people's stories. They are the backbone of the research, at the core of the films and woven through this book. Our priority was not the stories of the 'famous' Jews, or Jews in positions of authority, but the ordinary extraordinary Jews I knew, and their friends. And the friends of their friends. I wanted to focus on the broad middleground of British Jewry – from the people who feel themselves to be strongly Jewish but recognise that they need to make some accommodation with British life around them, to the people who see themselves as secular and British, but are unwilling to let go of some lingering sense of their Jewishness.

Our other starting point was the Hebrew Bible. I had never much enjoyed the stories of the Bible as a child, and neither RE nor my *cheder* had succeeded in bringing them to life for me. Secular society and particularly politics reinforced my disdain as I grew up. Now I found in them a richness, a beauty, an ambiguity and a great challenge. I saw that Jacob, the liar and cheat, the one who had to wrestle with his guilt and with his past, had been the one chosen by God to carry the covenant, and it made sense to me. I understood his exile, and through him the Jewish exile; I understood our rebirth through the Red Sea, and the wandering in the desert.

It felt appropriate to examine our contemporary Jewish world through the lens of these themes: to make Jewish films, and a Jewish book, Jewishly. We wanted to challenge the prevailing split between the religious and the secular worlds that is characteristic of life in Britain, and in the British Jewish world also.

The Bible is the struggle of a group of people to comprehend the incomprehensible, using specific imagery and symbols to evoke and illuminate their experiences. In each generation of the people of Israel there were encounters with the transcendent, visioned and recorded almost unconsciously, then finding their way into the dream-memory of the people. Our collective memory contains a patchwork of forgotten, reworked and remembered holy moments, too awesome to be described in everyday conscious language.[1]

3

When Jews lived in a closed society the holy texts of our tradition were at the centre of Jewish life, and Jews wrote their lives as commentaries around them. Holiness, the aim of life, was in the Torah and the legal and homiletic and mystical literature of the people. From that external source of holiness they sought their own wholeness. But when the Jews emerged from the ghettos into the modern world, they entered the mainstream of European life with a creative vengeance. Our modern civilisation rests heavily on their contributions: Marx, Freud, Kafka, Schoenberg, Einstein, Chomsky . . .

A gap opened up, for most of us. The gap was between those ancient texts and our own lives; between the mythical world that nurtured us for so long, and the new realities – social, cultural, psychological – with which we are faced. For many Jews, Judaism has become peripheral to everyday life, the religious and cultural heritage of the past seeming to offer little of relevance in an increasingly complex modern world.

In Britain, in recent years, the gap could be seen to be an abyss. Perhaps one half of Anglo-Jewry find synagogues and other Jewish organisations of so little relevance as to decline membership of them altogether: the rate of assimilation appears unstoppable. On the other hand, those who are religiously observant are becoming more so.

The Bible has become a battleground. The root of the word 'Torah' means 'aim' and 'direction' – originally of archers aiming their arrows in the direction of the target. From there Torah comes to mean the teaching which helps us find the direction of our lives, where we are to aim in our search for holiness. But the arrows have become poisoned. In the fractious arguments which criss-cross the Jewish world, Torah learning is invoked as part of the barbed weaponry of internecine strife.

I have two images of Anglo-Jewry. One is a picture of a community turned in on itself, like a boxer in a crouch, defensively strong, and yet gasping for air. And the other is of a community unsure of its own true value and richness, looking on helplessly, unable to withstand the waves as they gently wash the castle away.

Secular and religious Jews see one another in polarised stereotypes. For the religious Jew the secular world is a threat to learning and to authority, a world of unbridled hedonism, a world unregulated and hence lost. For the secular Jew, religion implies rigidity, superstition, backwardness, claustrophobia. A central purpose in book and films is to demythologise these stereotypes. To be religiously observant does not mean to stop asking questions, nor does it imply political conservatism. To be secular does not imply a denial of honourable living, nor a lack of concern for the human soul.

For some people, the external world, the world as seen by science alone, or in the play of ideas for ideas' sake, is intolerable. As Jung perceived, 'Among the so-called neurotics of our day there are a good many who in other ages would not have been neurotic – that is, divided against themselves. If they had lived in a period and in a milieu in which man was still linked by myth to his ancestors ... they would have been spared this division in themselves.'[2]

Disconnected from our mythological world, we are inwardly divided. And what we cannot face within ourselves, we act out in our communal disputes. The outer fragmentation of Anglo-Jewry is a reflection of a deeper, inner loss. It is one of the purposes of this book to explore this loss and its consequences for our sense of belonging.

We have structured both book and films around the themes of the founding 'myth'[3] of the Jewish people, as contained in the 'Five Books of Moses', the written Torah. It describes how one family, the family of Abraham, after much struggling, searching and suffering, evolve into a people whose exodus from oppression leads them on a journey uncompleted to this day.

We start in the family. The book of Genesis tells the story of the first Jewish family, the family of Abraham and Sarah. Only later does the family become a tribe, and the tribe a nation, with a religion and a law. Unlike the first family, there has grown up an idealised model of the contemporary Jewish family which few actual families can pretend to live up to. The first section of the book sets these aspirations against the reality of contemporary Jewish family life, the pressures upon it and the pressures within it. We look at how the strains are passed on between parents and children, and how they exist between men and women.

Our second section picks up on our existence as 'strangers in a strange land'. It harks back to the times when we were slaves in Egypt, and exiled to Babylon. It looks at our history and our consciousness as Jews in the secular and Christian culture of Britain; it examines the bargains we struck to protect ourselves, and how those bargains in turn shaped our own sense of identity. It looks at how the dark cloud of the Holocaust shaped Jewish awareness, and what that means for how we deal with anti-Semitism today.

The third section of the book, 'Exodus', takes mythical liberation from Egypt as a metaphor for the theme of liberation in our contemporary experience as British Jews. Since the foundation of the state of Israel, and particularly since the Six-Day War in 1967, there has been a newfound pride and confidence among British Jews. We give our attention to this renaissance, in its various forms and with its sundry contradictions, focussing on the rebirth of Jewish consciousness. We look at what Israel means to us, and why we defend it or judge it with such passion.

The final section, 'Out of the Wilderness,' draws its theme from the forty years in the wilderness that moulded into a people the mixed multitudes who escaped Egypt. It treats this journeying as a metaphor for our own personal spiritual wanderings: from the lows of fear and hunger and despair to those moments of revelation, as at Sinai, which are infinitely precious, but hard to grasp. In this section we leave the particularity of Britain and approach themes that are universal.

The rabbis created rituals and festivals whose meanings enable us to reflect on these themes, as we remember and celebrate the stories. So the festivals, too, thread their way through this book, not out of any didactic purpose, but because of the light they shed on our own lives. There is a rich and ancient ritual language in Judaism, honed and developed over the millennia. For those who live within the myth, learning is by doing, and understanding by experiencing. And there are the Jewish languages themselves. Yiddish or Hebrew words in this book that are italicised are explained in the glossary at the end of the book.

At one level, the ache and the fear and the emptiness in British Jewry is a product of the Holocaust. It is at the centre of our experience and casts its shadow over all Western Jews. The planned murder of one-third of our people bludgeons its way into our discourse, and our consciousness, whether we wish it or not. We can't understand contemporary Jewish families, our specific exile in Britain, Jewish politics, or Jewish spiritual wanderings without taking into account the Holocaust.

At another level, we want to honour Jewish creativity in the face of persecution, in spite of persecution, and when there is no persecution. The revelation at Sinai was a profound moment for the whole of Western culture. It asserted the equality of each person before God and before one another. It asserted the right of all people to a life of dignity, free from fear. It asserted our individual responsibility for our own actions, and also acknowledged our collective interdependence. The insights engendered by Sinai have become the foundation of our modern democracies. With wit, wisdom, and bloodymindedness, we celebrate our survival against the odds.

Paul Morrison
with Howard Cooper
September 1990

Part I
BEGINNING IN THE FAMILY

I
Jewish Families,
Jewish History

———————————✳———————————

When I was really young, every Friday night my uncle used to come round. And that was a big event because I'd be allowed to sit up late, sit around the table, and we'd always get into some discussions with him. I always looked forward to that because it was the one time in the week when everyone sat round together and it'd be quiet. We'd all be one.

I often think about those times as being very much a family occasion and that's what being Jewish is about. But there was no content! There's no real understanding of anything being very strongly religious about it. It was pleasant and family and warm and comfortable.

———————————✳———————————

I don't find it a great help to individuals — especially not single females. It's very much a family religion. One feels to a certain extent excluded from it. I'm not a great believer and in Judaism I don't really understand where religion comes in and where custom and some form of nationalism end ... All the Friday night ceremonies are really aimed at the family, and Judaism to me is a people — and I'm not certain I am wholly of the people, though I certainly am by birth.

The family ceremonies would be fine with a harmonious family. They're not fine when the family is not harmonious. They tend to become a hypocrisy and one tends to repudiate them. Judaism doesn't seem to me to include the mavericks, the people that don't conform to its hoped-for structure.

Jewish history is the history of Jewish families. Jewish history, Jewish family history, stretches back into mythological time:

Now the Lord said to Abram:[1]
'Go out from your country, and from your family and your father's house, to the

9

land that I will show you. And I will make a great nation of you, and I will bless you and make your name great; and be you a blessing ... and all the families of the earth shall be blessed in you.' [Genesis 12: 1–3]

Thus Jewish history begins with someone called to leave their family. A tension between the individual and the family is there in the beginning.

Abraham receives a promise: he will be the founder of a new family, a new nation. He hears that the nation has a destiny: the world will be blessed through this people. To achieve this, he leaves his family of origin and carries the blessing – and its burden – into the generations ahead. Scattered throughout the world, enduring the vicissitudes of time and fortune, we inherit the blessing. Or is it perhaps more truthful to say that it is only the *story* of the blessing that we inherit, to make of it what we can?

And sometimes now we may not even inherit the stories. Yet often, unbeknownst to ourselves, echoes of these ancient dramas reverberate into our own homes.

The opening book of the Bible, the book of Genesis, explores the experiences of one family, the family of Abraham, though several generations. History spirals on, with each character a link in a chain of events, the meaning of which is only glimpsed out of the corner of an eye. And all of our own lives are there: conflicts and love between husbands and wives; sexual intrigues; infertility; sibling rivalry; parental favouritism and its consequences; marrying 'in' or 'out'; the continuity of family traditions; the child who breaks away; the silences and evasions, the family secrets and the intrigues; hopes, fears, dreams, passed on by parents to children 'to the third and fourth generation'.

Within the Hebrew Bible there is no distinction between history and the unfolding saga of family life. One word threaded through the book of Genesis, the noun *toldot* (derived from the root 'to give birth'), contains a spectrum of meaning. It comes to signify 'offspring, descendants, generations, chronology ... history'. History is the story of those who are born, the relationships they form, the choices they make, the families they create or from which they break away.

Part of Judaism's divine conceit is this connection it posits between the apparently mundane events of family life and the supposedly grand themes of humanity's history. According to one non-Jewish observer, the Jews 'stand right at the centre of the perennial attempt to give human life the dignity of a purpose'.[2] In the past, the Jewish family was seen by both Jews and gentiles as a container in which that 'dignity of purpose' could be nurtured and expressed. Non-Jews continually refer to the warmth and closeness of Jewish families. We enjoy their feeling of our distinctive family life, for it corresponds to our own wishful thinking. That there are great strengths and much potential is indisputable. But there is a revolution taking place within Anglo-Jewish families. And as with many revolutions, there is much distress and not a few victims.

Modern Anglo-Jewish life contains some self-evident truths. The old stable pattern of family life – with an extended generational network spanning grandparents to grandchildren – is breaking down with a rapidity which leaves many bewildered and angry. Over the last decade the statistical litany has become familiar: one in three Jewish marriages ends in divorce; nearly 20 per cent of Jewish children experience the breakdown of their parents' marriage; one in three Jews who marry, marry 'out'; less than half the Jews who marry do so in a synagogue; each year Jewish marriages are outstripped by Jewish burials; the annual birth rate is roughly two-thirds of the death rate. Overall, Anglo-Jewry is an aging community shrinking numerically as the number of children born becomes insufficient to ensure the community's long-term continuity.

These trends are unlikely to be reversed. By the year 2000, if we continue to keep in step with the changes that are going on around us, it is possible that only one out of two children will grow up in a 'conventional family'.[3] It is a sign of our apparent integration into secular British society that our patterns of family life faithfully mirror those of the gentile community. Lifelong heterosexual monogamous marriage now seems a minority phenomenon. Non-adulterous lifelong marriage is even more of a minority phenomenon. From the ultra-Orthodox enclaves to the most assimilated suburban or rural milieux, all sections of Anglo-Jewry are subject to these pressures.

Chief Rabbi-elect Jonathan Sacks is by no means the only contemporary voice arguing for a return to traditional values in which 'the family is the crucible of the Jewish future'.[4] Yet no amount of moral exhortation will change what is now happening within so many Anglo-Jewish families. The crucible is already cracked. What we are witnessing is the degeneration of the Jewish family as an incubator of purpose. The family as the social entity that embodied and enacted the collective ideals of the Jewish people is being replaced by a fragmented individualism.

A gap has developed between the traditional ideals of what a Jewish family 'should' be, and how we actually live our lives. The idyllic scenario of the joyful Friday night meal, with relaxed family members celebrating together in Sabbath peace, rarely happens in reality. Instead, there may be exhaustion, rows and recriminations as the week ends and the accumulated frustrations spill out. There can be moments of respite, and some weeks are calmer than others, but then the bickering returns, or the angry silence, or the hurt withdrawal. Not all the time, and not all of this in every family. For 'all happy families resemble one another, but each unhappy family is unhappy in its own way'.[5] Anglo-Jewish families are suffering from a psychic fatigue, where the natural stresses of family life become strains which threaten to lead to fracture.

Each of us can create our own anthology: the father who cannot allow himself to see his grandchild because his son married a non-Jew; spouses looking for ways out of embittered marriages; the divorced men and women who feel they don't quite belong, or are a threat; singles searching for partners; the public emergence of our sexual minorities; the daughter not yet married; the post-Holocaust generation estranged when 'the fathers have eaten sour grapes and the children's teeth are set on edge';[6] what will happen when granny is not able to look after herself; the arguments over who to invite to the barmitzvah; the desire to escape from the claustrophobia; the pressures to succeed, or conform; the relatives one doesn't speak to; the '*broigus*'[7] over that business when . . .

This is not 'the Jewish family'. This is not how we like to think about ourselves. This is not how we want others to see us. Nevertheless, there is this intangible but pervasive sense in many contemporary homes that something has gone wrong – and Jewish family life is somehow being betrayed. Somewhere, a street or two away, we believe there is still a *heimishe* Jewish family living out the ideal. And, beneath it all, we feel that these things can hardly even be spoken about. Reticence about personal matters is normative English behaviour, and in Anglo-Jewry this is combined with traditional Jewish self-deprecatory stoicism in the face of hardship: 'Don't worry about me . . . it's not so bad really . . . it could always be worse . . .' But in the privacy of their homes some Jewish families are carrying levels of pain which those outside the family may rarely see.

Doctors' surgeries are full of Jews with what are often, at root, psychosomatic complaints – a proliferation of backaches and chest pains and tension in the neck. But who is on our back? and what is the source of our heartache? and who is the pain in our neck? Perhaps we do suspect sometimes that our heartburn doesn't come solely from the food we eat. And we know that the consulting rooms of analysts and therapists and counsellors are full of Jews who are depressed, Jews who are anxious, Jews who are neurotic, Jews with eating disorders . . . The ill-health of British Jewry is not only a metaphor.

That family life is vital for the future of Jewish life is undoubted. The question is: what kind of family life is this to be? For unless it can transform itself the Jewish family will increasingly be unable to live out the ideals – of nurture and respect, work, education and celebration – it has carried through the generations. How can we reformulate the role of the family – the incubator of purpose – in an evolving world?

With the dissonance between the idea of the family and its reality becoming increasingly clear, our problem is to separate the life-affirming aspects of the family from the dead weight of the past. Unless we ask these questions and respond creatively to them, the Jewish family will continue to fail those who look to it for sustenance and security. And thus it will fail in its larger purpose of carrying blessing into the society in which we live. The individual belonged to a family group and through that to a family of families – the Jewish people. The family was to be the epicentre of a holiness that was destined to radiate through the community into the wider society in which the Jew lived.

Yet at the heart of this, the texts of our tradition had planted a challenge: to live creatively. The balance in family life between sustaining what is of value from the past but reformulating it in response to the challenges of new times and settings was always going to be a difficult art to learn. For evolution to take place and the blessing to be realised, there must be adaptability. It is inevitable that the anachronistic and the harmful has to be discarded to make room for the creatively alive new growth. If the Jewish family is to evolve, something has to disintegrate, or be destroyed. This notion is embodied in the Midrashic fable of the young Abraham throwing to the ground his father's idols. 'There must be something else, more than this.' Monotheism emerges out of the debris of the smashed gods. Abraham understood that he had to join with the world outside his family without losing his distinctiveness. This became the Jewish task: to live in the world, maintaining inner continuity for the sake of humanity's evolution, development and change.

But continuity does not imply statis. In the past, the traditional restrictions of Jewish living – everything from what you ate to whom you slept with – were felt to serve the purpose of sustaining the covenant with which we had been entrusted. They were a source of nourishment and personal affirmation. But there are new freedoms now at work. What happens when the restrictions become repressive and the family begins to feel like a miniature totalitarian system? Once authoritarianism replaces tolerance and respect for differences, once the necessary adaptability feels too threatening, the family can no longer sustain its purpose. But how flexible can we afford to be? Where do we draw the boundaries? Can we now choose the restrictions rather than have them imposed on us?

We are being asked to take more responsibility for ourselves than ever before. This challenge is hard: when we look at what is actually happening to our families we see ourselves poised between evolution and disintegration. There seems no going back to those idealised families of old. Despite the fulminations of rabbis and the exhortations of communal leaders, we are going to have to learn to live with the complexities, the messiness and the diversity of the new realities.

Yet the paradox with which we wrestle is that Jewish history is composed of our failures. Time and again the Bible, particularly in the book of Genesis, shows how the failure of harmonious family life is woven, against the rational grain, into the mystery of the divine plan. Unresolved family dynamics, passed on through the children, are the foundation stone of Jewish history.

When Abraham placates Sarah's jealousy by favouring their child Isaac over the handmaid Hagar's child Ishmael, we then see how in the next generation Isaac's favouritism of Esau, and Rebekkah's favouritism towards Jacob, leads to deceit and enmity in the family. A generation later, Jacob's special, protective relationship with his child leads to the murderous jealousy of Joseph's brothers. One generation passes to the next the problems it fails to resolve. One generation passes to the next the problems it is seldom aware of and may never understand.

Our contemporary struggle with the conflicts and changing patterns of family life is continuous with this ancient drama. We do not know where the struggle will lead us; and we do not understand what this transformation means. But the end of the idealisation of Jewish family life may be the beginning of wisdom.

✳

It's assumed that the extended Jewish family will support its members in every way that's needed. The reality is that the extended Jewish family is now as scattered round the globe as any other family, so even if it wanted to help, it can't. People don't live in the next street any more. It means that when you've got an elderly couple, when one of them dies the other one is often left with no relatives living anywhere near them. There are young families that are single-parent families, without any grandparents nearby, so when there's a problem with the children there's no one to help out.

There are people who have been in long-stay mental hospitals who have been abandoned by their families. They come out and expect care in the community and there's no one there to give it to them. And there's all sorts of people in those kind of categories: there are young single people; there are young unemployed men and women. There's a lot of effort to imply that the Jewish community is all affluent and comfortably settled and we know from our work with the Welfare Board that that's just not true. Some of them are in considerable difficulties. Some of them are homeless. People may be surprised to think within our Jewish community that there are homeless people, but there are . . .

2
'All You Need Is Love'

---
*

I feel I carry some of the things that happened to my parents, which are still affecting me but not in ways that you can say. I just feel sort of wounded by it ... I think that I was cast in the role of being a good child, making everything all right in my family, making up for bad things and sort of restoring a whole family ... My parents are always pleased to see me and they get a bit hurt if I don't make a move to get in touch with them. That's a part of the role of being a very good daughter, a symptom that our family's okay ...

———————————————— ✳ ————————————————

I was probably over-anxious, quite protective, over-protective towards them, you know. Maybe imagining sort of anti-Jewish things where there weren't any. The slightest things I'm very sensitive to – not surprisingly – and I think we made mistakes. But who doesn't?

When we look around us at the shifting contours of Jewish family life we can sense changing expectations, the redefining of roles, the yearning for some security in the midst of the uncertainty. Yet most of the time we are too immersed in the stuff of life to see at all clearly what is taking place. Is it that something completely new is happening in Anglo-Jewry? Or is what we are now living through just another sharp curve on the spiral of the generations, the twists and turns of which constitute our collective history?

Contemporary Jewish novelists are adept at exploiting the convolutions of Jewish family life with all their sadness and evasions and humour. A reviewer of Bernice Rubens once summed up the basic premises of her fiction as follows:

a) Parents do not love their children enough;

b) Not being able to accept this, they blame the children for disappointing them;

c) The children feel terrible because the standards they try to live up to are impossibly high;

d) They don't work any of this out in time to prevent them from repeating the same syndrome with their own children;

e) All you need is love.

To this clutch of universal truths, Bernice Rubens adds another, more particular rule: f) If you are a child prodigy, or born into a Jewish family, it is worse.[1]

There is an ironic echo here of the Biblical claim that the 'sins' of the parents – perhaps 'failings' would be a more compassionate term in our context, for there is no blame involved – are visited on the children to 'the third and fourth generation'. This may have a particular relevance for that generation in Anglo-Jewry, primarily in their thirties and forties, who are the grandchildren or great-grandchildren of the immigrant generation into Britain.

The hardships experienced by those immigrant families have been amply documented. Fleeing from foreign persecution – or the fear of it; landing in an alien land to begin again a new life, with a new language and culture; the poverty and deprivations; the struggle to survive materially and spiritually.

16

Painful separations were part of the process. Often the young people who came had to leave behind them parents, siblings, even wives and fiancees. If they were lucky and made good they could bring them on later. You had to harden yourself to the loss, and to the loneliness. You yearned for a family that was whole and harmonious, but the reality was often painfully different.

Sometimes a man couldn't or wouldn't wait; or found himself a stranger to the woman when she did arrive. There were broken families, single-parent families and prostitution from the earliest days of the new arrivals. It was never one happy and united community.

Although our admiration for their achievements is boundless, the men and women working long hard hours in the shops and sweatshops and factories paid a huge price. The deprivations were not only physical. There was a tremendous, and largely hidden, emotional cost to being born one of six or a dozen children to an exhausted immigrant mother whose husband was away from dawn to dusk. Many of these strong, capable, resourceful women also had to work to survive. Sometimes they had to be more resourceful than the men, who carried with them the otherworldliness of the Eastern European *yeshivah* tradition.

How much real nurturing, how much undivided attention, how much unconditional love, was really possible in that fraught environment? The children of this immigrant generation often found that their parents were relatively distant figures. Much of the daily care was done by a maid, or an older sibling, an aunt, a grandmother. So they came to idealise their parents: my wise, authoritative father; my yiddishe momma, loved by everyone, who never raised her voice, whom nobody dares say a word against ... And in turn their parents came to idealise them – because they held the hope for the future, for another sort of life. This mutual idealisation was a symptom of the distance between them. The sadness at the absence of intimacy is being denied.

The immigrant generation gave to their children through their work, through what they provided. Chicken soup was the love-offering that solved everything. But the children bore on their own the burden of becoming British, of finding a sense of belonging, because finding an identity here as a Jew wasn't the sort of thing you could discuss with parents.

Theirs was a relationship built on a strong sense of mutual sacrifice. The parents denied themselves their immediate pleasures for the sake of the children's education and material futures. And the children sacrificed their childhoods. They found that they had to grow up early, and if they wanted to make contact with their parents it would have to be on adult terms – through helping out, through books, through religion. Yet they were of different cultures and came to live separate lives.

When the deprived daughters of the immigrant generation grew up and became mothers themselves, they had few inner resources to draw upon as to what 'good mothering' might mean – although, of necessity, this emotional deprivation is often denied. These post-war mothers gave up work in order to bring up their children. This was a part of the national trend, a fashion encouraged to make jobs available for returning soldiers. It was also a mark of the success of the sons of immigrants that they could afford to keep their wives at home. But for Jews it meant something else as well. It was a way of giving to their children the attention denied them in their own childhood. Women who had sacrificed their own childhoods for their parents, now sacrificed their adulthoods for their children. Without realising it they were projecting their own unmet needs and trying to look after themselves by lavishing their loving care on their offspring.

When the sons of the immigrant generation grew up and themselves became fathers, the model they had of fathering was equally deficient. Economic necessity had meant that most immigrant men had been largely absent from the home, so the next generation had no experience of a father actively involved in the rearing of a family. If there was an experience of father, it was either the idealised view mentioned above or as a distant and authoritarian figure: 'My father I never got on well with because he was so much older than I was, and a sort of heavy, lugubrious Jewish figure who wanted me to be Jewish and I just didn't want anything of it' (Jonathan Miller).[2]

After the war, as the old communities dissipated and extended families spread further apart, there was much work to be done in establishing normality. Men were preoccupied with earning a living, and Jewish women were suddenly on their own at home. They were lonely, and their anxieties had no outlet. Of course there was the telephone, and a real attempt to keep alive the kinship network by using it. But Maureen Lipman's satire on this phenomenon for British Telecom hides a painful truth. People were moving apart at a time when their needs for one another were greatest.

A post-war generation was born to needy mothers and distant, often passive fathers. These children became the inheritors of the insidious emotional deprivation. From their tenderest years this third generation grew up having to support emotionally their own mothers, who were suffering from a lack of uncorrupted affection from their own parents and now, additionally, from the failure of their husbands to provide active support and intimacy. And this third generation grew up trying to gain their fathers' non-judgemental love and involvement.

The burden of expectation placed on the post-war generation was large. Once again, the children would be the hope. The children would carry the dream. The children would make it all right. But these expectations were riven with contradictions. On the one hand the children were supposed to achieve success and security and acceptance in the outside world, and they were pushed hard in that direction. On the other hand they mustn't go too far from the confines of the family. The message was: stay Jewish, keep close, don't marry out. Jewish survival seemed to depend on it. And survival, just the physical flesh-and-blood survival of the Jewish people, was felt to be terribly important. After the Holocaust each Jewish life came to feel extraordinarily precious. There is a black humour in this: if even a knee was cut, an elbow grazed, it was a disaster.

The Jewish family became like a little hothouse. It appeared to offer safety, security, support. At the same time it threatened to explode under the pressure of the demands made upon its members. Parents clung to children but the children continually disappointed them or thwarted their expectations. Jewish children of the post-war generation talk of how their parents were always criticising them: 'I was good at tennis and very proud of it. But every time I came home from school and told my father I had won, he would make some disparaging remark: "What's the matter, did your opponent have two left feet?" I could never do anything that was good enough for him.'

The need of this generation of parents to criticise is familiar. Overtly or subtly the remarks are made, and a vicious circle is set in motion. In part the comments arise out of the enormous expectations on the children to succeed and to give the family the security and continuity it craves. And in part they are an expression of the parent's own lack of self-worth. Without the contact with their own parents that they needed, somewhere inside they still have the feeling that there must be something wrong with themselves. This is too painful to bear. The bad feeling has to be put outside. Without consciously meaning to, the child will be made to feel the unacceptable feeling that the parents cannot endure within themselves. Sometimes it is done through humour or a joke. But the feeling language required to make the real contact is not there. When they might have been reaching out to their child – and in a sense are trying to, though in a perverse form – all they succeed in doing is pushing their child away.

The only way out for the child is to cut off, to rebel, to break away. In the sixties, many children of that post-war generation found that there was life outside this psychological ghetto.

But as the generations of Anglo-Jewry roll on, the residue of the original deprivations remains in countless men and women. We become subject to unaccountable panic attacks or depressions or bursts of rage, or continual failures at work or in relationships – disparate clues pointing to a deeper malaise. These unresolved – perhaps unconsidered – cycles of deprivation have nothing to do with material or financial security, or the relative success of a family's assimilation.

When each generation keeps its anxious, controlling eye on survival, family members begin to experience themselves as parts of a single body.[3] Mental health practitioners who work with Jewish clients often hear this imagery emerging, especially when the 'wholeness' of the family unit feels that it is under threat: 'Intermarriage, the break up of a marriage, or even a child leaving home, is experienced, by one or more members, as the amputation of part of the body ... For the family who are over-identified with each other, this may be felt to be more than a rejection of values, rather a rejection of everything they "embody".'[4]

So the next generation's necessary separation from parents can become a deeply traumatic experience for all concerned. The over-enmeshment of Jewish families can mean that parents, while consciously wishing for their children's success and independence, may unconsciously fear or resent or envy it too. Feelings of emptiness, rejection or anger can be hard to acknowledge when one is supposed to want all the best for one's children. But these feelings need to be faced: separation involves loss.

A parent's difficulties in facing separation can lead to different forms of manipulative or controlling behaviour: 'My mother died recently at the age of ninety-four, and I loved her very much, but she never *never* let me go' (Bernice Rubens).[5] This characteristic difficulty for Jewish parents means that the children in their turn may find separation difficult because of the guilt feelings it arouses. If the children do assert their independence, they have to face parental disappointment. This is hard enough when it is spoken about openly, even harder when nothing is said directly. Then the parent may rely on a range of sighs, innuendos or tones of voice that may have become so habitual as to constitute a way of life:

My mother answered. 'Hello,' she said. Only someone who's heard my mother say hello will understand. The fear, the failure to which she resigned herself as the telephone rang. Hello, catastrophe, come to me. I've been waiting so long for you to come. And I don't have the strength to wait any more. Come, world, be real, beat me, sometimes the blow is easier than the anticipation. Hello.[6]

When children assert their own separate individuality there is a frightening awareness that has to be kept at bay – that *separation involves destruction*. In the absence of this awareness the child, now an adult, feels the need to continually pacify ('I wouldn't want to hurt them') and to 'make things good again' – that is, to keep the peace which is threatened by that assertive drive to grow up and be separate. When a parent can't let go, the child can only break away – or become depressed. This leads to the eating problems and disorders, the use and abuse of tranquillisers, alcohol or drugs, and the psychosomatic complaints that have become so prevalent in Anglo-Jewry. Self-destruction is the alternative to the destruction of the unconscious ties to parents.

The power of the feelings between the generations stretches from the cradle to the grave. Even after a parent's death the need for their approval, or a residual wish to meet their expectations, or a host of other influences from the past, can still blight a person's own quest for autonomy. In Jewish families free will is not so straightforward a notion as we would like to think. Frightened of our own failure to meet a parent's needs, we feel guilty about the secret aggressive impulses we feel against them – for we also love and need them.

Of course these dynamics happen in non-Jewish families too. But our historical experience – the struggle for survival, the sacrifices made, the hopes invested in the next generation – leads to a particularly atavistic impulse to keep the family together. The controlling Jewish parent is not only a stereotype. It is one response to our fear of helplessness and powerlessness. Often in Jewish families the pressures towards professional or business success – and academic or marital success for the children – are inextricably intertwined with a deeply-felt need for some kind of security in the face of the uncertainties of the world. Anglo-Jewry is still a frightened community. And our families carry the brunt of it.

Since the *shoah*, Jewish survival has not been able to be taken for granted. We glimpsed the abyss. The Holocaust has taught us that, for Jews, whatever the success we make of our lives, everything can be taken away in the twinkling of an eye. To live with this knowledge causes us too much anxiety to bear. We have to shut away our pain, our insecurity, our fears. We cannot allow those secret thoughts a moment to emerge. Through our controlling behaviour we maintain the comforting illusion that our destiny is in our own hands.

It is more than twenty years since Chaim Bermant, the man Anglo-Jewry loves to hate, diagnosed this underlying anxiety in the community. In his anatomy of British Jewry, *Troubled Eden*, he recognised our subliminal awareness that 'a few years ago one could be hunted down and destroyed wholly and solely because one was Jewish. The statistics, the names, the pictures which have become clichés, still evoke a shudder. The Jew who sees his small children splashing in their bath, or their sandals scattered about their room, cannot always keep the pictures of naked infants in the snows of Poland from his mind, or the mounds of shoes at Auschwitz. The six million souls excised from the Jewish people still cause phantom pains.'[7]

Nothing has changed, and the pain has not diminished. We just search for new ways to cover it up. Bermant shrewdly describes Anglo-Jewry's predilection for celebrations and parties for numerous causes and family events, during which 'there will be speeches and noise, as if all were determined not to hear themselves think, for when they do, the fare can acquire the taste of ashes.'[8]

Echoes of that trauma reverberate within us. We feel the fragility of Jewish continuity. And we feel it in our families. We feel that the continuity of the family is constantly under threat. A child leaving home; a youngster becoming less religiously observant – or more so; a student changing course in midstream away from what the family had hoped for; the choice of a different career from what had been expected; a change of career in mid-life; a non-Jewish partner; no partner at all. On one level this is a long way from the Holocaust. But when we feel deep within us that survival and continuity hang on a thread, we can react with defensive outrage to anything that hints of a departure from the behavioural straitjacket we feel our families have to wear if continuity is to be ensured.

'All you need is love.' And perhaps the courage and the honesty to face the pain of where we have come from, individually and collectively. We know that cycles of deprivation such as those outlined in this chapter are not a uniquely Jewish phenomenon. Yet their prevalence amongst British Jews demands our special attention and concern. These are our families. This is our history. We belong to these families and this history. And these families and this history belong to us.

3
Feeling the Pressure: Myth and Marriage

---*---

He: *There's* broigus *in every family – there's somebody who doesn't speak
     ...*
She: *You might have sat too near to the toilets at a wedding ...*
He: *Or else you didn't send them a nice enough present at the wedding, or
     barmitzvah, or whatever. That happens in every family. That is called
     tradition ... The Jewish people have come a long way. They've been
     wandering for how many years? And they've been through a lot in life.
     And I think they can take so much and then they snap. And that would
     be my definition of* broigus.

One of the central factors that makes the Jewish family dynamic distinctive
is the extent to which personal interactions are soaked in the mythological
dimension of Jewish tradition. Subliminally we feel that we are participants
in an ancient and sacred drama. The centrality of Jewish marriage within
our consciousness comes from the depths of this ancient Jewish desire for
continuity.

Already at a Jewish wedding new life is breathed into the old myth. The
happiness which is wished on the couple is, the marriage service says,
the 'happiness of Your creatures in Eden long ago'. The necessity, the
inevitability, of a man and a woman forming a bonded relationship seems
ordained from on high. No sooner have Adam and Eve become separate
individuals in the Genesis myth than their reunion is foretold: 'Therefore
shall a man leave his father and his mother and shall cleave to his wife;
and they shall be one flesh' (Genesis 2: 24).

Human loneliness is to be overcome through relationships. Com-
panionship, intimacy, sex – the human urge for closeness, for joining –
these needs are accepted, and valued, by the myth. But can Jewish marriage

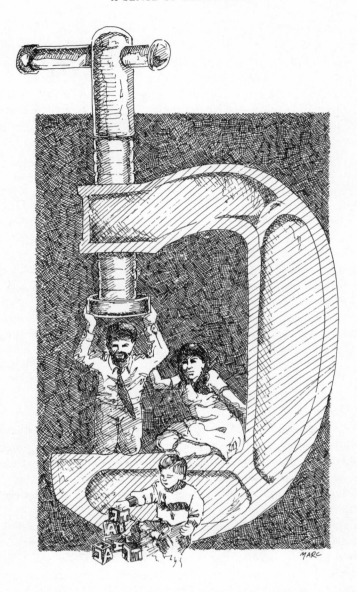

MARC

serve as the container for these fundamental human needs?

In the traditional portrait, it is the man who finds the woman. Yet the pressure exerted on the Jewish man to find himself a nice Jewish girl may well lead him in the opposite direction. We desire what we are forbidden, just like in Eden. The rebellious wish to break out of the claustrophobic circle may make the non-Jewish woman seem more desirable. 'When Esau was forty years old he took to wife Judith the daughter of Beeri the Hittite, and Basemath the daughter of Elon the Hittite. And they were a source of bitterness to Isaac and Rebecca' (Genesis 26: 34–5). *Plus ça change*. Staying inside the tribe can come to feel almost incestuous. After all, will not a Jewish woman become a Jewish mother? Yet the creative necessity of breaking out of the confines of the self-enclosed Jewish family is in conflict with the necessity for continuity.

If it is rare to find a Jewish family where the son does not feel the moral obligation at least to *try* and find a Jewish partner, the pressure on the daughter is perhaps even greater. From their earliest years Jewish girls are brought up to see marriage as the fulfilment of their womanhood. Any deviation from this norm can bring – for both parent and child – shame, disappointment and anger. A successful career seems no compensation for the absence of marriage. For the Jewish daughter knows in her heart (her mother has told her in a thousand spoken and unspoken ways) that without a man she is only half a woman.

The modern single Jewish woman begins to feel in a debilitating double bind. She thinks, or is told, or feels – though she may try to push the feeling away – that of course she 'ought' to be married. But for her own self-esteem, isn't a successful career important as well? The doubts set in. Perhaps she shouldn't over-emphasise her commitment to work. She'll pay the price for her assertiveness or her intellectual abilities – after all, what husband wants his wife to be more intelligent or successful than he is? A variation on this theme can become part of the married woman's dilemma too. Like a juggler with too many plates in the air, she will have to conjure with family commitments, work, keeping her body in good condition, household chores, her mother . . .

The pernicious pressures to conform to the traditional *mores* can have unforeseen consequences: there emerges a hard-to-pin-down but pervasive underlying emotional distress – feelings of emptiness, worthlessness, hollowness, an inability to enjoy life, or develop intimate relationships. Single men and women may push away these feelings while the search is on for a partner. But the search is often lonely and a quiet desperation may set in.

The proliferation of 'singles' events in the Jewish community; the charitable or social functions with the discreet (or barely concealed) hidden agenda of finding a mate; the 'lonely hearts' columns of the *Jewish Chronicle* and *Time Out*; even the re-emergence of the traditional *shadchan* who will help to arrange introductions – in all of these there is of course the genuine human need for committed relationships, for intimacy and friendship and warmth. But the specific backdrop of Jewish family life with its own innate expectations creates an additional pressure which many find soul-destroying. In the frenetic search for a marriage partner, the real needs of the individual can often become obscured.

And if an eligible partner is found, there can still be the illusion that they will be able to meet all the needs of the other: physical, emotional, intellectual, spiritual. We sense that no one partner can fulfil all of this, and yet so often there is the childlike hope that they can. When they fail, the disillusionment can be enormous, though it may take time to seep through. Meanwhile the frustrations multiply and the feeling grows that something is wrong. Often the woman knows it first: 'I can't talk to him'; 'He doesn't understand me'; 'He feels so distant'. The man is defensive or irritated: 'She seems to demand so much'; 'She's never satisfied'. Sex becomes a battleground. The Jewish marriage has left Eden behind.

And then there is the question of children. 'Be fruitful and multiply' is the first Biblical commandment. Although in rabbinic law this responsibility devolves upon the man, it is usually the woman who feels the emotional pressure. When she is going to 'start her family' is a subject of intense, sometimes barely hidden, speculation by other family members. A woman committed to her work, or who delays her first child for several years, or who is in a relationship where conception may not be possible, faces the anxious disappointment of parents who may see the lack of offspring as a reflection on themselves. When continuity is at stake, the mythic and private dimensions of Jewish life fuse.

Jewish tradition has created a sustaining framework to accompany the individual from the cradle to the grave. From circumcision to shiva, from baby-naming ceremonies to tombstone consecrations, we move through a series of family gatherings where emotions dominate and years of suppressed feelings may find their outlet. The emotional lives of Jewish families of course have much in common with the emotional interactions of non-Jewish families. Love, care, concern, sadness, jealousy, bitterness . . . these are universal. But the heightened emotionality and tensions of the Jewish family are nowhere more evident than in the fraught dramas surrounding events which carry, overtly or covertly, a Jewish resonance – whether it is a *seder*, a Friday-night meal, a birthday, an anniversary, or that symbolic inauguration of the marital relationship: a Jewish wedding.

The joy, the celebration, the unrestrained delight, the love shared in anticipation of more to follow – the Jewish family is never more aware of itself as the carriers of future hopefulness than at a wedding. We dance, we sing, we let go of some of our inhibitions. We rejoice in 'the voice of joy and gladness, the voice of the bridegroom and the voice of the bride'.

But the other side of this is less comforting. Jewish weddings can be highly unrealistic affairs. So much is passed over in silence, so many feelings

26

present that cannot be spoken or that come out in distorted ways. Married couples with their own unresolved issues. The divorced – who've seen it all before. Single women who dread the 'please God by you' that will inevitably come their way. Often there can be as much hidden pain as open joy at these weddings.

The number of synagogue marriages declines by the year. Is it any wonder, when the pieties of the occasion so clearly fail to address the realities of how we now live? Often, for example, the fiction is maintained that the couple have not been living together before the wedding. Everyone knows it's not the case but the performance requires the traditional conventions to be upheld. Who, we wonder, is being protected?

Previous sexual partners are a taboo subject. So too is the cost of the wedding, which will be prohibitive, but is borne with stoical good humour by the bride's parents, anxious to do what they consider best for their daughter, though perhaps even more anxious to be seen to be doing their best. Bankruptcy does not automatically follow – though it has been known to happen. Jewish marriages are no laughing matter: there are traditions to be maintained, family honour to be satisfied. It feels important to 'do the right thing'. But trying to do the 'right' thing can lead to certain complications.

As the day draws nearer the opportunities for *broigus* multiply: who to invite? (do you have to invite them because they invited you?); who to sit with whom? (ex-partners not at the same table); what to wear? (youthful mothers must not quite outshine their daughters). The relationship with in-laws-to-be becomes strained; the tensions between mother and daughter heighten. Everything has to go right and there's so much to arrange: the flowers, the table plans, the hairdresser, the clothes, the video, the cars, the caterers, the band, the bridesmaids, the cake, the ring, the photographers, the synagogue ... the list is apparently endless.

A Jewish wedding becomes a military operation. In the *mêlée* of activity the feelings of the embattled couple can easily become lost. No wonder there is such a problem about intimacy in Jewish marriages. When we consider what is involved in preparing for 'the big day', who is actually paying attention to the inner needs of the two individuals supposedly at the centre of all this busy-ness? Where is the quiet time to sit and speak of their fears and hopes, their need of each other and their families or friends? Who is there just for them, without a hidden agenda of their own, so the couple together or separately can speak their innermost thoughts about this crucial enterprise they are undertaking? So many expectations flood into this marriage, their own and their families', how do they begin to sort out what on earth is really going on?

If they are very fortunate they may have a rabbi who knows how vital it is to listen to them rather than to preach at them. The laws of *kashrut* and the *mikveh* are all very well, but when a couple actually does not know how to relate to each other in a personal way and as equals, no amount of kosher living will fill the gaps between them.

A therapist or counsellor will know this, but it is not as yet Jewish law that a couple must come to understand something of themselves first as individuals before they engage in the fraught attempt to understand their partners. The broken glass at the end of the marriage ceremony is a potent reminder of the potential fragility of the marital relationship.

This is true of all marriages. But the emotional configurations of Jewish families add their own dynamic. The weight of the myth, the traditions, the expectations, the enclosed and often repressive insularity of Jewishness, can hang like a yoke around our necks. With the strains this imposes, the Biblical epithet we have inherited seems rather apt. Any osteopath will confirm it: we are a 'stiff-necked people' (Exodus 33: 3).

---
*

He: *There's so much pressure in life today. I think you need so much money that the husband and wife have got to work. We all want better. Whatever you've got you want better.*

She: *If you've got a semi you want a detached. If you've got a small detached you want a bigger detached and then you want a bigger house. And if you go on holiday once a year you want to go away in the winter as well.*

He: *You've got to. Otherwise there's no point in working. You've got to go for more and more and more. You've just got to keep going and you've got to build your life. You've got to just get bigger and bigger and try your best and work harder and the rewards come ... It must be in your genes. It's instilled in you and it'll be instilled in the children as well. They don't see anything different.*

---
*

One of the problems is we have four separate independent lifestyles going on in the same house at the same time, which causes enormous problems, particularly if the children do require, or suggest, that we should take them somewhere. It can get very chaotic. All sorts of situations where there are two or three different meetings or work commitments on the same night – not to mention fitting in ordinary social life. It's a very busy household and we enjoy it, and in the sense that we've planned anything, we've planned to have a busy life.

Work has always had a high status within Jewish life and culture. From feeding the hungry to making the deserts bloom, Jews are the 'holy materialists' (Lionel Blue), preoccupied with work and dominated by the urge to achieve and produce. The resulting pressures on marital life are enormous.

Within Jewish tradition, the Hebrew word for work, *avodah*, is also used as a term for the service of God. In the past Jews believed that, through their work, they transformed the world in which they lived. The Jew was asked to make a 'leap of action'[1] rather than a leap of faith: God's work was done through human hands. Although in the long run work may be for the glory of God and the building of his kingdom here on earth, in the meanwhile we need to pay the mortgage; and give the children a good start in life; and feel our own sense of worth – often measured by how much we earn. But Jews are workaholics, and when the professional and career commitments are over for the day, the voluntary work begins.

Why all this Jewish busy-ness, the unrelenting pressure of activity? The explanations are understandable, familiar rationalisations. There is family tradition and peer expectations: 'I don't think it comes from anything other than a tradition of doing something in the community – which my parents did, and I'm sure my grandparents did, and which all our friends do . . .'

There are Jewish values involved: 'It's Jewish to think that charity of some form is essential. I was certainly brought up to think you never refused any request for charity, so I suppose you can extend that to giving your time or your effort rather than just giving a donation.'

There are personal needs to be met: 'Partly I suppose it's a sense of relative power. I actually enjoy committee meetings. I enjoy chairing meetings. What I really get is the sense of achievement of doing things that I can't otherwise do, because it is different from the work that I do and if you can achieve something outside your work it's almost like having a second job. You start a project and you finish it. In a way it's as challenging and exciting as anything you can do in life . . .'

There is too the sense of personal responsibility for the collective well-being of those around us: 'Someone has to do the work and I can't turn my back on it if it needs to be done . . . We've had a lot of new needs that no one had recognised before at all: like the need for a children's home; or the need for a home for people with learning difficulties; and some of the particular needs that come out of closure of long-stay hospitals we're just now beginning to find a way to respond to. So it keeps on growing and you can't just say, "Well, I don't think I feel like doing this any more." Someone has to do it.'

It is undeniable that the needs described here must be met fully by any civilised society. The deprivation is real. The work is often vital: life-enhancing, even life-saving. Yet the needs are infinite, and the demands on time and energy are never-ending. Again and again we identify the needs we see in others. Jews have a longstanding and honourable tradition of affirmative action on behalf of the emotionally, physically or materially disadvantaged. We work bloody hard – for ourselves and for others. It may not be in our genes but it still feels like second nature to us. But there is another side to the story.

What is denied is that there is a price to be paid. Something happens in the family when all the needs are seen 'out there', so to speak. What happens to the more hidden, personal needs of the family members when all this caring for others is going on? Unconsciously we are often trying to take care of our own unfulfilled emotional neediness by taking care of others. Unless we recognise what we are doing, we will continue to put ourselves under intolerable pressure as we run around like crazy trying to change the world – when what we really want is something to change for ourselves, perhaps in ourselves.

In how many Jewish families is activity a substitute for intimacy? How often does work replace communication and playfulness, busy-ness edge out stillness, 'doing' and 'having' take priority over 'being' and being together?

When personal needs are ignored or denied by one or both partners then the frustrations, of necessity, emerge somewhere within the dynamic of the family. Sometimes it is the children who carry the strains:

'I don't really like it, not seeing my parents a lot. And I don't like being in the house on my own – because I'm the person who does least of the actual committees – but I think it's better to have experience of knowing what it's like without being comforted all the time.'

And:

'It's very chaotic! We've no idea what time dinner's going to be, whether there's ever going to be anyone in the house. We're used to not having parents in the house at all and just sort of fending for ourselves quite a lot – which is probably very good experience for going to university, and things like that.'

The teenagers rationalise that what's happening is good for them, and maybe it is. But the question remains.

An impoverishment in personal relationships underlies our hyper-activity. Work becomes a substitute for fuller human relatedness. And a denial of our own personal neediness lies at the heart of our enthusiasm for meeting the needs of others. 'Their need is greater than mine . . .' This is the story we tell ourselves. If we ever stopped for long enough to turn this round, who would there be, we wonder, who could really meet *our* needs in all their depth? Our need to share ourselves: moments of tenderness, affection, intimacy, vulnerability. Easier to make that phone call we have promised to do, safer to go off to our next meeting . . .

Our underlying neediness is diverted into continual frustration that there's 'not enough time'. We feel angry, but this is the most difficult feeling for Jews to accept in themselves. Jews don't get angry – they have *broigus*. But unexpressed anger permeates the marital and family life of Anglo-Jewry. One problem may be that anger is seen as a gentile emotion. Historically, Jews saw themselves as the victims of that anger. And if gentile anger wasn't directed outwards in the form of crusades and pogroms, then it was turned back inside their own families, where cruelty, violence and murder were felt to be the norm. Of course, 'Jews aren't like that.'

The truth is more uncomfortable. A Jewish social services organisation such as Norwood Child Care reports that 10 per cent of their referrals have been 'at risk of physical, sexual or emotional abuse'.[2] In 1989 that was nearly two hundred children. The truth is that Jews are 'like that'.

Not surprisingly, we don't like talking about our angry, violent or aggressive feelings, particularly in public. This makes it very hard to look at what Jewish families do with these more difficult emotions. It is too easy to use humour or irony as a way of disowning their reality. Angry feelings can't be dispelled by calling them *broigus*. If the Jewish family is struggling to survive it may be because there is a failure to recognise just how destructive is this underlying anger, often unconscious, in both women and men.

It is now becoming a truism to say that the frustrations of the Jewish woman have not been sufficiently heeded. Women know that internalising their anger by playing the victim, or the martyr, is a denial of their potential and their potency. That there is a surfeit of anger in Jewish women is clear: about the lack of male support; or the inequalities and unfairness of traditional roles or expectations; or how their own mothers undermine them through an unconscious envy of their daughters' freedoms and opportunities; or how their fathers were too busy to give them the necessary attention or feeling of feminine worth. The anger is immense, as is the hurt and sadness underneath – and the relationship with the partner can become a debilitating battle for control. Decisions about money, holidays, food, or sex can become entangled with an underlying struggle for dominance.

Jewish men, of course, have their own anger. Often it comes out as a resentment at a partner's wish to be looked after or provided for; or at what's experienced as the incessant demands of family life; or in frustrations at work or with colleagues. It can manifest in sexual impotency; or affairs; or drink; or gambling; or a withdrawal of emotional support or intimacy. Often, though, the anger is denied in other ways and becomes lodged in

31

the body: ulcers, cancers, heart attacks ... a catalogue of complaints from the irritating to the lethal. And indeed women suffer just as much from the somatisation of their anger, though depression is often an alternative route.

The future psychological health of Anglo-Jewish family life depends on us developing a much more sophisticated awareness of what goes on between the partners in a relationship. For if there is mutual incomprehension between men and women it can lead to an insidious process of mutual denigration. This subtle but perverse process is the snake in the garden that threatens to destroy the continuity of Jewish family life.

He: *I feel we've achieved almost everything I could have hoped for fifteen, twenty years ago. I am a partner in a firm which I am told has a reasonable reputation as a firm of solicitors. I'm involved in as many organisations as I want to be, probably a lot more than I want to be, so that takes up all my time. So far as I am aware I have no enemies; I have a lovely wife; I have two lovely children — they are both intelligent — and I don't know what else I could have asked for. I can do financially most things I want to do. I can go on holiday when I want to; I can go to a restaurant when I want to; I can buy most of the clothes I want to. I don't really think I could have achieved much more if I'd chosen to. And that may sound extremely satisfied and extremely complacent and I'm sorry if it does. But I am satisfied. There's no point in pretending and banging yourself on the head if you're basically happy ...*

She: *I don't think I've come to a full stop or a permanent position in life in perhaps the same way. My roles change continuously all through my life because of both my career changes and changing family relationships. So I still see myself as in the middle of something. I'm doing lots of very satisfying and fulfilling things but they're taking up slightly more of my time than I really want them to. I feel that I'm missing out on some other things, like the people in the family — the children, the grandparents who I also want to make the most of while they're there. I'd like an extra day in the week — providing you don't tell anyone else about it. That would solve the problem ...*

4
'Today I Am a Man'

When I was barmitzvahed – which was just before the war, somewhere in May I think, beginning of May – I had to have tephillin *and all the rest, and say my prayers; and the funny thing is that when the war started, the first thing my mother packed to send away was my* tephillin, *with the prayerbooks and the candlesticks – which I never saw again because they never arrived. So I think that was the end of my religion ...*

There's a real sense of belonging when you realise that what you're doing is the same thing that somebody else has done, and somebody else has done, all the way back: and not because they felt like it or somebody suggested they might do it but because that was what God told them to do ... When I walk through the streets of Manchester with my kippa *on my head I get some funny looks and a few abusive remarks but that's the sort of thing you learn to live with. It's worth it because this is my destiny. There's no reason why I should be ashamed of it or try to hide it.*

There is a delightful scene in the Canadian film *The Apprenticeship of Duddy Kravitz* (based on the Mordecai Richler novel), where the Jewish hero Duddy, desperately trying to make a quick dollar, enlists the help of an older, eccentric, drunken English film-maker. Duddy's plan is to make a film of the barmitzvah of a distant relative. He sells the idea to the proud father of the barmitzvah boy and to the out-of-work gentile film director whose previous work has been somewhat more avant-garde than Duddy has realised.

When the screening eventually takes place – before an invited audience of expectant friends of the barmitzvah family – the film begins conventionally enough: we see the inside of the synagogue, the smiling faces, the Torah scrolls, the holy Ark, the *bimah*. But the musical accompaniment – Beethoven's Fifth – is a prelude to what is to come: the film cuts to a circumcision ceremony, blood splatters the screen, Zulu warriors appear in full regalia, and tribal ceremonial rites are intercut with scenes from the barmitzvah ceremony.

The boy's father, cigar hanging out of his more and more astonished face, mutters to the rabbi: 'That's not what *I* saw in *shul*.' The barmitzvah film comes to its conclusion with scenes of the voracious guests to the party intercut with an Indian fakir eating razor blades. After the credits come up there is a stunned and embarrassed silence. Eventually the rabbi saves the day. He comments, hesitantly: 'A most edifying experience – a work of art'. The boy's father beams with delight: 'See how nice you looked,' he says to the rabbi, and acknowledging the relieved applause of the gathering and their approving comments – 'I'd love to see it again' – he adds: 'It cost plenty – don't worry, it's all paid for.'

We smile at this. We recognise ourselves in it. We recognise how much emphasis we put on the public face we wear, how others see us, how others judge us. We recognise the narcissism of conspicuous display. In order to keep the system going we have to cover up the reality, repress doubts about the validity of our actions and bury uncertainties about how we actually feel about what we do.

In the Richler scenario we see several faces of the Jewish male. There is Duddy the young entrepreneur, the budding businessman, the man who pushes himself forward, eager for success, keen to make good, investing his hopes in the gentile world. There is the father, all pride in his son's achievement but needing to show it in public rather than in private, anxious to make the right impression, deflecting attention from the essence of events to the trivial, using humour to avoid the pain, hiding his feelings even from himself. There is the rabbi figure, saving the day with his politeness and his optimism, displaying that passive Jewish male ability to avoid confrontation by smoothing things over, not making a fuss, keeping the peace, at the cost of the truth. And there is the barmitzvah boy himself, the absent presence at the heart of the scene.

Barmitzvah is the initiation rite through which Jewish men enter adulthood. The density of feeling surrounding it points towards the tribal nature of male Jewish identity. Among the Masai in Kenya, teenage males are taken away some months before the initiation ceremony which introduces them into the community as full adult males. They are taught the history of the tribe – which they learn to chant and repeat until they know it by heart – as well as techniques for survival, how to be a responsible adult member of the community, and how their awakening sexuality fits into family life. It is a complete education in becoming a man, which culminates in a ceremony in front of the whole community. This includes a 'sermon' from the tribe's leading wise old man, often punctuated by cries of 'Quiet there!', 'Let him speak', and 'Stop talking while he's speaking!'. We do not seem so far from home.

Some may feel upset or angry at the implications contained in juxtaposing these primitive, mythic ceremonies of African tribesmen with our own Jewish sophistication of Torah and table plans. But barmitzvah (literally 'son of the commandment') is our own rite of passage for the thirteen-year-old Jewish male. Girls now have their own equivalent (batmitzvah: 'daughter of the commandment') and particularly within the more egalitarian, non-Orthodox world are encouraged in this. The equivalent Orthodox ceremony for girls (*Bat Chayil*: 'daughter of worth') is a gesture in the direction of female equality. But the emotional energy surrounding tribal continuity continues to revolve around the males – and this is the case across the religious spectrum. Traditionally the boy becomes an autonomous Jewish entity on that day. Full adult responsibilities (*mitzvot*: 'commandments') devolve upon him from that day on and for the rest of his life.

Of course it is often a weight too much to bear, a relic of the medieval world where adulthood indeed began in teenage years – before there was such a thing as 'teenage years'. Yet thirteen is the age dictated by tradition, and generations of boys have passed through this Jewish trial-by-family in the presence of the assembled community. So much is felt to be at stake in the boy's performance that we are inhibited from looking rationally at the potentially destructive elements within a system which requires such obedience from its followers. If nothing else, adulthood is about learning to exercise responsible individual choice. For many youngsters the barmitzvah is experienced as the antithesis of this. No wonder it induces in them such rebelliousness.

Barmitzvah exercises such an emotional stranglehold on Anglo-Jewish family life that it threatens to suffocate any hopes for the learning of the real adult responsibilities which are so vital for the future psychological and spiritual health of the Jewish community. Our thirteen-year-olds know this, intuitively, but what they well understand is ignored, denied, repressed by the adult world around them. This is how many Jewish men are inducted into the adult world: caused to deny their own awareness in the face of family and tradition.

———————————————————*———————————————————

One day my parents went up to the Hebrew classes and they said to the rabbi there: 'We would like to take Ricky to the cinema.' And he looked at them and said: 'Ricky who?' And my father was just shocked ... What I used to do was play football and then I'd run out from the football pitch to the Hebrew and I'd get there just before everyone else came out – and this went on for years ...

I had to promise them I'd go to Hebrew and I had to learn my barmitzvah piece in about six months, parrot-fashion, because I couldn't read Hebrew ... But the barmitzvah became quite important for me. I realised my family had all kinds of expectations: I felt that I had to fulfil something. So I put myself totally into it ...

I can remember being called up and afterwards the rabbi blessing me, putting his hands on my head and saying, 'Yivarechacha Adonai V'yishmarecha,' which is a blessing, and suddenly it was alive up in the window and I felt like this light came down on top of me. I can remember thinking, 'My God, what's happening?!' and just being totally bathed in light. Whether it was sunlight or what, I don't know. I can just remember walking down afterwards in a kind of daze, not feeling any more religious, but having been bathed in light. It was kind of profound and after that I can remember never ever wanting to go back into a synagogue again.

The preparations for the barmitzvah day start months, sometimes years, beforehand. Halls have to be booked, caterers arranged. The boy begins the long struggle to master the required but alien words. As the day approaches anxieties increase throughout the family. More often than we can call coincidence, boys become ill in the week preceding the event. Nerves are on edge. Feelings run high. In the synagogue itself, absent grandparents who did not live to see this day are very present. The whole of the extended family, from around the country – nowadays from around the world – are gathered there. It might be the first time in years. And it will possibly be the last time for some of them: the elderly members, or the younger members who will intermarry and be lost to the family and the continuity of Jewish life.

Primitive feelings predominate as the transition to adulthood is acted out. There is the mourning for the loss of childhood. Symbolically, the umbilical cord is being cut – and the ties to the parents. The parents realise that they too are getting older: this is the day on which our baby becomes a man. Barmitzvah acknowledges potency; and the physical survival of the group.

At the centre of it all there is the passing on of wisdom from one generation to the next. In reading from the Torah, the boy signifies his connection with past and future. The necessary illusion of continuity is enacted before the assembled gathering. The Torah scroll is an unknown, essentially mysterious object for most Jews today.[1] They rarely touch one. They will probably never read from it – except the men on their own barmitzvah.

As the family and the community listen to the young man they realise, usually, that they do not understand the Hebrew. In more ways than one, it is indeed a foreign language. Yet the young man-child standing in front of his family and the congregation is being initiated into the tribal wisdom. It is a sacred moment. He recites or chants the magical sounds which he has been rehearsing for months. The tears flow from the faces of the family and the whole ceremony is quite cathartic. There is a power and a mystery here which goes to the heart of Jewish identity.

The barmitzvah is so significant an event in Anglo-Jewish families because it is the declaration by the parents that they have succeeded in holding together the fragmented tradition. The boy is at the pivot of Jewish continuity. These same passages have been read from the Torah for two thousand years and speak of events even older. The Torah has provided the security for Jewish life wherever Jews have lived. Its observance and study were the basis of Jewish identity for millennia. It is the symbol of Jewish survival, Jewish security, Jewish life itself. It is the 'Tree of Life' (*Aytz Chaim*). Generations have loved it and lived for it. And generations have been martyred for it. Now our son has it in his hands. Reading from the Torah, he focuses the psychic reality of Jewish existence, and at least for a moment the survival of the people is ensured. We have a future. Perhaps the Messiah will come after all, after all that we've been through. If not in our generation, then in the next, because at least now there is a next generation.

Of course the party and the presents overshadow much of this for all concerned: 'Actually, we've decided to forget about the mitzvah and concentrate on the bar.' And all the emotional dramas preparing for the event help deflect us from the deeper issues that are evoked as the boy takes his place on the stage of Jewish history. Many guests will ignore the ceremony in favour of the party. The party has become 'the barmitzvah'. In the absence of insight into the soul-sustaining core of transcendent meaning contained within the time-bound rituals, we are caught once more in the trap of glamorous display.

Yet in the midst of this chaos of redefined priorities what happens to our trembling thirteen-year-old barmitzvah boy? Barmitzvah symbolises the coming to an end of one part of life, childhood, and the beginning of a new cycle – the teenage years, adolescence, the beginning of separation from home and family, the start of the journey into adulthood and some kind of maturity, the move into society and the wider community where life will have to be lived in all its fraught complexity. What kind of preparation have we given him? What kind of nourishment has he received from his education in what it means to be a Jewish man?

Times are changing and there are of course Jewish youngsters around us who feel proud of their achievements and secure in their Jewishness. But this is still the exception. If he leaves *cheder* the day after his ceremony, more often than not a boy's Jewish heritage consists of his ability to mouth some traditional formulae, some dos and don'ts, and a vague awareness of some stories that he never quite understood. Stuck with a child's view of the Bible and a child's image of God, in adult life he is blocked from any more sophisticated or mature approach. His intelligent adult consciousness, well able to master the intricacies of computers or law or medicine or business, regresses in panic when confronted again by the emotional destiny of feeling bound up with matters Jewish.

He becomes cynical, sceptical or dismissive about religion. He develops strong views about Judaism: it is good for children and necessary for the simple-minded. If he is married, he may tolerate – but possibly scorns – his wife's interest. But then it is crucial that his son becomes barmitzvah. After all, he had one himself, didn't he?

These are the defences against a tremendous amount of pain and insecurity wrapped up in those childhood years. Sometimes the sadness of these experiences becomes transformed into humour. It is a traditional Jewish way of dealing with pain. Consider the description by Howard Jacobson, the Anglo-Jewish novelist, of his own experience of Jewish education:

Although I was taught Hebrew every Tuesday and Thursday evening throughout the entirety of my childhood and youth, I never came close to mastering a word of it. The teaching was partly to blame because it was propagandist and emotional: I didn't find that it helped to have the rabbi cry when I made a mistake.

But I wouldn't have got on with the language however it was taught. I hated the primitive, Asiatic look of the script: I was unable, on aesthetic and neurological grounds, to recognise or reproduce the characters; and I resented in my soul being required to sway and incant. Read aloud, Hebrew sounded to me like a perpetual wail for the dead.[2]

There is pathos as well as humour here. We can take seriously the 'resentment in the soul'. It has afflicted and continues to afflict multitudes of Jewish youngsters. Jewish men still carry the repressed anger of what was inflicted on them as boys – and the guilt about their failure to live up to what was expected of them.

Much of this guilt and resentment is denied, and then projected: onto the synagogue with what is felt as its overweening reverence for tradition; onto Judaism with its heavy dependence upon and veneration of the past; onto Jewish ritual with its dogged exactitude and detailed requirements; onto the Jewish God, protecting but exacting. How often all of these are experienced within as parental authority, parental demand, shadowing the boy in the man throughout his life.

What energy and patience it takes to develop a feeling and thinking and responsible adult relationship with what one knows has formed one's body and soul. This is a challenge many Jewish men prefer to avoid. How much easier it is to act it all out, to run away like the Biblical Jacob, in an attempt to leave it all behind. So often the Jewish man absents himself from involvement in Jewish life, or his connection remains determinedly peripheral. The illusion is that the issues will go away, or be resolved, by his non-involvement. He has left the tribe. Nothing more is demanded of him. Thank God. Which of course he does not believe in.

Except that the pain remains. Except that in the unconscious, the tearful or frightened or rebellious little boy still stands on his barmitzvah day, overwhelmed, confused, betrayed; thrust into adulthood before his time. In reality there is no escape for the Jewish man. Perhaps after all that is the real reason for circumcision, to remind the Jewish male day after day: 'This is what you are, whether you wish it or not. Your body carries the reminder of the ancient and eternal covenant until the end of its days, whatever your mind wills. So, do not delude yourself – your psyche too carries its own indissoluble imprint of history and legend.'

In spite of himself, Jacob became Israel. The trickster, the manipulator, the heel, becomes the one who strives with God, on behalf of God.[3] In this struggle, which is the struggle for transformation, for consciousness, there is a continual ebb and flow of victory and defeat. The body is marked for life with the covenant; and for the soul too there is no rest, no escape. Only death provides release from this drama.

For those for whom this spiritual/mythic language still feels alien territory, we can transpose this challenge to the Jewish man into a secular guise. Jewish family life is determined by what happens between the sexes. So we need to know who we are and how we are experienced, as Jewish men. Often we are felt to be manipulative, egocentric, domineering, authoritarian. We can be over-ambitious and greedy; we want our own way; we have to be right; we know best. Our *yiddishe kop* enjoys having answers and rationalising and giving opinions. Argument and debate is the wellspring of Jewish male self-assertion. But if Jewish men can learn to develop some neglected aspects of themselves, then maybe the Jewish family has a chance of surviving in good psychological health into the next century.

And that means learning that there is strength in our abilities to be receptive, sensitive and intuitive. And it means enjoying our innate capacities to nurture, to dream, and to play. It means developing an integrity in our emotional life so that we can respond fully to what touches us and moves us. It means understanding how to be authoritative rather than authoritarian. And it means concerning ourselves with honesty rather than self-deception, real truth rather than what we would like to be true.

Jewish men are well-placed to begin this project. Many of us have the experience of not fitting comfortably into the role model of the beer-drinking, sport-loving and domineering man of countless television advertisements; or – closer to home – of not fitting comfortably into the expectations of the wider culture as they are expressed at school, or at university. The models of achievement for Jewish men seem not to be the same as for the wider society. They are more complicated and variegated. There is the model of the Torah scholar, dedicated, soulful and often unworldly, that comes from the ghetto. There is the model of the immigrant generation: hardworking, thrifty, aggressive in business, professionally scrupulous. There are cultural models that emphasize charity and generosity, respect for women, and the centrality of the family. There are the models of excellence, the message that says Jewish men have to be twice as good as non-Jewish men, to survive, to succeed. There are models of failure – drunkards, gamblers – dangled before us to show us what might happen if we let go of our drive, our push, our reliability and respectability. There are models where wit is valued above muscularity. And more recently there has been the model, from Israel, of the easy-going and handsome soldier, short-sleeved, with his Uzi slung over his shoulder.

Because we don't fit easily into the common male culture, some Jewish men have been in the forefront of the attempts to redefine and reshape masculinity over the past twenty years. We have participated in men's groups, uncovered our more vulnerable and emotional sides in therapy – but we were always closer to those sides of ourselves, our volatility simmering away – and willed ourselves into taking on greater shares of housework, cooking and childcare. (This was tough, as our sense of fairness came into direct contradiction with all that early training in success and doing better than . . .)

We have also looked at our relationship with other men, and tried to understand how the drive for success can divide us, and prevent us from developing deep and sustaining male friendships. Characteristically Jewish men use contact with other men (and work) as an escape from the family rather than as a source of contact and nourishment in its own right. There's a pattern of woman-centredness that seems to go back to the story of Jacob and Esau, that seems to hold for many Jewish men. Rebekkah encouraged Jacob to steal his brother's blessing. Jacob's envy made him listen to his mother, and the ensuing rift between him and his brother lasted the best years of his life. He needed to separate from his mother, marry (twice), and separate again from the bonds of his father-in-law before he could grow up sufficiently to face his brother once more, and for the rift to be partially healed.

The family of Isaac and Rebekkah, Esau and Jacob, is familiar in other ways too. The blind Isaac, feigning unawareness of the drama being played out around him, seems to stand for generations of withdrawn Jewish fathers, physically absent at work or study, or emotionally absent in subtle ways. The respect and deference that many Jewish men offer to women is superficially very attractive. But it can also be misleading. Contact with these men is difficult. It can be hard to find the firm ground beneath.

At root these are issues of self-worth and self-respect. Culturally Jewish men have always been grappling with experiences of rejection and denigration that have dug deep into the collective psyche. Our self-respect is hard-won, and when we find it, it glows with the heat of our long struggle. We have reason to be proud of our heritage, with all its contradictions, and of ourselves when we grapple with it. As we grow up and forge a new relationship with Isaac and Rebekkah, and our brother Esau, we can come to appreciate the blessing, and create a model of manhood that is worthy of it.

I'm unusual in the Jewish community. There're not so many of us who actually use our hands. There's all the solicitors and doctors and dentists. I think we're looked down on a little bit, but job satisfaction is worth an awful lot more than money. I'll never be wealthy but I measure my wealth in having four lovely kids. They seem to be very happy, contented children. And they're going to do in their professions what they want to do and get satisfaction the same as I am ... I'm not a religious person but the rest of the family are and it's a very nice, happy atmosphere. It's very satisfying.

5
A New Consciousness

---------------------------------✳---------------------------------

You still get the guilty Jewish mother feeling when sometimes you can't make the school play, or you can't see your kids singing in the Shabbas *service, and it's a shame. I hate it sometimes. I don't hate work but I hate the feeling that I'm up, and then get them off to school, then a day's work, then come back, see to the kids, make your dinner, get the kids to bed and then sit down and start again the next day and it's not easy, it's not easy. It's – bloody tiring, very tiring ...*

---------------------------------✳---------------------------------

Throughout history men, because of their superior physical strength, have been able to keep women in their place because they've been afraid they will take over. Of course in a lot of aspects women are much cleverer. I feel that women see things much more clearly. Women are capable of doing at least six things at once, whereas I find that men can only concentrate fully on about one.

---------------------------------✳---------------------------------

I'm the only person who will actually take responsibility for collecting or delivering children; or ringing them from halfway up the M1 to say I'm stuck in a traffic jam and I can't get back to take them to guitar; or will they ring the teacher and say they're going to be late. It's because I'm the only person who will actually do that. I mean, if I ask Colin on the odd occasion, if he says he's leaving the office I'll say, 'Great, could you come by and collect a child.' But I couldn't rely on him to remember it every day. If anything more important happens he'd forget. So it has to be me.

This is the chapter that no Jewish man will ever get right. For millennia, with a few exceptions, descriptions of Jewish women's experience were written by men. It is only in the last fifteen years that Jewish women in Britain have begun consciously to reappropriate their own experience. And so there is a certain riskiness, even temerity, in men attempting – again – to speak of women's experiences as if they understood them. And yet, with due hesitancy, we wish to celebrate the emerging new consciousness which is set to transform the Anglo-Jewish world.

After the War something rather remarkable happened to the image of the Jewish woman. A negative stereotype seemed to take over popular consciousness. The Jewish woman of the tradition, says Anglo-Jewish novelist Rosemary Friedman, was 'metamorphosed . . . into a domineering, guilt-ridden matriarch who lives her life for and through her children':

She is either a well-intentioned smotherer, who transmits a love of Judaism to her children while controlling their lives to such an extent that her sons may find themselves incapable of forming satisfactory relationships with women, or a misunderstood figure who exhausts herself in caring for those around her while neglecting her own emotional needs.[1]

But you don't have to be Jewish or a mother to be a 'Jewish mother'.[2] To manipulate, and provoke guilt in others, through self-abnegation or overprotective control is not a Jewish (or female) monopoly. Yet the roots of this perception go back a long way. The Biblical Rebekkah is the definitive version of the controlling Jewish woman. Modern Jewish women recognise the picture – in their own mothers, and perhaps in themselves: as in the Bible, the emotional currency of food becomes the focus of her creativity, and her power. Food comes to represent comfort and security, but is also a locus of struggle. 'Eat – but stay thin,' mothers said to daughters. 'We will control you by not eating,' they replied. And surrounding it all, the anxiety about survival. For food meant more than security – it meant life.

As we saw in Chapter 2, behind the need to control there are doubts about self-worth and the difficulty for the woman in acknowledging and expressing her own needs – or even in feeling she is allowed to have needs. In the 1980s, however, other kinds of 'Jewish mother' emerged, including our own home-grown variety of the Jewish American Princess: the mother who doesn't cook, who lets the au-pair or nanny look after the kids, who wants to have a good time, who wants to be pampered . . . and whose life, underneath, is empty. They want to 'do something' but, again, self-worth is the issue. In whichever version we know her, the 'Jewish mother' is not a figure of fun, but of sadness.

Perhaps the contemporary reversals in perceptions of the Jewish mother is an inevitable consequence of a long-standing idealisation to which the

Jewish woman has been subjected. For nearly three millennia, from Biblical poetry through rabbinic homilies to medieval folk tales, the Jewish woman was eulogised in story and song, right up to the self-denying 'yiddishe momma' of the 1930s – she who gains pleasure not from the material world but from the smiles of her children.[3]

That the Jewish woman was synonymous in the past with the Jewish wife and mother goes without saying:

> A woman of worth, who can find her
> for she is more precious than rubies;
> Her husband trusts her in his heart . . .
> every day of her life she does him good, not harm . . .
> Her children stand up and honour her,
> and her husband sings her praises.

> [from Proverbs 31]

Although the elision between 'wife', 'mother' and 'woman' has begun to be questioned by modern Jewish women, this Biblical passage became a central part of Jewish liturgy, recited by the husband in front of his wife and family every Friday night at the Sabbath table. It still remains a part of this service. The rabbis of the Talmudic era could not find words enough to sing her praises: 'Whatever blessing dwells in a house comes from her'.[4]

A thousand years later, the major medieval mystical text, the Zohar, goes so far as to suggest that the indwelling presence of God, the *Shechinah* (seen as the 'feminine' aspect of God), is dependent on the Jewish woman for its continued existence in the Jewish home and family: 'The chief influence transforming a man's house into his home is his wife. The Shechinah will not forsake his house if his wife keeps it according to the ways of Israel.'[5]

Jewish women still suffer from this idealisation. Wherever we find someone being idealised we should be on the alert for what is thereby being denied. And when we see the Jewish woman being put on a pedestal it is precisely to keep her at a distance. For the shadow side of this idealisation is the long-standing fear in Jewish men about the power of Jewish women.

In a recent article supporting an increased involvement for women in Jewish life, Rabbi Jonathan Sacks remarks that women 'hold the future of Judaism in their hand. If they feel excluded by it, they have the power to destroy it by simply turning away.'[6] Such power Jewish women have, who would not be afraid? In the past this fear led, in its most extreme form, to the identification of the woman with the 'evil inclination', or with the woman being personified as Satan.[7] Although far from being a normative view, this represents an undercurrent in traditional male Jewish thought. It is woman who leads man astray. And in particular it is her sexuality which is distrusted: 'Rabbi Hisda said: A woman's leg is a sexual excitement ... Samuel said: A woman's voice is a sexual excitement ... Rabbi Sheshet said: A woman's hair is a sexual excitement ...'[8]

Male fear of the qualities inherent in the Jewish woman is epitomised in the legend of Lilith. With this story Jewish tradition created a graphic representation of those characteristics the Jewish woman would do well to avoid: independence, aggression, self-assertiveness.

In its popular form the story tells how, when God created Adam out of the dust of the ground, Lilith was given to him as a wife in order to dispel his loneliness. Adam and Lilith, however, did not make a happy couple. She too had been created out of the earth and therefore considered herself Adam's equal. She insisted on enjoying full equality with her husband. She refused to obey him. She would not accept the missionary position in sex.

They quarrelled until, in a moment of rage, she uttered the ineffable Name of God and flew away from Adam, vanishing into the night. Adam complained to God, who sent three angels to capture her. They found her by the Red Sea and threatened that if she did not return, hundreds of her demon children would die daily. Lilith preferred this punishment to living with Adam. She takes her revenge by injuring human babies – boys during their first eight days, and girls until their twentieth day. After this, Eve was created to be Adam's companion. And she knew her place.[9]

Lilith is a symbolic figure intuitively known to Jewish women. As psychotherapist and novelist Alix Pirani says:

Every woman knows that she is capable of killing her baby and of being killed herself, in childbirth. Every birth destroys something in the mother, every mother at some time hates her child. To idealise the Jewish Mother, or the gentle loving qualities of the Shechinah, is to conceal this truth. That increases guilt-feelings and self-hatred. Post-natal depression is where Lilith is met and denied. She knows that hatred, murderousness, death, are as real in us as love, generosity, life. When we fully know that, we can choose life, choose love. Lilith's vital role of transformation is to bring us through amorality to morality.[10]

A revolution is going on in Jewish consciousness as it comes to re-evaluate the role of women, yet Anglo-Jewish men are still frightened of women's power. Although this is not a phenomenon confined to the Jewish community, male fear of the creative and destructive potential of women has specific resonances in a Jewish context.

Traditional Jewish expectations of women still cut across the new ethos. For men, the world of work predominates: 'I work ridiculous hours. That's nothing to do with being Jewish. It just happens to be the way I organise my life.' In spite of the disclaimer, this drive to succeed, to prove oneself out there in the world, is characteristic. In doing this, Jewish men relegate the world of the family to the woman. After all, is not this her traditional domain?

———————————————————————*———————————————————————

'I have to confess that it's my wife who phones my mother every morning and probably sees her as often as I do. It's she who buys the birthday cards for the children, for the cousins and for the aunts and for the uncles. It's she who replies to the invitations to weddings and barmitzvahs. And it's she who makes most of the social arrangements as to where we're going to go and such like. I'm quite happy about that. Whether she's quite happy with it is another matter!'

Sharing in the contemporary re-evaluation by Western women of what they wish for themselves in terms of work, sexuality, relationships and status, a generation of Jewish women have reasserted their desire to be more than Jewish wives and Jewish mothers. Jewish women now expect of themselves – and want their men to expect – that they will pursue their own independent personal or professional interests outside the home.

As the Lilith story illustrates so well, when the woman's strength, equality, authority and potency are denied, she becomes – necessarily – destructive. Being rejected causes her to turn her energy into that which must destroy in order to create something new. The anger in Jewish woman at the repressions to which she is subjected – whether it be in the family or the community – is an inevitable consequence of a system of traditional values which seeks to assign a place to her without recognising her own autonomous desires.

The lack of equality in the religious sphere does not need detailing here. Whatever the theoretical apologias given for their 'separate-but-equal' status, many contemporary Jewish women feel marginalised by the male hegemony over Jewish practice. This spills over into the secular sphere and creeps into the dynamics of family life. For contemporary Jewish family life to work, we need more than the Shechinah. We need the creative energy that Lilith represents: 'The more you banish and deny her, the more destructive she will be to achieve the inevitable transformation . . .'[11]

Lilith appears in many guises. Consider the following dream, of a young Jewish man:

I am watching the marriage ceremony of a young Jewish couple. The Chief Rabbi is conducting the ceremony. In the middle of it the woman starts arguing with what is happening. The Chief Rabbi ignores her and continues the ceremony. This seems wrong to me. A certain traditional phrase is reached in the service, but instead of it being 'this great people' what I am surprised to hear is the phrase 'this dead people'.[12]

In time-honoured Jewish fashion – from the Bible to Freud, and beyond – we pay attention to the imagery of dreams and wonder what they may be saying to us. At a Jewish marriage ceremony, at the birth of a new Jewish family, the (male) religious leader of the community authoritatively pronounces the death of the people. But before he reaches these fateful words the woman starts arguing with what is happening. What is liberating here (and perhaps shocking for those over-identified with the patriarchal tradition) is to see that it is the woman who voices the life-affirming dissent: 'No, I cannot continue with this.' She realises that if we continue what we are doing – the outer ceremony of Jewish living, the set rituals of our lives – but ignore what is actually happening to the people involved, then our reputed greatness will be exposed as a hollow sham. The woman wishes to introduce a new consciousness, and she will not stand by passively. It is a matter of life and death – not just for herself but for the whole people. She must insist on being heard.

For at least two millennia Jewish creativity has rested predominantly with men. They have argued with the old words, and wrestled with them for new interpretations to fit changing times and different situations. Their genius has sustained us through time. But now the woman wants to break through the established ritual, the way things have to be done, the words we always repeat, the forms we have inherited. It often seems that Jewish men would prefer to ignore her. It threatens us, makes us feel insecure: we would have to change if we listened to the voice of the woman.

The Jewish world – and in particular Jewish family life – will be transformed when the Jewish woman finds her true voice, speaks the knowledge she possesses, expresses fully the reality she experiences. At a certain point, Jewish men will have to develop a capacity for silence and within that attentive silence learn to hear (*Shema*) the voice of Jewish women; we will have to wrestle, fully and seriously, with what one of our leading feminist thinkers has expressed as follows:

At the moment in spite of what we share as Jews, to speak of Jewish culture, Jewish tradition, Jewish religion is a serious misnomer ...

Judaism can have no pretence to being a universal religion, Jewish culture cannot think of itself as a truly human culture, until they have opened themselves to, and faced the challenge of, the individual and communal self-understanding of women as women. Both Judaism and Jewish culture will, sooner or later, have to come to terms with the full weight and complexity presented by the lives of women – our particularity, our differences, the specificities of our experience with each other, with God, and with men. None of that can be articulated for us, understood for us, judged for us, defined for us, or explained to us, by men.[13]

Jewish family life has a future only if a new consciousness is allowed to surface in men as well as women. There may be family memories of the pious household of old where no harsh word was ever heard, where a spirit of gentleness and reverence ruled, where the man's wages were handed straight to the wife, where the doors were ever open to those in need, where the Sabbath was a foretaste of the world to come. One wonders though: did these families really exist? Our nostalgia is understandable but misplaced.

The Jewish marriage ceremony is called, in Hebrew, *Kiddushin*. Its root meaning is 'sanctification', 'holiness'. Matrimony as a holy venture, a religious/spiritual undertaking, is now a somewhat rare event. If Jewish marriage is to be maintained as *Kiddushin*, what must first be sanctified is what takes place between the couple. In a way this has always been true. But now it seems that it is not sufficient for Jewish legalism alone to dictate the rules of marriage. There has to be another basis for the holiness.

The new rules for *Kiddushin*, for holy living as a couple, need to be formulated in the relationship, free of external demands, free of parental pressures, free of peer-group expectations. Parents will need to understand themselves well enough not to live their lives unconsciously through their children, expecting them to fulfil all the unmet needs within themselves, wanting them to achieve all that they have been denied. Inner frustrations and doubts will have to be faced, not projected into the next generation.

The new rules for *Kiddushin*, for santification of the relationship, need to be searched out by the couple for themselves, with all the honesty they can muster, with all the vulnerability they can allow themselves to show, with all the self-disclosure – in fear and trembling – they can reveal to each other.

The new rules for *Kiddushin*, for the spiritual venture which marriage and committed partnerships will need to be if they are to survive our beleaguered times, will have to be developed with an openness and a self-awareness which is long overdue. It may even now be too late for a reconstituted *Kiddushin* to evolve and survive the disparagements it will receive in the conformist hands of the proprietors of the established conventions. For the new rules for *Kiddushin* will inevitably have to recognise the plethora of committed relationships now possible outside the boundaries of traditional Jewish norms. The only relevant criterion will be the inherent internal sanctity of these relationships. This will be the hallmark of the new *Kiddushin*: a spiritual integrity based on self-knowledge and knowledge of the other. And being single – with or without a partner – will be a source of pride, not cause for feeling a failure.

Each generation will have to learn to see what is happening to them, and face the pain of separation from parental wishes, face the sadness of failing to meet the expectations, summon the courage to say no to the unrealistic demands. The Jewish family will survive through the integrity of its individual members sensing the inner authority to find their own truths; and gaining the inner freedom to become autonomous Jewish men and women capable of a living connection with the past, yet aware of the challenges of the present, and open to the dizzying uncertainties of a future when the capacity to take personal responsibility for our actions in the face of the collective pressures around us will determine our Jewish survival.

6
The Blessing of Abraham

The portrait of the Jewish family in these chapters may have seemed undeservingly harsh or gloomy. We may prefer to speak of all the acts of generosity and love, of care and compassion, that Jewish families are also capable of: the selfless devotion to aging parents or sick children; the hand stretched out in genuine concern to one in distress; the financial sacrifices and the anonymous donations; the daily acts of kindness, of tolerance, of devotion to others; the capacity to be there when it counts; the small gestures of personal concern which nobody notices but which constitute a person's righteousness.

All this is the unspoken holiness of Jewish families. We know it. To know it may even embarrass us. We may want to diminish its significance: 'It's just what anyone would do.' We know the blessings we are capable of bestowing on others and our tireless capacity for self-sacrifice. This is our people's inheritance, our collective 'family tradition'. It may also be our own family's tradition. The nobility of purpose of the Jewish family cannot be gainsaid.

Yet in countless ways we have begun to recognise the darker side of the Jewish family. We see and feel the heartbreak which lies just below the surface. Unless we face the pain of what is happening in and to the Jewish family the heartbreak will only deepen, the wounds tear more deeply as we continue to deny the truths we know but wish we didn't. We need to learn how to understand a little better what it is that we do. The Jewish family can be redeemed only to the extent to which it sees itself.

Beneath the veneer of knowingness and apparent sophistication there seems to be much confusion about what it means to 'be Jewish'. Unresolved – maybe unasked – questions about the purpose of being Jewish lie just beneath the rim of our consciousness. And they haunt our modern Jewish families. They are at the root of much of our disharmony, inveigling themselves into family dramas and communal disputes alike.

Deep within us there is an awareness that we have lost something. The loss causes an inner discontent, some lingering, gnawing, aching dissatisfaction with what we have or what we are doing. The search for what we have lost drives us on, relentlessly. We feel we had something once that gave us meaning, gave us purpose, gave us a deeper satisfaction than the latest fad, or gadget, or project. What was it?

> I think I have lost something on the way,
> What it is I do not know.
> Shall I turn back? It is so far off now.
> Yet it is a pity to let it go.
>
> I have lost something, but do not know what.
> Is it anything of worth?
> I shall let it lie – for the day is short,
> And vast is the earth.
>
> Already the shadows fall from the trees.
> Long falls my shadow.
> My heart is unquiet. It cries – turn back.
> My loss torments me so.
>
> So I stand still in the midst of the road,
> Tormented, doubt-tossed.
> I have lost something, but do not know what.
> But I know that I've lost.
>
> ('I've Lost': Abraham Reisen)[1]

An awareness of loss is already the beginning of a new stage on the journey. To 'stand still in the midst of the road' is already to acknowledge that all our manic activity avoids the central questions. Part of the unceasing pressure to maintain the continuity of the Jewish family – survival at all costs – comes out of our confusion about what it is all for. We can be so busy trying to ensure that our children do not 'marry out' that we fail to address the larger issues. Anglo-Jewry seems terrified of these questions. Like the Biblical Jonah, we would rather flee to the other end of the world – on a package holiday to paradise – than stand still and attend to the voice of our own questions. Yet we long to hear.

The kaleidoscope of our identity forms shifting patterns in front of our bewildered eyes. Is it a racial inheritance – or a self-chosen ethnic identity? Does it require synagogue affiliation, or does identifying with Maureen Lipman suffice? Is support for Israel relevant – and do financial contributions count? Is being Jewish constituted by our moral standards and ethical behaviour? Or is it to do with the food we eat – or choose not to eat? Is my Jewishness defined by whom I marry? Or if I marry? Is it connected to belief in God? Or following the *halachah*? Or reading the

Jewish Chronicle? Or is it a sick feeling in the stomach when you hear the word 'yid' on the tongue of a stranger?

What constitutes our Jewish identity is, in the end, a very personal response we formulate for ourselves. The criteria we use may be rational or emotional. Usually they are a mixture of both. More often than not the Jewish values we hold, and the attitudes and beliefs we adopt – even though they may change in the course of a lifetime – are determined by experiences we have already long forgotten.

There are two components to Jewish identity. Unless one is a convert to Judaism, there is an unconscious core which develops in childhood; and an outer identity adopted later in life which rests upon this earlier base:

'The unconscious core of Jewish identity is established by identification of the young child with the parent; his need for generational continuity; his sensitivity to the distinction between family and non-family; his acceptance of group myths; and his use of sensitivity to language, names, dress and ritual as a means of establishing identification with the family and community.[2]

To express this in a different way: we imbibe our Jewish identity at the breast and at the Friday night table; in the meaningless prohibitions and the excited festive preparations; in the joyful singing or the joyless chanting; in the insistent regularity of family celebrations – or the absence of any family with which to celebrate. Our identity is formed out of a multitude of moments, events, experiences – unique or repeated – that make us who we are: 'I would never have dreamed of speaking to my mother the way you speak to me...'; peeping out of the protective covering of daddy's *tallis*, the closest we ever felt; the embarrassment of that aunt's pinch-on-the-cheek at how much we've grown, *kayn'aynhora*; that time your spilt the wine at seder night; the times you were dragged to *cheder*, or *shul* – or denied access to Jewish books; that nauseous feeling on the barmitzvah day – or not having a barmitzvah because of the war; the nervous banter of one's first *shiva* – is it allright to smile or do you have to look depressed?; being taught about the untrustworthy '*goyim*' and the wicked delights of '*shikses*'; the *shul* our family never go to; the part of the family we don't talk to; the hushed tones or angry rebukes about the one who married out; the silent exchange of parents' glances about that event that cannot be talked about.

Our earliest years are still alive within us. As part of the secret bedrock of our Jewishness we each will have our own private collection of moments and memories – half-buried, half-remembered, or seared inside our skulls. These strange hieroglyphs are the hidden language of the soul. They are the Jewish family inheritance that underlies our own quest for an adult Jewish identity.

———————————————————*———————————————————

If children are pushed too much into religion – and I've seen it, I've seen it myself – they rebel and they'll go the other way. And that I don't want ... I think you can show them the way and help them and hope that they'll take it up. That's a lot better than indoctrinating them, pushing and pushing and pushing. You can't do that because it doesn't work. You've got to let them, not make their own minds up, but show them the way and then they know that they're Jewish ...

One common cause of tension in Anglo-Jewish families is over that tendentious issue of how to transmit a Jewish, and particularly religious, identity to the children. Beneath the surface contradictions reign. Parents realise that they cannot push religion into children or children into religion: they rebel. (Of course we feel we can push them into schools. And careers.) But can you freely let them make up their own minds? Who knows what they might decide to do if left solely to go their own way? In some undefined and nebulous way, parents feel they have to 'show them the way'. But what is this 'way'?

For Jewish families across the religious spectrum, the answer to this might seem relatively straightforward. The Hebrew word *halachah* – often understood to mean 'Jewish law' – comes from the verb meaning 'to go'/'to walk'. *Halachah* is thus the 'way' we are to proceed in life, walking within the moral and ritual framework of Jewish tradition. These guidelines are constant, and constantly evolving. Jewish ideals are incarnated in Jewish actions.

Even Jewish families who choose to remain outside synagogal involvement might wish to make their children familiar with aspects of the tradition which they as adults have largely abandoned. A lack of personal commitment is no bar to the desire that the children inherit a way of life that, although it holds little meaning for the parents, is still seen as necessary for the next generation. What we so often hear is the wishful refrain: somehow, by 'showing them the way', the children will 'know they're Jewish...' Yet we know that the mere repetition of our pious formulaic hopes cannot make our wishes come true.

It would be too easy – and unfair – to dismiss these parental attitudes as hypocrisy. There may be a lack of insight as to why it is so important that the children follow a Jewish way of life, but there is an integrity in the passion for survival. There is an integrity too in sharing the importance and satisfactions of a personal faith and demonstrating that faith through actions which flow from it. And there is also an integrity in honestly admitting one's doubts as to the validity of Jewish practices, or one's questions about religious belief. What is dishonest is to pretend belief when there is none, to expect children to adhere to Jewish ways that no longer make sense to the parents, to expect the next generation to answer our questions in their lives.

Jewish families have to confront the religious and spiritual dimensions of Jewish identity. This is our central dilemma. But because an understanding of the purpose of Jewish survival requires a soul-searching which it may be too painful to undertake, the confusions of one generation are passed onto the next – a dubious inheritance. Our desire to concentrate on efforts to counteract what we perceive as an erosion 'from within' (assimilation; outmarriage) and the threat of destruction 'from without' (anti-Semitism; anti-Zionism) is understandable but misguided. *In order to survive we need to look beyond survival.*

Jews know that their identity has, in the past, been dependent on the maintenance of a particular religious tradition with its ethical requirements and its ritual practices. Freedom of thought went hand-in-hand with obedience in action. The mind could soar to the heights and explore the mysteries of the universe, but one's feet remained in this world. The *mitzvot* were pragmatic, prosaic reminders of one's responsibilities in community and family life.[3]

We know that without the religious adherence of generations of our forebears we would not be here to ask our own pressing questions. For our millennia-old intellectual and religious and cultural traditions to survive, we recognise – though we may fight what we know – that there needs to be some substance to our Jewishness. And in our hearts we know that enjoying Jackie Mason's humour, and bagels on a Sunday morning, is not quite sufficient to maintain this distinctiveness for very much longer.

In the third section of this book we will look at some contemporary responses to the search for a positive content to our Jewish identities. But here we need to spell out the underlying realities as they affect the Jewish family, and are reflected in it. For many Anglo-Jewish families face a real dilemma: living still, and inevitably, in the shadow of the Holocaust, unsure of their own beliefs and values – or secretly insecure even when professing a clear commitment to a 'Jewish way of life' – many parents find it almost impossible to help their children formulate a vibrant and honest response to the central questions of Jewish purpose.

Understandably, when personal beliefs are hazy and insubstantial, perhaps based more on nostalgia or wish-fulfilment, the focus shifts from the *purpose* of Jewish survival to the survival itself. Survival without a purpose holds little attraction for the next generation. Inevitably the questions come to be voiced, with frustration or anger or despair: why bother? why not walk to freedom?

There is a strange contradiction in Anglo-Jewish family life. On the one hand there is a deep conservatism, a wish to maintain the continuity of the old ways. Statistical research about the Jewish community is scarce, but what studies there are help illuminate the dilemma. Adult interviewees reported that what was handed down to them by their parents as the most important attributes of Jewish life were, in order of importance: 'Marrying a Jewish partner, being successful in one's occupation, being financially successful, being religious, and being active in the Jewish community.'

A longing for acceptance, or approval, or security, can certainly lead Jews towards embracing these parental values. But the contradiction is that although continuity is desired, the purpose of being Jewish seems to have gone missing. 'No wonder,' comments the clinical psychologist who quotes this study, 'increasing numbers of young people find little within their Jewish identity and cultural awareness to provide a meaningful identity or one that can withstand the unbearable nihilism of our recent history.'[4] They have found that the emperor has no clothes. This is not just youthful rebellion. Growing numbers of Jews of all ages are refusing to acquiesce to the accepted norms of how Jews are 'supposed' to lead their lives.

Yet the urge to break away is a perennial theme. In the Biblical myth the sisters Rachel and Leah angrily left their father Laban's home to make a new life for themselves.[5] Their flight from home has been repeated in every generation of the Jewish people. Jewish history is also the stories of those who don't, or won't, fit in: the rebels and mavericks and those who, like the patriarch Jacob, run away.

The drama of our lives is continuous with the sacred dramas of old. There is an Abraham in us all, waiting to be called out of our family of origin to explore new ways, for a new age. And there is a Rachel and a Leah in us all, parts of us that have to separate from the parents (outwardly, but more importantly – and problematically – inwardly). We then have to find our own way through life, with all the attendant anxieties – in spite of parents' wishes and hopes and expectations. And sometimes to spite their wishes and hopes and expectations.

After the war my immediate reaction was to get away from the family. I had to find out for myself what it was all about ... In order to try and understand it, to see it in perspective, to see what was good about it and what wasn't good about it, I took this very personal journey away from the family. Of course I

created another family and I'm still totally obsessed by family ... If the family breaks down then everything falls apart. How do we continue with our lives unless we have some ideals? If we allow cynicism to take us over then of course we're destroyed ...

There is a story within the Biblical tradition which dramatises the dilemma of how to integrate both continuity and adaptation into family life, without sacrificing our children on the altar of ideology. The story is read in synagogues on the Jewish New Year. It tells of the binding (and release) of Isaac by his father Abraham.[6]

The story disturbs us. It has the quality of a dream – or is it a nightmare? – with the beautiful rhythmic Hebrew prose conveying in simple detail the preparations for a murder. Form and content are in radical disharmony. With seductive artfulness our narrative beguiles us into listening to how the unthinkable comes into being: calmly, logically, thoughtfully, meticulously, the story unfolds before our disbelieving eyes.

We see the preparations being made and the journey commences. We hear the conversations on the way, between father and son, between Abraham and his servants. We look and we listen and we are hooked by the horror of it all. We sense the madness beneath the surface but we ignore it. At first we suppress our questions, but soon they grow insistent. What kind of God is this that tests a person by asking them to commit a murder? What kind of man is this who complies without resistance, without a murmur of dissent? What kind of innocence – or naivety – is this in Isaac, so passive in the face of his fate? As we read the story we are carried along, fascinated, and with the complicity of the voyeur we push away our doubts, our shock, our wish to cry out: 'Stop this! It's enough! This is crazy!'

We choke back our disgust, our disbelief, because – just perhaps – we recognise something of ourselves inside this story. Don't we recognise the blindness in following a way we know will only end in disaster? And don't we glimpse, as the tension of the story mounts, our own murderous impulses? Don't we see mirrored here a grim reminder of the impossible-to-talk-about hatred that every parent feels at some moments for their child? This is the great test for us, truly a divine test: can the inherent aggression that is part of the fabric of family life (every family's life), can that destructive potential be understood and integrated, or does it get denied, then unconsciously acted out?

We may murder the souls of our children more often than we dare admit. It our fascination with this story – and our upset, or our dismissal of it – we catch the echo of our own hidden, shocking desires. We need this story for its cathartic power; by speaking the unspeakable it releases us from the prison of our own repressed thoughts.

And instead of the knife descending, when the angel speaks and cuts through the murderous fantasy and blesses Abraham and his descendants, we breathe a sigh of profound relief. Somehow we feel that we too have been spared and blessed. And that is not just because we identify with the victim who is saved. Relief also comes because we have had a mirror held up to our own destructive potential, and by acknowledging what we too are capable of we are released from its power over us.

The blessing of Abraham has to be carried on by Isaac. For this to happen Isaac must be unbound. Symbolically, each generation holds the knife which can destroy, or release, the next generation. Each generation in Jewish history has had to learn to tolerate the departure of the succeeding generation, the carriers of the blessing who will transform it in the carrying. The story intuits that we are not allowed to sacrifice the future on the altar of the past. When one generation holds on too tightly to what it believes it has to do – what God, or tradition, or the law, or the community has dictated to it – the future is threatened and the blessing is in danger of disappearing, for ever.

As our dismaying century draws to a close and we remain unsure of what the future holds for the Jewish family, we can also look back and recognise that we have been here before – and not just in mythological time. At the beginning of the century the Central–Eastern European capitals of Vienna, Prague, Budapest and Berlin were centres of rapid Jewish assimilation and urbanisation. As in Anglo-Jewry now, Jews had a high profile in the cultural, intellectual and professional life of their host communities.

When Professor Hugo Bergmann – a Czech Zionist and liberal, later to become head of the Hebrew University in Jerusalem – wrote in 1914 to a colleague in Berlin, he was concerned that Jewish abilities 'have proved only in the smallest degree to be a blessing to society':

These gifted Jews are pioneers of atheism and materialism, revolutionaries and demagogues ... Jews – including even women – march at the head of the agitation against marriage and the family, participating as leaders and led in all the perversities of contemporary, urban society. What is the cause of this value reversal within three generations among members of a race whose family life was pure and chaste? It is the sad consequence of the fact that the Jews have lost their psychic balance...[7]

Somehow, the Jewish family, and thus the Jewish people, survived this loss of 'psychic balance'. Perhaps it is the fate of every generation to feel that all is crumbling around them, and that the past was so much more secure than the bewildering, unsettling, anxiety-producing present that insists on moving provocatively into the uncertainty of the future.

But being a Jew is not only about survival. It is also about purpose. It is about what we have to offer to the world. And what we have to offer is our capacity to hold the tensions between opposites: to keep memory alive, without dwelling only in the past; to keep hope alive, without becoming omnipotent; to see the present clearly, with eyes that are thousands of years old; to live with enjoyment and enthusiasm here and now, while keeping one foot in eternity; and to take responsibility for ourselves without denying our dependence on each other.

This is the blessing of Abraham. And the Jewish family is the womb in which the blessing grows – or dies.

Part 2
EXILE

On the strength of four virtues were the Israelites redeemed from Egypt: they did not change their names; they did not change their language; they did not speak evil; and they did not give up their moral standards.
(Midrash on Exodus 12: 6)

7
Keeping the
Flame Flickering

---✳---

It was just scary entering this non-Jewish world. I didn't want to, I didn't go about saying to people, 'Oh look at me, I'm Jewish, and now I'm working with you, or mixing with you.' I just felt that people knew that I was Jewish by the way I spoke, the way I looked maybe, and I just felt I wanted to be like my non-Jewish workmates and people I met during the course of the day. I don't know why. I still don't know why I felt like that at that time, maybe because I was a teenager and had ideals as teenagers do, about everybody being your equal and there isn't any such thing as religion and we should all be the same ...

---✳---

We are a modern orthodox Jewish family. We live very much in this world through our particular work as a doctor and a dentist, but at the same time we lead a traditional orthodox life. We don't ever work or do anything which would impinge on our orthodoxy ... At home I've always worn my kapple, *always. As far as possible I would always have my head covered. And when I get to within quarter of a mile of my practice I would then remove it ... in certain parts of my work I would feel very uncomfortable if I was wearing a* kapple. *I would become so self-conscious I feel it would actually restrict my natural flow. I don't want people looking upon me as, he said x, y or z and he's a Jew or he's Jewish, what do you expect, etc. So I'm just happy not to make anything of it. Maybe that is my own inadequacy but that I feel is the reality of living in a non-Jewish environment.*

The Jews have over three thousand years' experience of exile – far more than we have of being rulers of our own land. Indeed, there is a strong case for saying that power has with notable exceptions been a corrupting experience for the Jews; our kings and priests have been no less tyrannical and immoral than other kings and priests. We have learnt to make a virtue out of powerlessness; and notions of human equality before God, of democracy and freedom, and hence of resistance to unjust rule, are deeply etched in our religion and traditions. The notion of the one and universal God, as opposed to the God of a particular people and place, was a notion born of statelessness.

We have thought about exile, wrestled with it, become experts in it. We have hated it and longed for redemption and release from our bondage, longed to be back in the milk and honey of the promised land. And we have revelled in it, and taken pride in our skill at bridging two worlds, at the way we have enriched our own tradition and enriched at the same time the culture of our sojourning. Exile has known the Jews' greatest creativity. And also our greatest shame.

Abraham, the Jewish founding father, was asked by God to leave his home and family to go to Canaan and there to settle and begin anew. Jacob's dream, in which the covenant with God is reaffirmed, takes place in flight from his home. Joseph and his brothers are reunited in Egypt. It is as though every step in the founding of this dynasty takes place as a dislocation – progress requires a wrench from the home turf. Generations later, we became a people, in a strange land, as slaves in Egypt. We receive the Torah in the wilderness at Sinai, and in the traumatic dislocation of the exile in Babylon we create the framework of our religion, one whose very rules and structures and meditations are transportable.

The Word, rather than the place, or even the temple, forms the sustaining core of Judaism, and the word is God's word. 'What kept this people together in exile is precisely the fact that its sacred scriptures do not celebrate empire, but explore the meaning of exile.'[1] And the other side of this exploration is a vision, the vision of the promised land, the vision of the ingathering of the peoples, at a time when peace, harmony and justice reign upon the earth. For one of the conditions of exile, always, in its finest moments or its worst, is longing. And its antithesis, almost, is belonging. And belonging requires a relationship to a place, somewhere to put roots, land.

In more recent centuries we have become used to thinking of exile as being both an outer and an inner condition. The Hassidic tradition also emphasized the importance of inwardness: 'The real exile of Israel in Egypt was that they learned to endure it' (R. Chenoch of Alexander, 1798–1870).

But the interiorisation of exile is hinted at from the very beginning. We learn in the book of Exodus how the multitudes that escaped slavery in Egypt hunger wistfully for the fleshpots from which they have fled, rather than face the uncertainties of survival in the desert. Better the cramped soul that you know than the terrifying demands of the infinite. It is this learning to endure, the living-with, the taking for granted of some fundamental displacement of self, that is the core of our exploration here.

And what makes the condition of exile hard to recognise or appreciate in Britain is that we are not living in a totalitarian state. We are not in slavery. We are not threatened by genocide. We do not even suffer daily abuse, or systematic discrimination in all but a few areas of public life. Relatively speaking, for the last three hundred years the Jews of Britain have enjoyed a freedom that few other countries could emulate. We have reason to be grateful.

And yet the freedom has a price. In that very gratitude of many Jews in this country is a feeling of otherness. Of not belonging. Of not quite being accepted. The hurt is aggravated by the fact that the very condition of the freedom is to keep quiet, not express the pain, not be rude to the hosts. So the wound festers.

It is a mark of the century we live in that we have to use phrases like 'mild anti-Semitism' to describe our particular experience of British contempt. The horror which we escaped is so awesome that it becomes easy for us to deny and minimise our own real pain.

An example of this is related by a North London Jewish couple, now in their seventies, communally active, professional people. The man had long been active in Rotary, partly as a way of mixing in a non-Jewish world, partly for all the usual reasons – business, social, charity. They were staying outside Manchester with a non-Jewish couple while attending a Rotary conference, and the weekend was about to get under way. The couple were driving them out to their home.

'I never realised that Manchester had such nice suburbs,' the Jewish woman said.

'Oh, you wouldn't want to live here, though,' said her non-Jewish host. 'It's all rich Jews round here.'

They said nothing so as not to 'embarrass their hosts'. The rest of the weekend passed without them revealing their hurt.

We cite this story to show how we are caught in our own fear, how we rationalise it, and how deeply ingrained is the habit of non-assertion, to the point of being unrecognised for what it is, and well beyond the point of its usefulness. The Manchester couple deserved to be told a thing or two about Jews, and deserved to face their embarrassment. Perhaps it might have been of help to them. An opportunity was missed here, for the Jewish couple to stand a little taller. Very few of us who grew up as Jews in this country, particularly of the pre-war and immediately post-war generations, can put our hand on our hearts and say that such lost opportunities are not a familiar fact of our lives.

Such habits don't come out of the blue. They aren't intrinsic to Judaism or to some notion of Jewish character. They have their roots historically in the Christian teaching of contempt for the Jews that has dominated Europe for the past millennium. We have kept our heads down because it helped us survive.

The problem for many Jews in Britain now – and indeed internationally – is that we find it difficult to acknowledge when times have changed. The habits of caution are deeply embedded, and we aren't sure whether it is real anti-Semitism we are responding to, or imagined anti-Semitism. The long-lasting organ of the Jewish community – the *Jewish Chronicle* – seems to play on these fears. Where other papers attract their readership with gossip, sex and violence, the *JC* features news items about anti-Semitism on its front or back page almost every week. It seems to operate on the principle that there is nothing like a good anti-Semitic daubing to keep the figures up, and to keep the Jews Jewish. (This is not to invalidate the offence those daubings give, or the need to monitor and protest at what is happening, particularly at a time when European fascism is on the upturn.) The habit is so deep that we only know who we are when 'they' are against us. We don't know how real the threat is.

We have the choice to be outspoken about ourselves and our Jewishness. That in itself might be an effective answer to anti-Semitism. As Jackie Mason, the Brooklyn ex-rabbi and comic observer of cultural mores tells us, it is only the Jews who tell him his show is 'too Jewish'. The gentiles have no problem with it. The problem is our problem in knowing how to be, after being schlepped about on the tides of history for the past three thousand years, miraculously surviving, and deeply uncertain when we are next going to be sucked back into the crashing waves.

The low profile is self-defeating in other ways. Keeping ourselves secret, separate and mysterious fuels non-Jewish suspicion and fantasies. If we say who we are and expect to be responded to, we are joining in the world, presenting ourselves as human and vulnerable. We cease to be nameless 'other'. There is a great ignorance about Jews, which helps feed anti-Semitism. There is also much unmet curiosity. People in Britain want to know, by and large. And still we don't tell them.

We scarcely know we are doing it. The rationalisations are manifold. 'People can tell I'm Jewish anyway, so I don't need to talk about it.' 'Nobody wants to know our private business.' A young Jewish television researcher recently told of how he was leaving a job he'd been in for a year in order to go onto a series with a Jewish theme. At the farewell lunch someone he'd been working closely with over that year asked him, 'Does that mean you're Jewish, then?' He was shocked to find that what he had assumed was blatant was completely unobvious, even to people relatively close to him. Even he, a young man fluent in Hebrew and active in the

Jewish Youth movements, had learnt to 'pass', without even being aware of it.

Some of us take pride in our secrets. 'Nobody in the room knows I'm a Jew except me, and they won't know unless I tell them.' 'I bet I can tell who else is a Jew in this room, and the gentiles won't have a clue.' There's that moment of relief and warm recognition when you are discovered in the crowd. And yet there is something stale and distasteful about the cosy secret, like clothes worn too long in a smoky atmosphere, that require a fresh breeze blown through them.

It was striking how little film archive of Jews in Britain we were able to uncover during our research. From all the years since the invention of film – the years of mass immigration from Eastern Europe and settlement here, the years of the First War, the roaring twenties, East End creativity, the depression, anti-Fascist struggle, refugee arrival, the Blitz, Jewish units in the British Army, the move to the suburbs – from all these years of huge drama, upheaval and change for British Jews, there is scarcely any film footage in any of the major libraries and collections. In the vaults of Pathé, Movietone and the COI, Jewish life remains substantially undocumented. There are a small number of novels, an even smaller number of feature films, and poetry and family photographs in profusion. The more private the medium, the greater the selection.

Partly, of course, this reflects the limited power of Jews. Those who ran and owned the popular media, including the news media, weren't interested. But this was also our own choice, out of a reticence born both from our experiences in Europe, and from our specific Anglo-Jewish history. At bottom is a real reluctance to believe there is anything to show, anything to express, anything to reflect. A real fear that if we come into the open, there will be nothing there. A loss of faith and confidence in ourselves that is an enduring legacy of the Holocaust.

Once a year, into the empty space, sidling into our self-doubt, with its wonderful, cheerful and hopeful face – and without the veiled threat that Easter brings – comes Christmas. At Christmas more than any other time we are faced with living in a culture which is Christian at its root. We are bombarded with television programmes, advertising hoardings, shop windows that carry the message of the joy of Christ's birth. Jingles and hymns, Christmas trees and gifts, Father Christmas at school, the nativity play, the carols, the office party – all reiterate the theme. We can tell ourselves that this is Christmas paganised, secularised and commercialised beyond recognition – Christmas without Christ. But still it is Christmas, and we have to decide how to accommodate to it.

To make it a family day? To give presents or not to give presents? To give presents but not to have decorations? To have decorations but not have a tree? To have a tree but not to let the children go to carol service? To ignore Christmas but to upgrade Chanukah, the minor Jewish festival that usually precedes Christmas by a few days, and sometimes overlaps with it? To go to Eilat for two weeks and not have to think about it?

How we relate to the conundrum of Christmas is likely to be some sort of indicator of how we strike the balance between our Jewishness and the culture around us. Most of us will make some sort of 'improper' compromise, because there are aspects of Christmas that we have come to enjoy, and we'll find ways to justify it. Franz Rosenzweig makes a useful distinction between assimilating *to* one's own culture what seems relevant and meaningful from another, and assimilating into another culture, such that one's own sense of self and history disappears.[2] It's doubtful that he had Christmas in mind when he developed this distinction. Nevertheless, one way to make the burden of choice lighter is to strengthen our understanding of Chanukah, for it is one of the two festivals in the year – both winter festivals – that explore the theme of exile, exile from Jewish meaning and purpose. The other is Purim.

Chanukah comes at the darkest moment of the year, close to the winter solstice, on the 25th of the Jewish lunar month of Kislev. It lasts for eight days, so that in the middle of the festival the moon disappears altogether, to return only for the last two days. Even if the festival were to take place on the solstice itself, it would not be darker, since the moon might be full on such a night.

Most of us know Chanukah as a festival of lights. It's the festival when we light the eight-branched candlestick, one candle on the first night, two on the second and so on until on the final night, the eighth night, the night beyond creation, all are glowing brightly. It's a festival about keeping the light of God alive, the light of the soul, the light of the true self, when the weight of the world threatens to extinguish them.

In Albert Square in central Manchester the lights of the Christmas tree are echoed in the lights of a large Chanukah menorah, courtesy of Manchester's Lubavitch Hassidic community. Ironically for people wrestling with the relationship between Chanukah and Christmas, the story that Chanukah commemorates is not to be found in the Jewish Bible, but was preserved as the first and second books of the Maccabees as part of the Apocrypha within the Christian Bible.

The story is that of a struggle for religious freedom. In the fourth century BCE Alexander the Great with his Greek armies conquered the Near East, including Israel. After his death this empire split apart, and the land of Israel came under the control of the Seleucid dynasty, which ruled the region of Syria. In the year 167 BCE the king Antiochus Epiphanes

decided to force all the people under his rule to Hellenise. Observation of the Jewish Sabbath was outlawed. So was circumcision. Traditional temple worship was replaced by the worship of Greek gods and the sacrifice of pigs. Some Jews adopted the new forms, others refused and died as martyrs.

One day the Greeks came to the village of Modi'in and set up an altar. A Jew was ordered to bring a pig to be sacrificed to show obedience to Antiochus' decree. Mattathias, an old priest, became enraged at the Jew,

67

and killed him. He and his five sons then fought the Greek soldiers, retreated to the mountains, and began a guerrilla war against the Hellenists, the Syrians and the Jews who supported them. Mattathias died in the mountains, and the mantle of leadership passed to his son, Judas Maccabeus, who defeated Antiochus' armies through bravery and cunning. Finally, he and his followers liberated Jerusalem, and reclaimed the temple from its defilement by the Greeks. They created Chanukah – literally meaning 'rededication' – as an eight-day festival in imitation of Sukkot, the eight-day harvest festival which they had been unable to celebrate while hiding in the mountains.

It was not until the rabbinic period a couple of hundred years later that the final part of the story that we now regard as traditional was added on. It tells how, when the Hasmoneans liberated the Temple, they could only find one small cruse of oil with which to rededicate the temple. Enough to burn for one day. But when they lit the Temple menorah with it a miracle occurred, and the menorah burned for eight days.[3]

From this point on, the rabbis tended to emphasise the later, Talmudic addition to the story and to minimise the military victory. Themselves living under Roman rule, they may have felt obliged to censor a story about a small number of Jews staging a successful revolt against a powerful enemy. Nor would they have wished to encourage another disastrous uprising like that of 70 CE, which resulted in the destruction of the Temple, or 135 CE, the Bar Kochba rebellion, which resulted in wholesale massacres of the Jews. Indeed, the Maccabees themselves in the end had become corrupted as leaders, choosing puppet subservience to Rome.

The rabbis would have been aware of the pitfalls of these various arrogances and misjudgements. So they chose to emphasise the redemptive aspects, the theme of keeping alive the light of truth in the darkness of spiritual desecration, the need to trust in God to keep the oil alight. For them, it wasn't a struggle against a Pharaoh, a cruel and tyrannical slavedriver, for human rights per se. It was a religious battle, a struggle for the right to pray in one's own way to the god of one's choice. It was about maintaining faith under the rule of the 'other'.

When the early Zionists rediscovered the original version of the story in Christian texts in the nineteenth century, they switched the emphasis back again. They re-identified with the Maccabean guerrillas and saw in them Jewish Garibaldis, Tom Paines, and other populist-nationalist folk rebels. They turned them into heroes of secular Zionism. And now the Israelis too re-emphasise the wit of a small army faced by apparently impossible odds.

Thus are Jewish festivals, and particularly this one, pliable, capable of adapting their message to new times and new situations.

How we choose to see the story today, in Britain, poses the question of how well we feel ourselves accepted here, how free to tread our own path as Jews, how respected, how appreciated. And it raises the question too of how well we respect and appreciate ourselves, and the people of other faiths and cultures around us. Are we the Jews who 'bring the pig to sacrifice', colluding in our own oppression? Are we under any compulsion to compromise our Jewishness? What battles do we fight in our own hills? What is the light that we might want to keep alive?

What follows is a kind of journey through British Jewish identity, from the first arrival of the Jews on these shores with William the Conqueror, until the early 1960s.[4] We hesitate to call it a history, as it is an account told without the discipline of historical scholarship. Inevitably, this makes it more subjective than one would hope a good history would be. But it has the depth both of our personal encounters with the historical material and our encounters also with the people whom we interviewed as witnesses to history. It is a narrative which we have chosen to recount under eight headings, reflecting the eight lights of the eight days of Chanukah.

Rabbi Jose said: 'I was long perplexed by this verse: "And you shall grope at noonday as the blind gropes in darkness [Deut.28:29]." Now what difference does it make to a blind man whether it is dark or light? Once I was walking on a pitch black night when I saw a blind man with a torch in his hands. I asked him: "Why do you carry the torch?" He replied: "As long as the torch is in my hand, people can see me and aid me"'.
(Gemarah, Tractate Megillah 24b)

Exclusion

I don't go out of my way to make a big thing out of my Jewishness, because of the anti-Semitic association of Jews and money. Because of the system which we dentists work under, where one is always charging, one cannot do any item of treatment without mentioning money. I would be very sensitive to the nuance of a patient who would pick up on something like that, you know, who would say something about Jews and money and it's allright for you or etc., etc. So even when I discuss my own academic interests on my course of Jewish studies, I don't tell people the true title of my course, because I don't want to get into a discussion on it. So if they ask me what I am doing, I give a bland title . . .

The old Anglo-Saxon stereotype of the greedy, grasping Jew dates back to medieval times. The first English Jews come in the wake of William the Conqueror. They came under royal protection, with only those rights that royal licence gave them. Unable to practise a trade or to own land, moneylending was among the few ways Jews could earn a living, and indeed they were welcomed to practise this. A few Jews achieved wealth as they helped to manage the finances or the estates of local fiefdoms, and eased the wheels of debt. Their vulnerability and their position as outsiders made them reliable and perhaps pliable creditors. The majority of Jews were very poor. Yet in the eleventh and twelfth centuries relatively settled communities established themselves in most of the major cities – London, Cambridge, Bristol, Lincoln, York. Under Royal protection there was freedom to practise their own religion, and as in Spain there were occasionally public disputations with prominent Christian theologians, intended to prove by argument the weakness of the Jewish faith. But the Jews were not easily persuaded. Jewish difference, and the increasing dependence of individual nobles on their Jewish financiers, could not long be tolerated. In the turbulent jockeying for power in the feudal order and the zealous Christianity that was to unify Europe behind the crusades, the Jews made an easy target. We became the crusades' first victims.

The ritual murder accusation – that the Jews murdered Christian children for religious purposes – originated in England. Later the charge was refined and extended: the blood of those children was said to have been baked into Passover *matzahs*. The accusation has persisted well into this century and is associated with the Christian doctrine of Jewish culpability for Jesus' death.

In 1190, at the start of the Third Crusade, scores of Jews were murdered in towns as diverse as Lincoln, Bury St Edmunds, Oxford, and most spectacularly at York, where hundreds of Jews took refuge from the mob in Clifford's Tower, the castle keep. Royal protection counted for little when royalty was as fanatically Christian as Richard I, and many Jews took their own lives, men, women and children, rather than surrender to the mob. The remainder, who were promised freedom if they agreed to Christian baptism, were instead cruelly put to death.

The next century saw increasing insecurity and poverty for England's Jews. They were stopped from practising their sole trade, usury, and progressively stripped of their possessions. In 1290, the English had the dubious honour of being the first of the medieval monarchies to expel its Jews.

While there is little doubt that, as in Spain and Portugal, Jewish families remained in England and practised their Judaism behind the veil of official baptism, there is virtually no recorded indication of Jewish presence in

Britain for almost three hundred years. It was not until the revolution under Cromwell that it was possible to be a Jew openly in England once more. In 1656 Menasseh ben Israel, an extraordinary statesman, businessman and Judaist, a friend of Rembrandt, led a group of Dutch Sephardi Jews to petition Cromwell for re-entry. These descendants of Jews who had previously been expelled from Spain and Portugal were admitted for religious and commercial reasons. By 1657, the first Jewish synagogue had been established, in Creechurch Lane in the City, and others soon followed, including the still standing Bevis Marks in 1701.

Since then the Jews have enjoyed a freedom and security in Britain almost unparalleled in the rest of the world. Yet still the sense of being here on sufferance remains, and seems to have bitten deep into the collective unconscious of Anglo-Jewry. Many Jews persist in talking about non-Jews as 'the English', or as 'our hosts'. While in part this sense of rootlessness is the result of the successive migrations and persecutions of European Jewry of the past eight hundred years, in part it is a phenomenon with specifically British characteristics.

Englishmen of the Jewish Persuasion

Compared to the autocracies of Central and Eastern Europe, eighteenth-century Britain offered a relatively benign haven for the new arrivals, whether wealthy merchants or the desperate poor. Economic liberalism, the spread of capitalism and trade, meant new opportunities in trade and finance for the relatively mobile Jews, chafing at the restrictions imposed by semi-feudal orders. Nevertheless, it was made difficult for new arrivals to naturalise, and unnaturalised Jews were excluded from the artisans' guilds, from owning land and from public employment. For the poor hawking – reselling old clothes – or peddling along the hills and valleys became the prime ways of making a living. So the Jews became more visible, and their settlements spread throughout England and Wales. Attempts to make naturalisation easier and fairer for a small number of Jewish merchants – the 'Jew Bill' of 1753 – led to anti-Jewish riots in major towns, and the bill was rescinded.

The eighteenth and nineteenth centuries saw the development of, on the one hand, a small settled and wealthy community, consisting of the descendants of the original Sephardi families, supplemented by a number of established families from Germany (the first Ashkenazis), and on the other hand, a much larger and growing group of urban and semi-rural poor. The tension between the settled and the newcomers, in the face of English exclusivity, shaped the culture of Anglo-Jewry.

The great Jewish families of the nineteenth century – the Rothschilds, the Montagus, the Waley-Cohens – were in appearance and outward manner indistinguishable from their English counterparts. They were 'new rich', but they could hold their own in all but parliamentary suffrage with the best of the land. They owned fine houses. Their children had the best education. They had the ear of princes and statesmen. But their acceptance had its price.

The British Jewish community deemed its relationship to the general society to be governed by a form of contract, in reality informal but to the leading Jews having the force of law. The terms of this contract were that the community was to forswear any national qualities, and adhere to a definition of Jewishness as different only in its religious rituals and beliefs. In return, gentile society would award the Jews civic equality. As a result, the community felt that any deviation by them from this strict contract, in other words any assertion of national rather than religious identities, would result in British society likewise abrogating its side of the bargain, and removing the civic equality it had previously bestowed.[5]

As Israel Finestein says, 'That established Jewish community attached to Jewish emancipation a quasi-messianic character. It was perceived as meeting an historical need, rectifying unjust anomalies, reversing past errors in Jewish–Christian relations and reaching a millennial solution to the "Jewish question". With this philosophy they combined a profound sense of gratitude to Britain, a firm belief in the essential liberality of the aims of British foreign policy, a conscious preference for all things English and a ceaseless concern to justify in the public mind the wisdom and propriety of Jewish emancipation.'[6] In 1858 Jews were finally admitted to Parliament, after a long and difficult campaign culminating in the right not to be sworn in as a member on the New Testament Bible. Sir David Salomon had already been elected but in effect had been prevented from taking his seat by this rule.

Jewishness became a matter of private religion alone – and Jewishness as a cultural, ethnic or everyday matter of religion was squeezed hard. Judaism had become Christianised, or rather Protestantised, and the spiritual arena separated from daily life according to the demands of liberal capitalist society.

The few exceptions to the rule somehow served to reinforce it. While it was necessary for Disraeli to have been baptised in order to reach the pinnacle of political success, he nevertheless took pride in his Jewish bloodline, and his genius was commonly ascribed to his lineage. He didn't hide his Jewishness, so much as redefine it racially and biologically. Respect for 'Jewish blood' was fashionable for a period, but tinged with envy and distaste. By and large the maxim stood: it was time to be an 'Englishman in public, a Jew in private'.

———————————————————*———————————————————

I realise now that I must have been very conflicted. My life at home was extremely Jewish and we were brought up in a very strong Jewish tradition. We kept all the dietary laws. We went to synagogue. We learnt Hebrew. We celebrated every Jewish festival. And at school it was if my Jewishness didn't exist at all ... We used to have such a strong emphasis on Christmas and for instance when I got to secondary school and we studied literature that was one of the hardest things for me. Nobody paid any attention to the fact that lots of the books that we studied were really offensive to us. Nobody ever said, 'You might find this book very difficult', or 'You might find this portrayal of a Jew very offensive.'

I think it was very odd, because many of our parents were prepared to fight for our religious rights. For instance, I left school on Fridays early in winter so that I would be home before the Jewish Sabbath ... The only thing that people cared about was the outward trapping. We were definitely given the message that fighting for anything Jewish was okay if it was religious, but not if it was anything deeper.

The emerging Jewish institutions reflected the bargain. The Board of Deputies of British Jews, founded in 1760, was modelled on Parliament. The Jewish Lads Brigade was modelled on the Church Lads Brigades, and, no less than they, saw its task as educating its young people as upright and loyal citizens, equipped to fight for king and country. The Jewish Board of Guardians was modelled on the church charitable institutions. Welfare for the poor was contingent on their taking steps towards behaving as upright Englishmen. The established synagogues amalgamated into the United Synagogues, in imitation of the Anglican Church, and intended to make united representation to English authority. The institution of the Chief Rabbinate, representing a degree of centralisation of rabbinic authority hitherto unheard-of in European Jewry, was modelled on that of the Archbishop of Canterbury. The Very Reverend Herman Adler, Chief Rabbi 1891–1911, became known as the 'West End goy'.

Added to this a plethora of educational and charitable institutions was formed, designed to minister to the needs of the new poor and at the same time encourage them to conform to the niceties of English life: the Jewish Ladies' Visiting Association, the Jewish Working-Men's Club, the Jewish Soup Kitchen.

'In Anglo-Jewish philanthropy it is possible to detect a modicum of disinterested benevolence, a protective and supportive sympathy, a desire to help co-religionists integrate comfortably and quickly into Manchester society and so escape the hostility, anti-Semitic or xenophobic, of a wider society. But the new agencies were more evidently the instruments of class control in a communal setting, designed to protect the status of the communal elite at the expense of the culture of the communal poor.'[7]

Incorporation

The waves of new immigrants fleeing persecution in Russia and Poland from the 1870s onwards posed a threat to the hard-won status of the older families. The newcomers brought with them the languages and culture of the tiny country *shtetls* from which they had come. They maintained their national identities – groups of 'landsmen' would tend to live close to one another, and to pray and study together in *chevras*, tiny rooms built onto the back of the house. And they maintained their East European Jewish identities, speaking the Polish, Russian, or Lithuanian variants of Yiddish, which was the common tongue of all the Ashkenazi Jews.

———————————————————*———————————————————

Every Saturday in the year I spent two or three hours in synagogue. Now, unlike Protestant churches, for me the synagogue was a very picturesque affair. It was very dramatic. There were all these men shrouded in these tallisim, *their praying shawls, falling and swaying to and fro, and above them the cantor, who would be on the platform, what they call the* bima. *These men had good voices. They would improvise music and it was very emotional, extremely poignant. There were certain passages which everyone knew and everyone chanted out loudly so that it was quite an uproar. There was always this almost Oriental atmosphere. So on the one hand you have this devout atmosphere. And on the other hand you had this very informal business of people walking in and out chatting, very conversationally, usually about what they call* geschafte *in Yiddish, business affairs.*

Certain times of the year, certain festivals, the rabbi would come in front of the Ark, face the congregation and deliver himself of an oration. Generally this was to do with the persecution of the Jews and the hope that next year we're all going to be in Jerusalem. That was the dream. They would give orations that were so powerful, with dramatic pauses and gestures and twitchings of the prayer shawl, and the women, who were always sitting in the gallery, never with the men below, separated, they were crying, crying out quite loudly and men too were sobbing, very emotional. And totally un-English. You don't let youself go like that – nothing to do with what English worship in a church would have been like. Or for that matter a liberal synagogue.

Many of us today can still sense that we come from a culture that is more emotional and expressive, passionate and full of longing. We locate it inside us and often it only emerges fully when we are away from England, in Israel or perhaps New York, and the veil of Britishness we have grown up with falls away. In this period, the foreignness of the new arrivals was palpable, and shocking to the established elite.

Many Jews at the turn of the century congregated in the anarchist clubs and reading houses and shared the ideas of socialism and syndicalism which made sense of their poverty and powerlessness, and gave them a vision of the future. Few could relate to the austere, cathedral-like synagogues of established Jewry.

The British working class was deeply ambivalent about the new arrivals, even the most radical of the trade-union organisers like Ben Tillet seeing them as threats to the English working man. The popular press, then as now, played up the fears of the 'alien invasion', and anti-Semitic stereotypes of the dirty, thieving, penniless, foreign-born Jew stealing jobs and women have a familiar ring. The very poverty into which the immigrants were forced came to be held against them.

Against a background of mounting anti-foreign hysteria, the established Jewish families trod carefully on the tightrope between the desire to aid their fellow-Jews, and the fear of offending the English 'hosts'. Unwilling to allow them to become a burden on the British state, help was provided, conditional on assimilation to English manners and customs.

Samuel Montagu founded the Federation of Synagogues, to provide small orderly synagogues affordable to the Jewish working class and to wean them out of the *chevras*, the newly-forming Jewish trade unions and anarchist meeting places.

The Jewish Free Schools were established. On the one hand they were invaluable in giving the newcomers the basic rudiments needed to hold down a job. On the other hand the schools were unswerving in their basic purpose: to create respectable English citizens. The pupils were to speak English, and encouraged to adopt English names, with or without parental approval. They learned English manners, 'discipline' and etiquette. They learned English literature, history, geography, songs and games, and they celebrated Empire Day and May Day festivities – and Christmas.[8] The use of Yiddish was banned from the schools, and in the space of a generation Yiddish was lost as an everyday spoken tongue, for all but the ultra-Orthodox.

This process was not without its opponents. A protracted struggle was fought over many decades for the hearts and minds of the new arrivals. Many parents still insisted on sending their children to the orthodox *chederim* for their religious education. And they clung to the familiar *chevras* for prayer, and to the informal support of family and friends, rather than face the conforming pressures of the charitable institutions.

The pressure to Anglicise was beautifully satirised in the 1890s – originally in Yiddish – by the poet-writer Israel Zangwill.

My brothers, sisters newly here,
Listen to my wise oration,
You can live without the fear
Of hatred and repatriation,
All you have to do, I bid,
Is stop acting like a yid.

Endeavour to be strong and fine,
And live just like the English do;
If you live like Eastern swine,
Our nightmare, left behind, comes true;
The man who lets his earlocks dangle,
Makes us all go through the mangle.

Marriage must be civil, legal,
When you pray keep silent, still;
In the West End it's so regal,
Elegant and such a thrill;
God does not care for your ilk,
Unless your tallis is made of silk.

Ei, ei, ei is so demeaning,
English voices sing so sweet;
Ei, ei, ei, is so unseeming,
Oi, oi, oi, an ugly bleat.
Pom, pom, pom, is rude and crazy,
Try instead Tra La or Daisy.

Do not disgrace yourself at table,
Gorging every Jewish dish,
Strive and try when you are able,
To eat some tasty fresh fried fish,
Eat like they do, don't forget,
And Christmas pud will taste good yet.

Don't play cards for lots of money,
Working every day and night,
I'm a fine example, sonny,
Of dignity and what is right,
Tailors should sit still at home,
Not work their fingers to the bone.

Accept from me this invitation,
My advice is so well-meant,
We must have assimilation,
Men like me in Parliament,
Follow me and do what's right,
And may your strength be well upright.

Chorus
Yes, we would love to be MPs
And we will learn to do all this,
We will say, 'How do you please,'
And cultivate communal bliss,
We will change our ways and struggle,
To eat our Christmas pudding right,
Put away our Yiddish kugel,
Read our Milton every night,
We will call Rev. Adler 'chief',
And nobody will come to grief.

As British fears about the level of immigration rose, the Jewish establishment supported attempts to restrict it. The British trade unions also, by and large, opposed the arrival of foreign workers. The outcome was enshrined in the Aliens Act of 1905, which satisfied chauvinist fears but in itself did no more than slow down the level of immigration, and make the Jewish community formally responsible for the well-being of the new arrivals. The Jewish Board of Guardians – the main Jewish welfare organisation – arranged the repatriation of thousands of Jewish families back to the Eastern Europe from which they were fleeing, or paid for them to be sent on to Australia, South Africa or America.

Recently settled Jews had ambivalent attitudes towards the First World War. On the one hand, they were being asked to join an imperialist war for a country and king which were unfamiliar to them, ambivalent about them, and whose names many were unable even to spell. In Eastern Europe Jews had suffered deeply from discriminatory induction into the tsar's army, and the political education many had received in the East End made them unlikely to be enthusiastic about conscription into the British Army, to fight quite possibly against other European Jews. The sense of an international working class had an immediate ring of truth about it for Jewish working people. Numbers of Jews avoided the army, sought conscientious objector status for as long as it was possible, or joined in the small Jewish pacifist movement.

On the other hand, Jews wanted to belong, and belonging meant taking patriotic pride in fighting for the British. Jews joined up in numbers that were proportionately greater than the general population. (They were also less likely to be in trades – like farming – that would give them exemption.) The painter-poet Isaac Rosenberg joined up partly out of sheer economic necessity, and his surreally honest poems witness the war from the non-heroic stance of the private soldier, in contrast to most of his English contemporaries.

By the time the war was well advanced, and the young Jewish men had died in their thousands along with the youth of a whole generation, British Jews felt they had staked their claim to belonging here, and staked it in blood. Despite a revival of anti-alienism – there was an attempt to blame Jews for the ravages of the war, which led to anti-Jewish riots in South Wales in particular – the deference of the established Jewish families was beginning to be questioned. With it came a realisation that efforts to assimilate had gone too far, and were in danger of destroying the very identity of the people for whom preservation had initially been sought.

Among the newly wealthy of the Polish and Russian Jews were some who were prepared to join the campaign to press the British government for a Jewish homeland in the Palestine mandate. The older families by and large resisted and opposed the Zionist movement, fearing accusations of dual loyalty. For the first time the Jewish community had shown itself divided over an issue which asserted Jewish nationalism, and not just Jewish religious difference. At the same time the Jewish Free Schools modified the focus of their syllabus. The Jewish holidays were celebrated, and more emphasis was placed on Hebrew teaching and Jewish learning.

Between the wars it is possible to identify a more determined Jewish spirit in the East End of London and in the working-class Jewish districts of North Manchester, Glasgow, Leeds and Liverpool. Yiddish theatre and newspapers survived. There were Jewish boxers, Jewish gamblers, Jewish prostitutes. At the same time many fled what they experienced as the stale air of the study-house and embraced the new secular cultural opportunities that were opened up to them – in art, poetry, literature and politics. People were coming up against a new world and the old rules were in question.

———————————————*———————————————

I was an avid reader, I read anything. I was gradually drawn into what was known as the rationalist movement. They were agnostics who met in a place, South Place behind Liverpool Street, and they sang secular hymns of all things. So by the time I was confirmed, barmitzvah boy at thirteen, nominally I was still Jewish, nominally I could read Hebrew and all of that but I'd become sceptical. I couldn't have any real belief in it. Things that I was reading in the outside world were so contradictory that I shed it all, much to the horror of my parents and my rabbi. I ate things which were not kosher. My mind was absolutely avid for new horizons, new things to fill it. It was a blank. If you leave a religion, have a blank, what fills it?

The Jewish trade unions thrived among the impoverished Jewish workers. Many Jews were attracted to the left and to the Communist Party. Some on the left saw universal values as supplanting Jewish ones, and felt cultural Jewishness to be sufficient, and religious Jewishness to be irrelevant. Others, particularly in the Workers' Circle, sang Jewish songs and took up Jewish causes, but at the same time subscribed to the ideals of socialist internationalism.

———————————————*———————————————

As far as we were concerned being a Jew didn't necessarily identify with religion. We thought of religion as being prejudiced, it hampered us because when we were involved with things that affected Jewish working people the religious authorities weren't on the side of the Jewish working class. When they asked the Chief Rabbi to preach his sermon against the sweat industries, against all the conditions that they were up against, he refused even to do that ...

Other Jews began to look to socialist Zionism as an expression of their ideals and a way out of the struggle for identity in a country where the pressure to assimilate was still great. The dream of a new land where social justice and democracy would prevail and where the freedom to be Jewish would be axiomatic began to capture people's imagination.

We had a glorious past; and here were people who had gone to Palestine, were re-establishing a homeland in a very special way, not just in the towns. But particularly the kibbutz, the communal settlements, were really socialist idealism at its very very best. And people were tilling the soil, all those romantic ideas of the new type of Jew, and proving they could do it.

Many Jews were touched by one or other of these competing ideologies. But for most the main preoccupation was fitting into the new land.

We wanted to be accepted. We wanted to get on. You know, the Jewish thing is your son to be a doctor or a lawyer and so on and there was pressure for education. And to get on in the world here in England one had to accept the English way of life. And perhaps you didn't do all the [religious] things that you ought to. When you had awkward names, you changed your name, you Anglicised your name.

My father was a master tailor and he didn't want me to go into tailoring. So the pressure was on me and my younger brother to go into the professions. When we were at school there was a great keenness on us to do homework before we went out to play with our friends, to get on. The school report was under great scrutiny at the end of term, and really also to grow up as responsible human beings so that we could hold our heads up in the English community around us.

We wanted to be like the people around us, didn't we? We wanted to sort of sink into the background, not be too prominent. We used to have tea and supper. Well we'd seen that other people don't do that. So when we came home from work we had a high tea and then a light meal afterwards, changed it a different way. But we still couldn't go out with anybody that wasn't Jewish, not if our

*parents knew. You'd be very careful to hide that ... and hoping in our hearts
that nobody'd ever see us in town.*

School was the key experience. For many it was where they first spoke
English. It was where you first met 'them', the others, the goys. If Jews
were there in large numbers it would be easier to maintain your sense of
your Jewishness than where Jews were a minority. In non-Jewish schools
there was little respect for Judaism and Jewish culture. You had to fit in.
And that meant learning the language and codes of the non-Jewish world.
Christian hymns and prayers. The English language, English writers and
poets. Sports and games – cricket, hockey, football – of which Jewish
parents had no experience. History and geography that placed Britain at
the centre of the world. The few images of Jews that cropped up in
literature – Fagin, Shylock – were likely to be derogatory. But the complicated feelings that these images might induce in young Jews weren't on
the agenda.

By and large the derogation was of a subtler kind: the slow drip of
omission. For gentiles, Jewish lore and learning weren't worth knowing
about. How could Jewish children maintain a belief in the value of their
own culture if nobody ever showed curiosity or interest in it?

The Jewish Bible was called the Old Testament – its stories were a
precursor to the birth of Jesus and the arrival of the New Testament, which
put the final gloss on it. In the light of New Testament mythology, the old
myths were reshaped into neat moral tales about what good Christians do
and do not do. The ambiguity was gone, the sense of the Bible as a store
of questions, a source of argument.

To expect otherwise would be unrealistic. The notion of a multi-cultural
syllabus was not to appear until the 1970s. The theological reappraisal of
Christian arrogance and derogation of other faiths began at about the same
time. It's as well to be mindful of the generations of English Jews who
grew up in imperial Britain in an atmosphere that was fundamentally
contemptuous of Judaism, as it was of all foreign cultures, despite the
liberal ideologies. It's an open question as to how much the 'backwardness'
of which many young Jews of these generations accused Judaism was
intrinsic to Judaism's own clash with modernity, and how much was learnt
self-denigration.

Judaism also was tied up with the past in a foreign land, and for people
trying to establish themselves here, it could be seen as a waste of time, a
hindrance. If you ran a shop or a stall or even a sweatshop, you needed to
work on Saturdays. For the children of immigrants, even their parents

were a source of shame and embarrassment and of confusion in their dealing with the new world. Often they were tugged between their loyalty to the older generation, and the need to keep them at arm's length in public. These people, a generation or two away from the *shtetl*, had no doubt of their Jewishness. Why did they need to worry about what would happen a generation or two later?

Finally, Jews in Britain were trying to find their way in a tight, but not impermeable, class system, which owed its survival to a certain degree of porousness, but in which the codes of entry were strict and entry itself was limited and conditional. Occasionally, where Jews couldn't play the game – in large areas of the City, for example – they began to invent a new one. In retailing, in garment manufacture, Jews were at the forefront of innovation.

Jews sent their children to elocution lessons to take the edges off the influence of the working-class neighbourhoods they had grown up in. They struggled to send them to the best public schools, the best that would let them in. They sought acceptance, and they sought security.

I was admitted to a school of art and lo and behold I went from the East End working-class area to a middle-class English school of a totally different kind of discipline and was taught the elements of drawing, of crafts of all kinds. And there I met people I had never met before. They were the English middle class. And above all I met something that really rather terrified me, it took me years to overcome: the English middle-class girl, full of self-confidence as I was not. And to get used to their ways and their charm and all the rest of it was a great struggle for me.

The backdrops of the 'Boris' wedding photos that were so popular and fashionable among Jews of the thirties are very revealing. They represent a combination of Hollywood romance and upper-class English country-house living, glitz and sophistication, that had to be part of the British Jewish dream. And with it those Jews who could began the move out of the confines of Whitechapel and Mile End and Redbank and the Gorbals into the leafier suburbs north and west.

In all these circumstances, the wonder is perhaps not how much was lost of Jewish life and culture, but how much was zealously retained.

Fascism

In the worldwide economic depression of the thirties, anti-Semitism was on the increase, and the stories began to filter back to Britain of what was happening to the apparently secure and assimilated Jews of Germany.

---
*

I was never told I was a Jew. The first time it happened, I was five or six. I was playing on the streets and children said to me, 'You can't play this game if you are a Jew.' So I said, 'What is a Jew?' They said, 'A Jew is somebody who doesn't believe in God. I said, 'Oh, I believe in God.' 'Oh well, you can play with us.' And then I told my mother and she became very concerned and my father told me the following week, 'Well, you are Jewish, and Jews also believe in God.' And that was my first introduction to being Jewish.

Later, I went to a Nazi grammar school. We had lessons on race and there were three Jews in the class and we all three Jews had to get up and the teacher started to compare our skulls with those of the German pupils. And I remember, I had to go to the front and he started to measure my head. At first I felt very, very scared but the teacher, he patted me on the head and said, 'Don't worry, it's not your fault that you are a Jew.' And then he tried to show us with photographs that our skull was different from their skulls. I had the reaction, 'What a shame that I can't be Aryan like the others.'

---
*

The big boys were throwing stones at me on the way to school and away from school, and I knew that if I had been hit nobody would help me at all.

This was the beginning of a great deal of pretending. After 1933 my father lost all his money. I was continuously afraid that we were going to starve, but again it was something I couldn't talk to my parents about.

As often in history, it was resurgent anti-Semitism that served most forcibly to remind the Jews of their Jewishness. What was happening in Germany was happening in a milder but still frightening form in Britain. The Jewish working-class communities of Britain began to organise their own defence, uniting where they could with non-Jews. Some of the framework of organisation was provided by the trade unions and the Labour and Communist Parties. Much of it was a spontaneous, grass-roots outpouring of anger against anti-Semitism, which became a battle to deny the Fascists, defended by the police, a platform.

---

*

Toward the outbreak of war I got involved in anti-Fascist activities. There were a whole lot of Fascists, some blackshirts that used to speak at Hyde Park Corner and Tower Hill. The Board of Deputies, I think it was, were organising classes in public speaking and sending out teams to heckle them and speak against them. We spent about half an hour learning to pitch our voices to speak outdoors and learning to be amusing and to stimulate emotion and then the people who'd actually been out on the job came in. We heard all about the latest insults. The place crackled with insults and people shouting them round the place and finding the answers to them and I think everybody enjoyed it very much. I met other Jews and I think for the first time I really liked and admired them as Jews. I never had before.

Committees were set up to protest against what was happening in Europe, and to help the first refugees from Germany. Jewish defence groups, young men willing to 'take on' the Fascists, sprung up in most major cities. In Cardiff local young men asked for a Jewish unit to be formed in the British Army, to give them the fighting skills needed to defend themselves. They were aware of what was happening in Germany, and 'wanted to make sure that it wouldn't happen here'. This was to underestimate the severity of what was happening in Germany, and what was required to prevent it. After the battle of Cable Street, Oswald Mosley, leader of the British Union of Fascists, was successfully discredited, and his strong-arm tactics eventually turned the British public against him.

Yet while few people ever voted for Mosley, the underlying attitudes he represented were pervasive. Anti-Semitism was fashionable in its upper-class version no less than it was on the streets, and even writers like H. G. Wells and T. S. Eliot made barely concealed attacks on the Jews. It pervaded the Foreign Office and the Home Office. Britain in the thirties consistently refused to let in significant numbers of Jewish refugees from Nazi Europe. Harold Nicolson, who headed a campaign during the war to admit Jewish refugees, spoke of his personal distaste for Jews even as he supported their admission, showing the deep ambivalence of the British at this time towards the Jews. The Jewish establishment, tamed by its own fears of resurgent English anti-Semitism and by its habitual caution, acquiesced in the policy that only those who were sponsored or could support themselves be allowed in. Only a small number made it.[9] After Kristallnacht in 1938, the rules were relaxed somewhat. The children's transports came in greater numbers. But before long German-occupied Europe had extended its grip over all major Jewish centres of population, and escape became virtually impossible.

Many Jewish families, especially those with family still in Europe, took in refugees, or helped in other ways. Most were preoccupied with their own struggle for survival. The East End, now often viewed through rose-tinted spectacles, was still an area of great poverty and hardship, and the economic depression had fallen on the Jews no less than any other social group.

As throughout Europe, few British Jews took Hitler at his word, and there remained an optimism that this bad period would in time come to an end.

The refugees who came here were completely displaced. Often they were young. Often they had come hurriedly with little time to prepare themselves emotionally, or to say goodbye. They left behind parents, family and friends. Sometimes they came with siblings, but often they were separated even from these. There was little recognition of the trauma of their departure, let alone curiosity about what they had endured under the Nazi terror. Habits of silent suffering that originated in Germany were compounded in Britain.

---

*

As far as the non-Jewish reception was concerned, bear in mind we were very poor conversationalists. Every time it was the same.

What's your name?

Where do you come from?

Is it true what they say about Herr Hitler?

And after, what do you think about England?

And after that the conversation stopped. Interest waned. We were looking at one another across a gap, across a valley.

---

*

It's dangerous to generalise but the Jewish population was both happy and embarrassed with us. On one side they saw us as poor little lost sheep and their emotions said let's help them. On the other hand Jews are neurotic and apprehensive and the last thing the Jewish community needed was some more foreigners, and particularly Jerrys. So therefore there was ambivalence. Yes, you are welcome. But how long are you staying? Are you going to move on soon?

With very few exceptions, all the refugees of this period describe the same sense of displacement. Despite individual acts of kindness and charity, they felt themselves to be unrecognised and unvalued. Their unexpressed rage and grief at being separated from their parents probably amplified their sense of distance from those who met them and took care of them. They would have felt that these were the wrong people looking after them. They would have withdrawn, or been angry at those who had unsurped their own parents. Few people in those days would have understood and accepted the burden of these feelings. In addition, they came from a different culture, as often as not an assimilated German one quite different from the orthodox religious culture that had emanated from Eastern Europe. Old snobberies and antagonisms were woven around the original bitterness and pain.

In 1941 the Association of Jewish Refugees came into being, and it seems to have been significant in providing a sense of community for the dispossessed.

Two events early in the war added to the sense of displacement experienced both by the refugees and by young Jews already here. The first was the internment, in 1940, after the fall of Holland, of most adult male Jewish refugees, and many females, in order to avoid the feared 'fifth column'. Those who had escaped the barbed wire in Germany found themselves behind it for months on end in the land of their saviours.

The inability of the British to recognise the distinctness of Jews and their needs was echoed in the mass evacuation of children from the heavily bombed cities. Many children found themselves billeted with families who had no appreciation at all of their difference. They were given bacon for breakfast. They were taken to church and Sunday school. They learned to love and appreciate the Harvest Festival and Christmas. Some children only came to be reminded that they were Jewish when they returned to their families at the end of the war.

For almost two years Britain waited for Hitler's threatened invasion. But for British Jews, the threat had a special meaning, as Nazi sympathisers here gathered names of prominent Jews, socialists and trade-unionists for Hitler's death-list.

Anti-Semitism in Britain had diminished, but not disappeared, with the advent of war.

---------------------------------*---------------------------------

When I went to school and we studied The Merchant of Venice *I sat in the middle of that class and I was Shylock. I could feel the eyes on me and I could think, 'Am I really Shylock? Is that what I am?' When we did* Oliver Twist *I was Fagin. The eyes were all on me. So this was the sort of thing one felt, that one was the odd man out, the foreigner, the stranger, and it made one angry because this was during the early war years when this country had gone to war with Germany. We were on the side of the angels and had gone to war with Germany because they practised racism and anti-Semitism and I was both angry and confused by the fact that I was being made the subject of anti-Semitism. People were going out and offering their lives against this. My father served in the First World War. At a later date I served in the forces myself.*

The war itself provided a diversion from anxiety. On the face of it, the Jews of Britain, like the Jews of every country that Hitler occupied, inured themselves against the fear of the possible consequences. 'Somehow or other it would be all right.' 'It couldn't happen to us.' Dealing with the Blitz and the war effort, daily survival, would have been enough in itself for the conscious mind to cope with.

There remains a gap that is hard to explain between peoples' conscious recollection of their experience, and what we believe to have been their experience from hindsight. Nowhere is this gap more acute than in British Jews' remembrance of their learning of the Holocaust.[10] The great majority of British Jews who went through the war as adults will date their first learning of the death camps and the gas chambers from the liberation of Belsen in 1945. Yet newspaper headlines of June 1942 in the majority of the daily papers of the time – *The Times, Guardian, Express, Mail, Telegraph* – as well as the *Jewish Chronicle*, attest to the mass murder of the Jews and spell out the means that were being used. Any reasonably alert and literate person would have had access to this information. It appears that it was unbelievable, unassimilable, until victory in the war had ensured that the Jews of Britain were not to suffer the same fate.

---------------------------------*---------------------------------

I had a very British war, not a Jewish war at all. As far as I was concerned we were absolutely cut off from the continent. I had no idea what was happening in Germany. I'm very glad I didn't because it's awful to know that terrible things are happening, and to be absolutely powerless to do anything about them.

I think those of us who didn't know and only discovered afterwards had more peace of mind than those who did.

The shame of powerlessness itself, the sense of impotence to affect the fate of fellow-Jews on the European mainland, must have helped to breed this strange selective amnesia.

✳

I sometimes read people say, 'Well, we didn't know.' I find it very hard to believe. There was a lot of information coming over. There were lots of photographs.

There wasn't much you could do. What could you do to prevent Germans who'd overrun the whole of Europe? Nothing you could do really. Except you raised your voice, you cried. For what good that did.

As has been well documented, Britain and the Allies, despite repeated requests, refused to take even those small steps towards the end of the war that could have ameliorated the horror for Europe's Jews – bombing the railways that carried the death trains, or the gas chambers themselves. Jewish passivity echoed official reluctance. And few Jewish lives were saved.

🕯🕯🕯🕯🕯

In the Shadow of the Holocaust

✳

There should have been a great overwhelming joy and release when the war finished. It happened for a lot of people but it didn't happen for us. It didn't happen for the Jews of the East End for the simple reason, of course, we got news of the Holocaust. So that all of us, whoever we were, were touched directly by it. No letters came from anywhere.

They were all dead.

Along with this comes Hiroshima as well, remember. They came together. It was as if we understood that we couldn't celebrate because Hitler wasn't the

end of something but the beginning of something else. A new phase had happened.
We were the first people to receive notice of that change.

We were brought up to believe that if you lie you'll get punished, that if you
cheat you'll get your comeuppance. God is good. Right will triumph over evil.
And what happened? It didn't work out that way. We were completely thrown.
Evil had triumphed. Dehumanisation had come to the surface. And I think
that's where the communities started to die. People were going in all directions.
It was at that point where people started to make separate lives for themselves.

It was too much to face, the Holocaust, and we didn't talk about it
afterwards. It was a freezing of the emotions. That was the beginning of the
disintegration of, if you like, the emotional community, as opposed to the
physical break-up. I think that that came first. When people started to move
off in various directions, the schism had already occurred.

We who grew up in the shadow of the war, grew up also into the frozen
despair, the loss of faith, the buried sense of grief and outrage that this
passage describes. But the language was not there, the words were not
used, and in their place came silence, a deep depression, and a mystery
that even now is only just beginning to be unravelled.

On the one hand we glimpsed the ferocity of Jewish suffering; there was
a dark message of silent pride in our Jewishness. On the other, there was
a desperate drive for security and educational success, careers, acceptance
in the English world. There was little sense of joy in Jewish history
or learning. Little sense of God. We felt a huge weight of undefined
responsibility, as though the burden for what had happened had been
passed to us. A deep sense of unease and disturbance surfaced in our
dreams.

✳

I don't remember being told about the Holocaust. I just remember feeling
incredible fear. I knew the stuff was around . . . I suppose I was about ten or
eleven when I had the dream first. It was a recurring dream and probably as
I dreamt it over the years it changed as I changed. I don't think I told anybody
about it. I think as a child I was a bit ashamed about it. It was about me being
in bed at night, safely, and we lived in a house and on my small room I had a
balcony outside. And the dream was that I was safely in my bed asleep and
suddenly the Nazis came over the balcony, there was a great deal of noise,
there was a great deal of light. They smashed down the door. There was

breaking of glass and they came and took me away and that's where the dream stopped each time. And I got to the stage where I was frightened about dreaming this dream and when I was little what I did was, I made myself safe. And the way I made myself safe was that I built a square of teddies and dollies around me and I slept in the middle ...

The new generation was to be protected from the anxieties of those who had lived through the war. It was to be given the best possible education, to be pushed towards secure, professional careers. For the older generation the priority was setting up a house, a family, establishing a career. In London, those who had ambition mostly moved northwest, or to the West End. You settled for the 'uncut moquet and the three-piece suite, hire purchase'. You couldn't ask the big questions about God or morality, because they only led back to the Holocaust.

The Holocaust cast its shadow over all Jews. It seeped into the fabric of all of our lives. And yet at that time, other than in fragments, it didn't and couldn't unify us. We were unable to drew comfort from one another. It shattered us, turned us on the defensive, pushed us inside ourselves, made us bitter and rancorous. We couldn't name the fear.

※

Not getting into the news, being quiet, keeping a low profile, not wanting to be ruffled by anything, not ruffling anything, just remaining to not make a noise and disappear. I suppose we were then colluding with each other to disappear into England and to lose our identity. However, enjoying being ourselves in private, at weddings and simchas and things like that, fine. But no longer do you have the candles in the window.

It needs to be remembered, also, that the end of the war, which was meant to signal the end of all wars and the end of anti-Semitism also, did no such thing. Within months Mosley was on the march again, and the struggles that Jews were waging against the British mandate in Palestine provided a foil for a renewed groundswell of anti-Semitism that was particularly English, and also international in its dimensions – pogroms and massacres of Jews continued, for example, in Poland in 1946. Once more the underlying doubts about our belonging in Britain were fuelled. British policy to Jewish survivors of the camps also raised questions for post-war Jews. What has become recently apparent – that it was easier for Latvian and Ukrainian Nazis to enter Britain after the war than for their Jewish victims – was then reflected in the harsh policy towards Holocaust survivors in British-zone Displaced Person Camps who wished to go to Palestine. Were the British really on our side or not? And if not, what could we do anyway but get on with our lives. The low-profile strategy prevailed.

The cracks started to appear for the new generation when they went to school. Many public schools at that time had Jewish quotas. You could choose to participate in the hymn service, making your own decisions as to whether there were words or phrases that you would mouth silently or not sing at all. Or you could sit and wait it out with the Sikhs, Jehovah's Witnesses and other conscientious objectors, and file into the hall just before the announcements. You could choose to ignore the occasional swastika, or the fact that it was usually a Jewish boy who was the victim of the school bully, or the teasing about Jewish wealth. It was hard to label this real anti-Semitism, when anti-Semitism could only be measured in terms of the murder of the six million.

And what of the six million? The pervasive message was that it was the Jews' own fault that they had died. That they had died because they didn't fight back. They went quietly to their deaths and colluded in their own destruction. Somehow or other, the shame attached itself to the victim and not to the perpetrator, the Hun, who was cunning and brutal and the worthy enemy of a thousand comic books.

The chameleon is the image that I have of that time, of having to change colour rapidly in order to fit in as far as one could and at the same time sometimes fiercely fighting to defend what was true for me and also defend others who I saw getting really harsh treatment in those circumstances.

We learned to be discreet about our Jewishness. We learned to defend ourselves with humour or through our achievements. Success would make us impregnable, or at the very least give us a margin of safety. We learned how to negotiate English reserve, English understatement, wry and barbed English humour. We found our heroes in the English eccentrics, the outsiders whom we also saw struggling with the rules that bothered us, the comics – Tony Hancock, the Goons, and later the Beyond the Fringe team.

Some of us with a spiritual bent flirted with Christianity. There was little curiosity about what it meant for us to be Jews, no sense that this was a part of ourselves that we might want to develop, or know more about. The only way to 'belong' at a religious level to the school was through Christianity. It was taken for granted that there was no alternative. For most of us, Judaism just wasn't on the agenda. As a repository of ideals, it was remote. As a way of life it appeared irrelevant.

For those of us who grew up in more orthodox homes, with a more defined sense of their Jewishness, the conflict took on sharper dimensions.

———————————————————*———————————————————

A Catholic girl once told me that I killed Christ, my people, in a very offensive way and I hit her and she hit me and we had a real fistfight surrounded by umpteen others. I'm quite ashamed of it now, but the school's attitude was horrendous. They wouldn't accept that I had been provoked. What I did certainly wasn't right but they showed no sensitivity to the fact that I had been very abused about my religion. I was deeply upset and went rushing home thinking my parents would support me. And they weren't prepared to make a thing about it. They just accepted that that's the way people think about the Jews and that's just what you have to put up with. I didn't like it at all. By the time I was about fourteen I'd picked up the very clear message that if I really cared about my Jewish identity I couldn't carry on living in England. It was as if I had to make a choice between becoming assimilated or being part of the Jewish culture which I absolutely loathed, which was ostentatious, flashy and not into anything thinking. It was as if the world of the arts out there didn't exist. I knew afterwards there was another world but I never met it growing up.

The Holocaust fed and amplified British Jews' insecurities. It created a pressure within families to stay close, and on children both to be successful and to conform. Survival became the watchword, and issues of meaning were postponed to safer times. For the refugees from Europe of the thirties and the survivors who came after the war, the pressures were similar, but multiplied many times. They were on their own, surviving in a strange land, learning a new language, struggling to build a new life. Gradually they had to come to terms with the likelihood that the parents and family they had left behind them in Europe had been murdered. Not for them the chance to earn a little money and then bring over their parents, like the previous generations of immigrants. They had to grieve on their own. They had to accept what kindness they were offered, find friends, love, family, work. They had to find acceptance. They had to survive.

------------------------------------*------------------------------------

It wasn't easy to establish yourself here. You became a little nobody and didn't have any money. You could work in a household. Or you could become a nurse. These were the two things open to you.

The English were like a different world. They spoke a language you couldn't understand. They'd say 'Do come to tea', or whatever, in a very polite way, and you knew they didn't mean it. You were so baffled and bewildered, and you felt very pushed out. You were the foreigner. It took me years and years to acknowledge that I was a refugee, I suppose I didn't want to be in a special category, so I said, 'Well, I left Germany, that's it.' They all seemed to be laughing and I didn't know what they were laughing about. So I just laughed.

For many of the refugees, coming from assimilated Jewish homes in Germany or Austria, where they had little sense of Jewish religion or ritual, it was no easier to find a place among English Jews than among non-Jews.

------------------------------------*------------------------------------

We had a very uncertain attitude towards Judaism and Jewish people. There was quite a lot of anti-Semitism in the German Jews, which was wrong but I do realise it.

The Jews I met all seemed so orthodox and that was something we found very difficult to accept. They had all sorts of customs and we just couldn't relate. And I was really resentful because I wasn't going to let Hitler tell me who I was.

I have a particular memory of people saying to me 'Well, you know, you abandoned Judaism and that's your punishment,' or something like this. It was like a completely different world.

Some refugees kept their distance from the religion, and even from their Jewish identities. They had never practised, and the Holocaust had destroyed for them the possibility of faith. It was too painful to be near a synagogue, because it evoked too much of what had been destroyed, too many dark times. The pain would be masked by rationalism, adopted by some as a moral faith in itself, in the hope that reason could stem the tide of future mass-murderers. It was as though belief itself was to blame for what had happened. And all beliefs held collectively, including Judaism, were now suspect.

Most of the children of these refugees grew up without an extended family. The sense of pressure within the family was even more amplified for them. The feeling of insecurity, of imminent flight, of not fully belonging, has been inherited.

Where their parents have remained unfamiliar with Jewish traditions, without a culture to pass on, they have also felt like outsiders within Anglo-Jewry, without a shared language: out of place in Jewish schools or Jewish youth movements, finding their cultural roots in Austro-Germany rather than further east, uncomfortable if called upon to attend synagogue – for a marriage, a barmitzvah, high holy days. Not wishing to face their ignorance or discomfort, they kept themselves on the margins of Jewish life, until perhaps their own children called them back, or they found that they were able to share common perceptions with other children of refugees.

Often the families that suffered most for their Jewishness ended least able to appreciate or enjoy it. The Jewish people were wounded. We needed healing, but within ourselves the resources were not available.

A New State

Into the despond came Israel. After the war the need for a Jewish homeland, a refuge, a state, a place where Jews could control their own destinies, was generally accepted by British Jews. Indeed, with the appointment of Brodetsky as president of the Board of Deputies in 1940, the older families had finally lost their hold on the Jewish leadership here, and the pro-Zionists gained ascendancy for the first time.[11] Israel achieved independence in 1948. For British Jews, and particularly those who had been Zionists before the war, this was a moment to be cherished, a hugely creative struggle for and affirmation of survival. Nothing could redeem the tragedy of the Holocaust, but the newly emerging state could provide comfort and more.

---∗---

As far as I was concerned this was the first time Jews could be represented on the world stage without having to kowtow or duck or run or fight ... We took an overcoat off, if you know what I mean. We were able to stand upright and look the world in the eye and say, 'We're Jews, we're proud of being Jews.'

How deep this went for many British Jews, it's hard to say. For many, the shock of the Holocaust was still too recent for the joy of Israel to be easily absorbed. (Of course, numbers of British Jews made *aliyah* to Israel in the immediate aftermath of the founding of the state. Here I speak of the majority who were not Zionists before the war, and for whom the founding of Israel was a fact to be reckoned with outside their immediate experience.) As people began to visit, so the 'dream' of Israel began to enter people's consciousness.

Israel became another place in which to invest hope. And once again, the hopes were out of proportion. Israel would be a haven for the Jewish people. A model of social justice, for Jews and Arabs. It would be truly a light unto the nations. A great social experiment, the kibbutz, would provide a vision of cooperative daily life. Jews would be rescued from their role in the diaspora as hunchbacked, obsequious, dependent, assimilated, backwardly religious traders and moneylenders, to become proud, upright, handsome and secular pioneers, farmers and soldiers.

Those who went to visit experienced the wonder of being in a country where the majority were Jews. They marvelled at the Jewish shop names. The fact that the dustmen were Jewish. The Jewish women in army uniform. The Jewish tractor-drivers and herdsmen on the kibbutz. All this did indeed give them a sense of wholeness and pride in their Jewishness.

And also they experienced the flip-side of the dream. The Israelis' contempt for the diaspora mirrored their own insecurity. If you wanted to be a real Jew you had to be in Israel. And yet the great majority of British Jews did not make the journey. 'I thought I'd go, but...' '– but then my mother died and my father was left alone.' '– but then I went to university.' '– but then I found out what I'd earn.' '– but then I was just establishing the business.' '– but my wife gets ill with the heat.'

The self-contempt and insecurity British Jewry felt as an outcome of the Holocaust got mixed up with a kind of deference to Israel. Israel was a wonderful place. All Jews needed Israel as a refuge. We'll go for holidays to Israel. We'll raise money for Israel. We'll *identify* with Israel. But we don't want to live there. And we feel somehow guilty and ashamed about that.

Israel is an issue we are understandably sensitive about. But we must separate the real relationship and the real achievements from what could be called the 'dream of Israel', which took on its own life, separate from the reality, and became a kind of substitute Jewish identity for many Jews here after war and the Holocaust. Later, as more young people made *aliyah*, or spent years in Israel studying or working, the links became more solid and tangible. But at that time, somehow we separated ourselves from the history and traditions of the Jews of Europe whence we came, and we invested our hopes in Israel. As we will see in the next section, support for Israel became a way of being Jewish.

We found ourselves in a double exile: exile from the promised land, and exile from the very culture which had grown up to sustain us in exile. This was not fertile ground.

Drifting Away

The defensiveness of Anglo-Jewry reflected itself institutionally. The vast proportion of the budget of the Board of Deputies of British Jews – the central body of communal authority – was focussed on defence.

———————————————*—————————————————

The Holocaust was one of the things which made the whole community pull itself in, draw itself together, encourage almost a ghetto mentality, as any persecution would ... We felt that if we didn't help ourselves no one else is going to help us, because that's been so much of the experience of our people through the ages. So I think it made the Jewish community much more self-sufficient and self-dependent.

When Jews were refused entry to golf clubs (or banks, or public schools, or departments of surgery), we didn't make a fuss. We didn't do what the blacks in America were to do a generation later, and demonstrate. The

offence was rarely so blatant, or so absolute. So we waited our time. Or we set up our own institutions.

The result was an Anglo-Jewry enclosed, provincial, obsessed by its committees and communal institutions; busy, dynamic and apparently empty. It was miracle enough that this community had survived at all. But for many it wasn't enough.

———————————— ✳ ————————————

I wanted to get away, and in so doing I hurt all of them. It wasn't known, to step outside, to maybe go with a shiksa, *not to be known as respectable, to go away for nights and not come back. And that was my own journey. I had to go through that in order to try and understand it, to see it in perspective.*

―――――――――――――――*―――――――――――――――

The thing that sticks in my mind is somebody giving the parallel of German Jews who felt themselves German first, Jewish second, and their subsequent fate, for their persecutors continued to see them as Jewish first and German second and they were led to the gas chambers because of their Jewishness. The implication being that should I feel myself secular, English, before I felt myself to be Jewish, then that might lead to similar problems, that I might be treading on dodgy ground.

That reinforced an army of shoulds that were thrown at us, explicitly or more often implicitly, like, you should marry, you should marry a Jewish girl, you should be involved in your synagogue community, you should have Jewish friends, you should be interested in Jewish things, you should go to Israel on your holidays. And at the age of twenty I needed a stronger justification for those things than the survival of the Jewish people alone. I needed to know what I was going to get from being Jewish.

The very defensiveness and insularity of large parts of Anglo-Jewry, its very desire to hold onto its young, was strangling them. Many of the brightest and most creative began to drift away, and still do. Few would describe it as a conscious move. They would say that they just happened to develop other friends, other interests. University, or careers, or social life, or marriage, just happened to take them in different directions. Judaism, Jewish life, Jewish culture, Jewish history just happened to take a back seat. Until the onset of children, or the death of a parent, maybe encouraged them to take an interest again.

Their idealism was invested in socialism, Third-World freedom struggles, feminism, ecology; their need for healing in therapy groups, analysis, holistic health, consciousness-raising; their spiritual growth in meditation, Rajneesh, the New Age – often with the fervour and excess of both youthful rebellion in general and the craziness inherited from the Holocaust in particular. There were a host of creative liberatory trends thickly populated by Jews, but never *as* Jews. The parents both despaired of and secretly envied their young.

The community became polarised, between those who saw themselves as being on the inside, and those who felt themselves outside, and drifting away.

Anti-Semitism: Sacrificing the Pig

We have no reason to view the movement away entirely negatively. The Jewish story is made up of periods of stultification and periods of rebellion – and the rebels initiate the renewal of the culture. But some of the post-war drift lacks the passion of rebellion. In the secular Christian culture of Britain, where the shift away is reinforced by negative stereotypes of Judaism and Jewish life, we are forced to be suspicious. Renewal can only occur when the forces that inhibit a strong Jewish identity are known and confronted.

Let's look at some of the negative stereotypes:

Judaism is backward. It has been superceded by Christianity/secularism, which are respectively a) more loving b) more rational.

Judaism is not concerned with spirituality.

Judaism is unchanging, just a lot of archaic and restrictive rules.

Judaism is the most patriarchal of the major religions, the most anti-woman. Indeed, the Jews gave the world patriarchy.

Jews ought to assimilate, and then there would be no more anti-Semitism. (This goes with various strictures about Jews being loud, ostentatious, flashy – i.e. more Continental in style.)

Then there are the old chestnuts about Jews loving money (materialistic is the epithet these days that describes the Jewish attempt to find material security), various versions of Jewish conspiracy theory ('Jews control the theatre/media' was strongly pedalled during the 'Perdition' controversy[12]), and Jews only being interested in their own. Add to this a few jokes about JAPs (Jewish American Princesses), Jewish control of banking and finance, and Jewish vulgarity; 'Zionism is racism'; and the complete absence of expressed interest in Jewish life or ritual, and you have a good enough recipe for Jewish self-hatred, or at least self-indifference.

Now is not the time to refute these stereotypes. We are a small way only along the road of rescuing Judaism from common perceptions of it. Christian contempt for Jews as a people has become unfashionable in educated circles. The contempt now tends to attach itself to the religion or the desire for national security expressed in the state of Israel. Few of us feel seriously threatened by anti-Semitism in a daily, physical, sense. But many of us have internalised attitudes to our Jewishness which are worth tickling out, because they undermine us if they are left to fester.

British Jews of the wartime and post-war generations have difficulty in dealing with anti-Semitism. The Board of Deputies appears always to be trying to minimise it. For example, recently the leaders of the Board withheld information from the public, and hence the Jewish community, about the vandalism of graves in Edmonton, which followed a series of attacks on Orthodox Jews in North London, saying they wished to avoid copycat incidents. Since such incidents have been a feature of British society on and off for the past two hundred years, it would have seemed that the cat was already out of the bag. In addition, the Board had been presented with evidence[13] that the attacks were imminent, and were part of an international anti-Semitic conspiracy. Days after the Edmonton attack came the well-publicised desecration of Jewish graves in the village of Carpentras in France.

The difference between the two leaderships' response is instructive. In France, admittedly responding to a more serious situation, the Conseil Représentatif des Juifs de France (CRIF) immediately called for a public demonstration, and for public expressions of support for the struggle against anti-Semitism. Two hundred thousand people took to the streets, including the French President, François Mitterrand, and the regular television programmes were shelved on all channels in order to show a documentary on the Holocaust. The French were invited to show their support for the Jews, and they did. Jews emerged feeling proud at having stood up for themselves, and well supported by the French people as a whole.

In Britain, we were encouraged to keep our heads down and hope that it would all blow over. Our major communal institutions didn't reach out to non-Jews for support. We didn't even let them know how we feel when our graves are desecrated. We just keep *shtum*.

It's a communal version of the story that began this section of the book: the couple in Manchester who went through the weekend not admitting to their hosts that they had been offended. But this is more complicated. At the same time as they protect us from knowledge of the worst anti-Semitic acts, the leadership and the *Jewish Chronicle* (not its organ, but a good indicator of what is going on in a certain section of British Jewry) are obsessed by anti-Semitism. They continually keep it on the boil. Not too hot, but not too cold either. Just enough to keep us worried, and keep us in the fold; but not as much as would make us want to do something on our own initiative that might upset the apple-cart.

What happens to us internally when we keep silent about these outrages? When we shrug them off, pretend that they are not important, pretend that we aren't affected? Our legitimate pain and fury become transformed into something else, something more destructive, even though we recognise it as a traditional response through the ages: on the one hand we end up feeling, as Jews, very superior to those who denigrate or attack us; and on the other, our repressed anger is amplified into a murderous rage, born of our shame and our humiliation.

As Jews we've always used the traditional notion of ourselves as a chosen people to defend ourselves against attacks. We know intellectually that our chosenness doesn't mean that we're better or superior, but rather that we have certain responsibilities in this world. But clinging to our specialness, secretly or openly, we gain comfort and consolation and a defence against the world outside. We look down at our persecutors – the Board dismisses them as 'hooligans' – and see them as victims of the cultural, social and educational malaise of the shadow-end of this century. Still, though, we end up being the victims of their frustrations and their anger. Feeling superior is, in the end, not a lot of good; it creates an aloof distance at which we can safely nurse our hurt, but no more.

We have to tread a very delicate tightrope as Jews who are also British. Our dual identity means that there are times when we are going to be experienced as different, threatening, undermining, outsiders. We can fall off the tightrope by pretending that we're just the same as 'them' and all these digs and jokes and insults and attacks don't mount up to anything. But we can fall off the tightrope the other way too. When every non-Jew becomes a potential threat, or when Christians en masse continue to be seen as our persecutors, or when our paranoia rises so much that the mildest less-than-appreciative comment about Jews or Jewish behaviour or Israel becomes an anti-Semitic attack, then we are failing to see another kind of reality, a difficult reality about ourselves. Sometimes we are the ones who are attacking; we are the ones who are persecuting; we are the ones harbouring the hatred, out of the store of rage that we have put away over the generations.

It is vital for our collective health that we recognise our anger, and find ways of channelling it constructively. The Holocaust came at the end of generations of persecution – real persecution, not fantasy persecution. And we are still suffering from the trauma of what happened to us collectively. In our souls we are all survivors, whatever our age, our background and our experience. And we are still mourning what we have lost, we are still hurting and we are still raging. We rarely allow it to surface. It is, understandably, much easier to project it unconsciously and see 'them' as the ones who hate.

There are elements in Israel acting out the aggression. The pent-up fury of generations says, 'Someone else can be the victim now.'

Sometimes we come to turn the anger against ourselves, or against other Jews. We experience it as shame, and doubt. We criticise ourselves for our inadequacy as Jews. Or we criticise others in the community. We bitterly attack Jews whom we experience as betraying the years of martyrdom.

Or we dissociate ourselves from the community altogether. We come to internalise the anti-Semitism. The names, some of them, begin to stick.

If we could face our pain and anger; our rage and our hatred; our doubts and insecurities about who we are as Jews, about our right to be here and stand up for ourselves, the problem of anti-Semitism wouldn't disappear, but it would be a lot easier to confront. We need neither fend away the non-Jewish world nor disappear inside it. We could joyfully embrace what we like about it, and without fear express what we didn't like. We could tell non-Jewish people about ourselves; we have made of ourselves a mystery, without meaning to.

Already over the past ten to fifteen years this process has begun. Many young Jews today exude confidence. They would find it hard to recognise themselves in this section of the book. No longer exiled from themselves, their exodus is under way. The next section of the book tells their story, and the story of others who no longer wish to hide.

---------------------------------*---------------------------------

For all that one doesn't want to, as it were, paint a picturesque panorama of the East End with its poverty and all of that, there was a warmth of community living which has gone completely out of my life. It's like the child's innocence has gone. It's a useless regret, but it's there when I think about it.

Intellectually, no regret at all. I married a woman who's not Jewish. No regrets, on the contrary. I have a child, a girl who has no notion of the Jewish religion at all, and I've cut that out too. There is something that nags at bottom that I can't give words to, and I don't want to appear mystifying or anything. There is something which is emotional, but it's not a regret about religion. It's more a regret about being with people, than religion.

About belonging. I don't belong. I don't feel like an Englishman, I don't belong. I accept it. There I am. So I'm not an Englishman. I count myself – what? – a European. I know it's a cliché, but that's how I feel.

Part 3
EXODUS

8
Exodus Past and Present

---*---

I was brought up in a very Jewish home but also a very English home. My father had fought for England in the First World War. He ended up as a major. He considered himself an English gentleman who was Jewish by religion and he believed to his dying day that the British would always keep their word. So when the Six-Day War came and I knew that there was a treaty in existence, I waited for the British army to walk in to help the Israelis. And I remember going out of my house to a shop on the day that the war started and I said to someone in the shop, 'But, we have a treaty with Israel, we have guaranteed their borders.' And the woman behind the counter said to me, 'You wouldn't expect us to send our boys out to help a lot of Jews, would you?'

That was the moment when I realised that when it comes to the crunch the Jews can only rely on other Jews. It made me even more aware than I had ever been before that I had a responsibility to all Jews everywhere, because I was in a very comfortable position, I was leading a very happy life, and I had to help others who need that help.

Since 1967 Anglo-Jewry has been experiencing a form of exodus. 'Exodus' is the Biblical paradigm for the liberation of a group following the oppressions of exile. In exile we live on the defensive and are subservient to others. Exodus speaks of our struggle to become free. In exile we feel that our lives are determined by how the non-Jewish world sees us – or how we imagine they see us. In exile we are divided inside ourselves, Jews in private and British in public. Exodus is a 'coming out', an assertion of pride. It speaks of our movement towards self-determination: deciding for ourselves how we will be Jewish in Britain.

The Book of Genesis tells of the vicissitudes of the individuals in a single family – the family of Abraham and Sarah. The book ends with the family in exile, in Egypt. But this exile is seen as part of a larger scheme of purpose. For it is only as strangers in a strange land that this family grows and multiplies and becomes a people. And this people Israel will become the people of God, a people who will transform human history – and who will, in turn, be transformed by history.

Ironically, it is Pharaoh who first recognised that Israel are now no longer a large family group but have become a 'people' (Exodus 1: 9). For this they will suffer. The Jewish people was forged out of the common experience of oppression. Our story as a people begins in shame:[1] the shame of living subject to the dictates of others, the shame of living without autonomy, the shame of knowing who we are only when 'they' are against us.

Nobody who has sat at a *seder* table, or picked up a prayerbook in the synagogue or for *kiddush* on Friday nights, could have avoided the omnipresent reminder that our peoplehood stems from our deliverance from Egyptian slavery. The texts of our tradition continually reinforce this message: you are the Jewish people now because you were once saved by your God from 'the house of bondage'. The seder ceremony is only one of a multitude of traditional ritual practices and ethical demands that are rooted in this memory – or are ordained in order to maintain this memory.

This emphasis on the Exodus story involves a threefold assertion. Firstly, and obviously: without this historical memory and experience there would be no Jewish people. Secondly, the deliverance of the people from oppression had an ulterior motive. Freedom from slavery led to, and was a precondition for, a new kind of 'service', symbolised by Sinai. The creation of a people was followed by a revelation to the people. Servitude to human beings was to be replaced by service to the Divine.[2] Time and again Moses's demand to Pharaoh, 'Let my people go!' is followed by the rationale, in the name of God, '. . . that they may serve Me'. Freedom entailed responsibilities. And this became the basis for the third assertion that emerges from the centrality of the exodus experience.

Our special knowledge of what it meant to suffer at the hands of others obliged the Jewish people to work for a world freed from such oppression. And this was to be done primarily through a scrupulous avoidance of all acts of oppression of their own. They were to model for all nations patterns of human interaction ruled by justice.[3] Thirty-six times the Torah repeats, in one form or another, the key sentiment that emerges from Israel's exodus: 'You shall not wrong a stranger, neither shall you oppress them – for you were strangers in the land of Egypt' (Exodus 22: 20). The constant reiteration of this message testifies both to its importance within the ethical system of the people, but also to an awareness of just how problematic it is for human beings to avoid oppressing others once they have a modicum of power.

All this may seem a long way from the burgeoning activity of post-1967 Anglo-Jewry. Yet the metaphor of 'exodus' can help illuminate the emergence of new and disparate assertions of Jewishness that have followed and been catalysed by the Six-Day War fought between Israel and the Arab nations. Since 1967, Anglo-Jewry has begun to discover that being Jewish and being British can be complementary rather than opposing expressions of personal identity.

The titles of the following chapters in this section correspond to four linked phrases from the Biblical exodus, recorded as God's 'promises' to Moses of His continuing involvement in Israel's history:

... I will bring you out from under the burdens of the Egyptians, and I will deliver you from their bondage, and I will redeem you ... and I will take you to Me as a people ... (Exodus 6: 6–7).

Later Jewish tradition utilised these phrases to justify the annual cele-bratory drinking of the four cups of wine during the Passover seder as we recall our exodus from the Egypt of old. To use them in the context of a contemporary, metaphorical exodus – a post-1967 Anglo-Jewish revival – entails certain ironies.

Firstly, there is the *chutzpah* of using Biblical formulations to frame expressions of Jewish identity that may be avowedly secular, and even anti-religious, in character or purpose. Clearly the post-1967 mosaic of Anglo-Jewish groupings asserting Jewish identity does not represent a religious revival in any traditional sense. Yet the sense of belonging this exemplifies, and encourages, seems to testify to the unique adaptive ability of the Jewish people. The affirmation of a hope-filled continuity of being, coming so soon after the despair of the Holocaust, bears witness to a creative life-giving spirit which animates our collective survival.

But liberation is not always welcomed or understood by those who hear about it. When Moses reported to the children of Israel his new awareness of the divine involvement in their history, the children of Israel remained unreceptive and unimpressed: 'they hearkened not to Moses due to impatience of spirit and the harshness of their slavery' (Exodus 6: 9). In our impatience and out of our insecurity we continue to oppress each other. Our sense of collective Jewish achievement in Britain is marred by our reluctance to listen to and learn from those who see the world differently.

It is hard to recognise that one is part of a larger movement towards a liberated sense of Jewish identity when one feels beleaguered even within the Jewish community itself. But there is probably no group within the community that does not feel under attack from another quarter of the Jewish world. We are quick to spot those with whom we disagree and slow to recognise the limitations of our own hard-won positions. Someone else is always doing it the wrong way.

A sense of crisis is never far below the surface, defying Anglo-Jewry's self-confidence to reassert itself. Just as the celebratory nature of the original exodus is far outweighed, in the Biblical account, by the grumblings and dissent of the Israelites once Egypt has been left behind, for us too the fissiparous and argumentative nature of the community can destroy our capacity to celebrate our achievements. Ironically, involvement in an 'exodus' seems to entail the failure to understand fully what is happening. Immersed in our subjectivity, our 'impatience of spirit' clouds our capacity to see.

And yet, within a plethora of contemporary settings, we are seeing new dimensions of meaning being grafted on to the traditional lessons of Exodus.[4]

First, there is the awareness that the oppression of that ultimate manifestation of 'Egypt' – the Holocaust – has not defeated us or destroyed us. What emerged from the rejection and subjugation of those events was not only disillusionment and despair, but determination. Part of our exodus consists of our sheer survival as a people: and, in addition, a new homeland, promised from days of old, has been born out of the ashes. The Jewish people have returned to history.

Secondly, although we may feel confused about the sources of contemporary revelation, there are new affirmations of Jewish life which defy the efforts to deny us our right to exist in this world. Not only the Zionist enterprise, but every attempt – religious and secular – to reassess or reformulate Jewish purpose is part of the process of revelation. The creation of post-war communities and institutions, the flowering of Jewish learning, our continuing artistic and cultural and political endeavours – all these manifestations of the spirit testify to our hopefulness. They are Sinai after our exodus.

And, thirdly, there is the continuation of the emphasis, in spite of what we have experienced, maybe because of what we have experienced, on *Tikkun Olam*: the restoring and repairing of our fragmented world. Our suffering is transformed, at its best, into commitment to others through our sensitivity to their suffering; into an identification with those who struggle, domestically or internationally, for their own freedom from oppression: political, material, or spiritual.

These new applications of the old lessons underlie our own Anglo-Jewish exodus.

———————————————————————————✳———————————————————————————

Liberation is always a process. I'm not sure that anyone is actually there. Feeling free to question, to struggle, to examine, to recognise that assumptions are there for challenging – that, for me, is to do with being on the road to liberation . . .

9
'I will lead you out ...'
Anglo-Jewry and Israel

The first Ashkenazi Chief Rabbi of Palestine, Rav Kook, once said that the Jewish way to spiritual renewal was to 'renew the old and to hallow the new'. He saw the devoutly secular Zionist enterprise as a disguised form of religious activity, 'a great positive force ... that, despite all estrangement, contains a vital spark of holiness'.[1] He recognised that wherever and whenever Jews take responsibility into their own hands for building their destiny, without embarrassment and without fear, there the holy work of Jewish living is being enacted.

In the years following the Six-Day War Israel seemed to me to be basically 'good': it represented social justice, it represented the possibility of a new Jew being created totally different to the image of the oppressed moneylender of European literature. My image of the diaspora was of a community that was living beyond its time, that there really was in the post-Holocaust era no future for European Jewry. Their future lay in Israel and I would become a Jew in the full sense of the word simply by living in a Jewish state . . .

Rav Kook's mystic understanding that secularism could contribute to Jewish redemption was articulated before the twin transforming Jewish experiences of modern times – the Holocaust and the establishment of the state of Israel. As such, it is a bridge between two distinct eras in Jewish history. In order to understand the significance of 1967 it is necessary to view it within the larger panorama of Jewish history – a story which we can talk about, thus far, as being a drama in three acts.[2]

The opening act of Jewish history takes us 1500 years from the exodus from Egypt to the destruction of the second Temple in Jerusalem in the year 70 CE. This huge swathe of time saw the creation of a distinctive people with holy texts and a sense of their own specialness. This insubstantial fragment of humankind, the Jewish people, felt themselves elected to be a 'light to the nations' (Isaiah 49: 6).

Latecomers on the stage of world history, their purpose on earth was to redeem humanity. In this singular task they were to be assisted by their God, who had spoken to His people at Sinai and subsequently through a series of prophets who had arisen at vital moments in the nation's history to rebuke, to warn, to cajole, to comfort, to mediate to the chosen people the wishes of the Holy One of Israel who was also the source of all that lives.

During this Biblical era the Jewish people, once freed from slavery, developed their nurturing covenantal relationship with God in the political context of – give or take periods of exile or dispersion – possession of the land of Israel. The Temple in Jerusalem, and the priesthood who ministered to it, regularised and institutionalised the contact between the people and their God. But the Roman destruction of the Temple, alien possession of the promised land, and the enslavement and dispersal of the people, saw the end of this first act of Jewish history. The ensuing crisis of faith and meaning ushered in the second act: the rabbinic era.

Over several generations the rabbinic genius transformed defeat into victory. God was no longer accessible in Jerusalem? Well then, He could be met in the synagogue, any synagogue, in any land. And not only in the synagogue. He too was in exile, as it were, but could be met through the prayers of the human heart. The sacrificial cult – the centre of Jewish worship – was no longer possible? Personal acts of justice, generosity and love were the sacrifices that were now required. Righteousness, ethical action, a multitude of *mitzvot* – these were to replace the formal rituals and pieties of old. God had abandoned His people? No: He had called them to a new stage of relationship and service, a new partnership. Through study of Torah His presence was restored. Through prayer He was present again. Through holy living the absence of God was refuted. The divine was to be encountered within the realm of everyday human activity.

All this ended in flames. The second act of Jewish history lasts nearly nineteen hundred years. It closes in Auschwitz.

The writings of Elie Wiesel contain one hauntingly memorable image which evokes the end of this era. It is the unbearable image of a child hanging on the Nazi gallows, still alive. After half an hour 'his tongue was still red, his eyes not yet glazed' and someone asks: ' "Where is God now?" And I heard a voice within me answer him: "Where is He? Here He is – He is hanging here on this gallows ..." '[3]

The post-war generations have had to wrestle with this question, born out of their disgusted horror. If our God is here we can only despair. If our God is not here we can only despair. But if this is man we must also despair. Yet Jews did not succumb to their despair. The third act of Jewish history emerged out of the despair and the powerlessness. Israel became the source of hope and of empowerment.

The knowledge that after four millennia we have been witnessing and participating in the beginning of the third act of Jewish history is sometimes too awesome to grasp. Our sense of time is often mundane and pragmatic, limited to the end of the day when we get the kids to bed, or our next birthday, or our last holiday, or perhaps, when we exercise our imaginations, some fleeting memory of our childhood. How can we possibly retain a sense of awe, or any sense of perspective, in a timescale spanning millennia?

Intuitively we have understood that something intangible but infinitely precious has gone for ever. We long for the certainties of old, yet know that we need to face the uncertainties of the future. Within weeks of the deliverance from slavery the children of Israel voice their fear of the future through their distorted view of the past: 'Would that we had died ... in the land of Egypt when we sat by the fleshpots and ate bread to the full! For you have brought us forth into this wilderness to kill this whole assembly ...' (Exodus 16: 3). Whatever we would like to be the case, there is no going back to our pre-Holocaust consciousness. Psychologically, we have begun the traumatic transition from 'exile' to 'exodus'.

For twenty years Anglo-Jewry, while emerging from the numbness surrounding our disbelief over the Holocaust, ever-mourning the losses, quietly rebuilding shattered lives in new suburbs, was also ever-mindful of Israel's fragile birth, its blossoming development, its confident death-defying, death-denying resurrection of Jewish optimism. The new experiment in Jewish self-determination was followed here with our own brand of restrained British encouragement, even a degree of genteel enthusiasm: our gentile hosts had taught us to be genteel in our passions.

Almost without our being aware of it, long-distance support for Israel became the unifying factor in our changed Jewish condition. Within a generation it seemed that the traditional priorities of Jewish life were turned on their head. In the past there used to be, preeminently, the collective belief in the reality of God and His mysterious yet guiding hand in history; secondly, there was the commitment to the study and observance of Torah; and, thirdly, there was the awareness of the Jewish people, *Klal Yisrael*, scattered throughout the world yet somehow united in purpose and destiny.

Yet the Enlightenment in Europe had severed the previous Jewish commitment to this traditional religious trinity of preoccupations – God, Torah and the people Israel. The forces of assimilation and secularism had led to massive defections from Judaism as well as to an engagement with diverse new movements of secular holiness – socialism, Zionism, Bundism, Marxism. Nevertheless, sufficient numbers of Jewish immigrants into Britain in the generations before the Second World War had retained enough of the vestiges of ancestral faith to maintain a distinctive Jewish connection to the old ways in a new land. God, Torah and Israel – the priorities of *shtetl* life – were transposed into British settings: some form of religious belief, some level of Jewish observance, some sense of Jewish community and the interdependence of Jews.

These were the residual truths lived by British Jews until the curtain fell on the second great era of Jewish history. In the years after the *shoah* we slowly awoke to the new priorities of the third act of our continuing drama. Out of our degradation there arose the conviction that dared not speak its name: the God of Israel, it seemed, had abandoned His people in their hour of need. God, the traditional hope and centre of Jewish life, had become discredited.

This cast a large question mark over the second priority of Jewish living – Torah. Some abandoned Jewish practices altogether and went the way of total assimilation: not now the adaptive name-changing of the previous generation, but the adoption of a thoroughly British way of life – remaining Jewish defied common sense. Although the majority of British Jews continued with bits and pieces of tradition, often half-heartedly, out of a vague sense of guilt or family duty, the Torah no longer had the power to rule Jewish life as it had in the past. So what was left? Only Israel, that brave new experiment in homecoming.

The old era's formula 'I believe in God' was replaced by the new incantation of Anglo-Jewry: 'I believe in Israel.' Before 1967, belief in this new force in Jewish history was still somewhat muted. The shadow of the

Holocaust continued to eclipse pride in Jewish achievements – especially when these Jewish achievements were in a distant land.

Despite the Zionist Federation's numerous *aliyah* campaigns, British Jews failed to translate their Zionist inclinations into actual emigration: a semi in the suburbs still seemed a safer (and more comfortable) bet than breaking one's back in the sun or the daily toil to maintain a tiny flat in brash and bustling Tel-Aviv. And we lived – not too comfortably, but comfortably nevertheless – with the guilt.

After all, we could always give money. And British Jews did give their money: either through what was then known as – with what seems in hindsight undetected irony – the Joint Palestine Appeal; or through the omnipresent blue-and-white collection boxes of the Jewish National Fund; or through the ubiquitous activities of the Federation of Women Zionists and WIZO; or through any one of the innumerable causes for Israel that enabled Jews in the diaspora to feel they were involved in the noble venture of building the new Jewish state. 'Maybe one day we will need it' was of course the hidden subtext of these activities.

Inch by inch Zionism was becoming the new religion of Anglo-Jewry. We could still be Jewish without the inconvenience of being believers in the old pieties. And here we were doing no more than follow the lead of the United States, which we knew had become the central force in world Jewry – whatever was happening in Israel.

In the post-War years in Britain we gradually evolved our armchair definition of a Zionist: someone who collects money to employ someone else who will try to persuade a third person to settle in Israel. But suddenly, in the spring of 1967, the joke was nearly on us. Within a fortnight, Nasser's rhetoric of 'driving the Jews back into the sea' was accompanied by a remilitarisation of Sinai (lost in 1956), the expulsion of the compliant United Nations forces and their replacement by a 100,000-strong Egyptian army, and military agreements with Jordan and Iraq. The world watched as a second holocaust threatened the reborn people of Israel.

The Six-Day War was more than a resounding military victory. It was more than the attainment, for the first time, of defensible frontiers. It was more than the conquest of the lands of the Biblical heritage, Judaea and Samaria, and the reunification of the ancient religious heart of Jewish life, Jerusalem. For British Jews it was the keystone in our changing attitude to ourselves as Jews. Our post-Holocaust shame was lifted. The ignominy of the victim was removed. Our irrational but pervasive sense of failure disappeared almost overnight. We felt proud to be Jews.

The gentile world looked on us with new eyes. No longer sheep being led to the slaughter, we gained a new respect in the world. We were seen, and saw ourselves, in a new light: the ghetto Jew had been reborn as the heroic sabra, daring, powerful and strong.[4] And British Jews felt they too could walk tall in the dazzling reflection of the Israeli strategy that had conquered the might of the Arab armies on every front.

Even more important than the reflected glory was the rekindling of our residual loyalty to the Jewish people. We had been tested and not found wanting. Not only did British Jews give their money – £16 million in June and July 1967[5] – but now they gave goods, clothes, medical supplies, blankets . . . whatever the need of the hour. They even gave themselves, standing for hours in queues outside the Jewish Agency, prepared to go and fight, give blood – or at the very least pick oranges. Religious and secular Jews were united, for a moment, in a sense of shared wonder and appreciation.[6] We repeated it again and again: *Am Yisrael Chai* – the people of Israel lives!

The euphoria was palpable. Communal halls were packed to capacity. Synagogues were overflowing. Within one week Jews discovered long-buried aspects of their faith: they were tied to their people with invisible cords of love and hope and concern; and it seemed that this time, miraculously – a word we thought had died from our tongues – God had saved His people. In amazement we realised that the drama that had begun with Abraham was continuing, in our own days still continuing.

This was the beginning of our exodus. Beneath the divisions and dissent we recognised that each individual Jew was involved in a spiritual identification with the Jewish people, as represented by Israel. Freed from the fear of destruction, liberated from the terror of a second annihilation at the hands of one whom we thought of as Hitler's successor, we celebrated our rediscovered sense of peoplehood.

Those halcyon days: when 'Zionist' was a word evoking admiration, rather than being a term of abuse. The third act of Jewish history concerns Jewish power, and what it does to us.

---------------------------------*------------------------------------

I was born in 1950, in the aftermath of the War. There was a problem for my generation then about Jewish identity. I didn't want the kind that I was offered as a child: the 'Hebrew classes' kind of Jewish identity felt really alienating. Habonim, the Zionist youth movement, seemed to offer some sort of alternative to that, a progressive way of being a Jew that was secular, and also culturally vibrant. There was a contradiction for me in that it was disconnected from the previous generation, but that also seemed a source of strength, making my own way as somebody Jewish . . .

Looking back, the Six-Day War seems like a huge watershed. On the way home from school I used to pop in to where we met, and people were volunteering. And suddenly I was excluded, because I was a woman, a girl. With hindsight that was a very clear expression of the sort of male-dominated militaristic culture that Israel was offering to diaspora Jews, which subsequently came into very sharp conflict with my socialism ...

The self-confidence of 1967 was followed by the shock of 1973 and the Yom Kippur War. Another victory, but this time with traumatic losses. A growing disquiet amongst some Jews about what it meant for Israel to be conquerors and occupiers was arrested for a while by Begin's brave ability to trade land for security when he met Sadat at Camp David in 1978. Sadat's courage cost him his life. Meanwhile, Israel's colonisation of the territories was stepped up. 'Never again!' became the watchword of world Jewry, with Masada the symbol of an ever-to-be-renewed defiance.

When our children made *aliyah* we were so proud – they had done what we could not do. We no longer felt the secret shame – just an undefined pain. The separation from the children made us sad, which we also had to hide. We were trapped by our own rhetoric. Subsequently, any attack on Israel, verbal or otherwise, was an attack on our children. Our natural parental protectiveness made us spring even more passionately to Israel's defence. Yet somewhere in our hearts we knew that we hadn't meant it to end up quite like this.

During these years Anglo-Jewry's commitment to Israel hardly wavered. The community said no to large-scale *aliyah*, but yes to holidays in the homeland. We joked about Egged busdrivers and El Al ('Every Landing Always Late') and thanked God we didn't have to live there. For Anglo-Jewry 'next year in Jerusalem' was quite soon enough.

Passive Zionism was a form of vicarious Jewish living that demanded little of its adherents. On the surface it seemed to give us a comfortable and positive Jewish identity. Yet in our hearts we knew that it was Jewishness at one remove. Like all idolatry it was attractive, but hollow. We colluded with the Zionist message from Israel: that diaspora Judaism was second-rate, irrelevant, doomed to extinction; we could send our money but that was no substitute for sending ourselves. In the end we were left feeling guilty and inadequate: really we should be 'over there'.

The third era of Jewish history demanded that 'Jews are forbidden to hand Hitler posthumous victories. They are commanded to survive as Jews, lest the Jewish people perish.'[7] For many, Jewish 'survival' was

equated with, and ensured by, unconditional support for Israel. Personal
Jewish identity was so wedded to the collective survival of the state of
Israel because we had no home-grown and substantive Jewish identity of
our own. Our confusion arose because it was so easy for 'Belief in Israel'
or 'Belief in the unity of the Jewish people' to become an ersatz belief, a
substitute for a more personal relationship to Judaism and Jewish life.

As the seventies went on, British Jews came to realise that their pride
in Israel was double-edged. While Israel was a paragon of the fortitude
and resourcefulness of the plucky underdog – so beloved by the British –
Jews here could retain their innocence. But as Israel began to lose some of
its moral stature in the eyes of the world, we British Jews began to
experience a deep confusion.

Our situation was complicated. We were justifiably appalled by the UN
General Assembly's 1975 resolution equating Zionism with racism. We
saw pro-PLO positions being adopted at home and abroad with no compassion for the history of the Jewish people nor any historical awareness
of how Israel had come into being. We felt anti-Semitism re-emerging as
anti-Zionism. We heard Israel being judged according to impossibly high
standards by those who did not care for us, or about the survival of Israel.

Yet we British Jews were also judging her, secretly, in the light of one
of the lessons of Exodus: compassion for the oppressed. And in spite of all
the nauseous anti-Israel propaganda, we knew that now the oppressed were
the Palestinians.

So, because we did not feel secure enough as diaspora Jews in our own
independent sense of Jewishness, there were few who could criticise Israel
supportively. We were caught on the horns of a profound dilemma, one
born out of the new realities. How could we retain our Jewish idealism – the
product of our historical powerlessness – while maintaining the pragmatism
necessary for our physical survival in a beleaguered state that was dependent
upon only recently-attained Jewish power?

The maverick American theologian Rabbi Irving Greenberg captured
the essence of our new reality: 'There is a danger that those who have not
grasped the full significance of the shift in the Jewish condition will judge
Israel by the ideal standards of the state of powerlessness, thereby not only
misjudging but unintentionally collaborating with attempted genocide.
Ideal moral stances applied unchanged to real situations often come out
with the opposite of the intended result.'[8]

British Jews lapsed into silence. This paralysis lasted into the eighties.
Some might say it has lasted into the nineties.

Despite the positive glosses put on Israeli policies and the attempts by
some Jewish establishment figures to demand Anglo-Jewry's unqualified
public support for whatever the Israeli government chooses to do, we know

that we are now a deeply divided community.[9] And we know, painfully, that we will continue to be divided – both communally and perhaps within ourselves personally – for as long as the *intifida* lasts and justice is denied to the Palestinian people.

Looking back, we can see that the watershed for Anglo-Jewry was 1982 and Ariel Sharon's deception of the Israeli public – and even the government – about the aims of the Lebanon war. His cutting off of supplies of water and food to besieged Beirut, and his indirect responsibility for the massacre by Maronite Christian units of hundreds of women and children in the Sabra and Shatilla refugee camps, caused us a moral disquiet which subsequent events have only compounded.

Understandably we abhor the propaganda which draws an analogy between Israeli attitudes to the Palestinians and the Nazi treatment of the Jews. But our passionate wish to defend Israel from these calumnies and to support her inalienable right to exist within secure and defensible borders is not helped by our awareness that there are political parties in Israel that implicitly favour the expulsion of Palestinians from the territories, and that, according to Lieutenant General Dan Shomron, the only way to stop the *intifida* is 'transfer, starvation or physical extermination – that is, genocide' of the Palestinian people.[10]

Is it any surprise that British Jews have been turning away from Zionism as the sole affirmation of a sense of Jewishness here in the diaspora? There is an underlying sense of shame that Judaism has lost its moral, its prophetic, drive. And then we turn our anger – which emerges when we deny our shame – against those who remind us of what we do not wish to know.

'I will bring you out ...' We no longer dare to trust this. The Hebrew word *bitachon* originally meant trust in God. In modern Hebrew it means military security. 'It is the secularization of this word which epitomizes the burden of contemporary Jewry.'[11] Yet is it possible to hold on to both meanings? History has created the miracle of a Jewish homeland. We insist that we will never be powerless again. But we can become just as powerless when we see Israel the nation-state as the *sine qua non* of Jewish living as when we refuse to see the centrality of a secure Israel for the fulfilment of our historic destiny.

Since the Holocaust it has been hard to imagine Jewish survival without the existence of the state of Israel. It has provided the glue which has kept us together. But the glue is coming unstuck. Israel risks losing the adherence of the Jewish people while it feels unable to learn and apply the still-contemporary lesson of Exodus: that identification with the oppressed is an ethical foundation stone of Jewish identity.

Without a morality of righteousness we are a people whose power turns perverse. It is not Jewish suffering which legitimises our existence in Israel but our historic covenantal commitment to holy living, to acting as a 'light to the nations'. Empathy with the rights of the Palestinian people is, in this profound sense, a truly *Jewish* response – born of our own suffering – to those who now suffer in turn.

We remember that exodus and revelation were followed, within the Biblical myth, by the trauma of the worship of the golden calf: our basic human need for the security of the tangible has always seduced us away from the idealism of the original vision. Perhaps, for a while, Israel became our golden calf, around which we danced attendance, offering it the gold of our hands and our unquestioning and obedient worship. And yet, to conceive of a post-Holocaust Jewish life without Israel would have been – and is – like imagining a body without a soul.

As Anglo–Jewry tentatively renews its own hopefulness, sensing its own inherent vitality as a community, we avert our eyes from gazing too long at a nation divided and in pain. Like so many in Israel itself we wonder at what happens to the soul of a nation brutalised by power and the perpetually re-invoked fear of the Holocaust.[12] Those who work for peace in Israel wonder what will happen if the spiritually-numbing attrition, this 'slouching towards Belfast',[13] rumbles on pitifully for years and years. Whatever attitudes the Palestinians adopt, the problem will not disappear. With empathy, we do share the pain – for Israelis and Palestinians – that political power has brought.

Meanwhile we continue to build here our separate identity as Jews. We are aware that whatever will happen in Israel will inevitably and necessarily touch us all, and perhaps, like Cain, mark us all till the end of our days. But, in the final analysis, the future development of Israel cannot determine how we will choose to lead our Jewish lives in Britain.

Consciously or not, Anglo–Jewry in the eighties and early nineties has drawn on more and wider sources of inspiration for our sense of belonging, our sense of a living and vital Jewish presence here in Britain. And this may be just as well, for we do not know what the nineties will bring. We pray for peace in the Middle East. We push away our underlying fury that time and again we have to justify our existence. We hope, fervently, that Israel does not act out generations'-worth of this pent-up Jewish aggression at being the eternal victims, but that it remains true to its historic and prophetic destiny: to be a haven for the persecuted, a sanctuary for the oppressed, a truly holy land, a source of pride for Jews throughout the world, a source of blessing to its inhabitants and its neighbours.

But, inevitably, we fear that our wish-filled dreams – impossible to believe in and impossible to live without – will once again be dashed to pieces on the rocks of *realpolitik*. Although we cannot foresee what monstrosities those in pursuit of the millennium might yet bring to birth, we do not have to be apocalyptic doom-merchants to imagine other crazed scenarios affecting Israel, any one of which would cast its long shadow over the new blossoming of Anglo-Jewry:

- Arab leaders with chemical and nuclear weapons, touched for a moment by a martyr's madness. A place in history for all time is only a missile away.[14]
- Or, in a crisis, a pre-emptive nuclear strike by Israel – aping God's fire and brimstone destruction of Sodom and Gemorrah – as the perverse fulfilment of the inner logic of Jewish history.
- Or Israel being 'rescued' from civil war by a military dictatorship, the culmination of Sharon's paranoid gangsterism.[15]
- Or the nascent Jewish proto-Fascist underground, biding their lunatic time, awaiting the day when, with a messianic glint in their eyes, a well-placed bomb at the Dome of the Rock would 'redeem Jewish land', prepare the ground for the rebuilding of the Temple – and incarnate a blasphemy so grave that hell would know no bounds.[16]

The third act of Jewish history is only just beginning.

***

Even today there's a shortage of voices on the English side of Jewish people who say: Look, we really do support Israel and do love Israel and we endorse Israel's right to defend itself – but we want to express our reservations about certain issues of Israeli policy ...

One has to tread this very difficult line: on the one hand saying what one believes about the situation; on the other hand defending Israel against the enormous number of unjust accusations that are brought against her ... I do believe that it's possible to strike that balance and that means basically speaking one's mind even though it makes one unpopular in lots of different circles. It makes one unpopular inside the Jewish community that you actually voice criticism. And at the same time it makes you unpopular outside, because when people think they've got a tame critic they can wheel out to endorse their criticism of Israel, they find he's saying, 'No. What you're saying is wrong.' So that you're saying to all the people who are expecting agreement, 'No, we've got our own way. The truth is much more complicated.'

10
'I Will Deliver You ...'
Anglo-Jewry's Religious
Revival

---
*

I'd left Israel in 1974 in the aftermath of the Yom Kippur war and found myself back in Britain, at university, and I couldn't work out what to do about being Jewish outside of Israel. I don't think it ever entered my head that I would stop defining myself as a Jewish woman. That was always taken as a given. It was more a question of what kind of Jewish woman and what kind of Jew ... It was a very slow realisation on my part that it's very difficult to be an identifying Jew in a positive committed sense outside of a Jewish state unless there is some kind of acknowledgement of the religious and spiritual aspect of one's Jewishness. It was actually quite a struggle to find out how to express it.

---
*

The people I went to school and university with were all sort of easy-going, happy-go-lucky partygoers wanting to have a good time. That's where I was too. I was just like any normal guy ... When I was twenty-three – I'd already started work by then – I thought maybe it's a good time to go and study something, to keep my brain going. I had friends who were already religious, so I was recommended to go to a shiur, *a lecture ... At first there was no struggle. What I wanted to do was have the benefit of learning about Judaism, taking on maybe a few* mitzvahs, *a few* halachas, *putting some commitment into them. There was no way that I decided that I was going to give up everything else and put my full commitment into Judaism. So I was really starting to live a double life ...*

I didn't want to give up all my hobbies and interests: I'd joined a band and music was definitely going to stay in my life. But slowly my interests started to fade away ... I suddenly realised that there is such a thing as looking for

121

your roots. And that gave me a lot more inspiration. After some time of part-time learning I decided to go to Jerusalem for six months – studying in yeshivah, *building up skills, studying till my heart was content . . .*

When I came back to work I had made a commitment to wear a kapple *all the time, and I'd grown a beard. So I decided I was now a fully-fledged religious young man. I think I was much happier as a person. I felt much more fulfilled. I felt that I was doing the right thing, as it were. I didn't feel that all my energies were going in all directions . . .*

Now I live in Stamford Hill. I'm married. I work for British Rail. My interests are very much around my home and my learning in Judaism. I met my wife through – I'll say this in inverted commas – an 'arranged marriage'. When we met through some friends we met for a specific purpose, and that was to get married and build a Jewish home. We were both at the same stage of becoming religious, both going in the same direction . . .

Freedom was a process of finding my own path. It didn't come until the latter stages of becoming religious, when I realised that I was free from wanting to be like other people; I just wanted to use my own talents and energy for fulfilling the word of God, in order to serve God the way God wanted me to serve him. Basically I do what I can, and God only wants me to try my hardest . . .

At the end of the last century Achad Ha-am, that prescient Zionist ideologue, recognised that the tide of secularism was washing away what had been, from the rabbinic era onwards, the major component of Judaism: its rootedness in religious belief and practice. Jewish survival, he believed, would come to depend on Jewish culture and a sense of Jewish peoplehood replacing God as the central focus of Jewish identity. Rejecting what he perceived as the self-defeating introversion of traditional religion and the self-negating option of assimilation, he envisaged Jewish life being revitalised by the establishment of an independent spiritual centre for the Jewish people. Through rebuilding Jewish life in the land of Israel, the diaspora too would be rejuvenated.[1]

And yet in the last ten years Anglo-Jewry has being edging away, slowly but subtly, with many an anxious backward look, from unswerving belief in Israel as the central defining characteristic of Jewish life in Britain. Sadly, but inevitably, we are coming to realise that our unifying slogans 'The Jewish people are one' and 'We stand by Israel' have begun to turn bitter in our mouths. The vision of Achad Ha-am has died on the streets of Gaza and in the villages of the West Bank.

Continually trying to defend the increasingly indefensible postures and policies of Israel has eroded the previously unquestioning belief of Zionist supporters. Caught between a passionate and loving commitment to defend the integrity and necessity of a Jewish homeland, and a reluctant awareness of the spiritual bankruptcy of Israeli government actions, British Jews have begun to move towards alternative sources of inspiration to feed the hunger in their souls. Jewish nationalism has failed us and many, it seems, are turning to – or returning to – religion.

It is as if, in some secret recess of our minds, we have been thinking to ourselves (thinking, because we dare not say it): 'If the purpose of Jewish survival is to have a state that tortures Arab prisoners and shoots Palestinian children, then there has to be something else. If my sense of being Jewish requires my acquiescence to oppression and involves me in defending the oppressor – what hope can there be for me? Four millennia of Jewish struggle to survive, four millennia of a unique Jewish creativity transforming the world – and it has come to this? God knows, there must be something else . . .'

And amazingly, it appears, there is something else. Tentatively, fragmentarily, hesitantly, like a guilty partner after a failed love affair, we are turning from our beloved land and returning to our Beloved One. Where once we felt that we had been abandoned, we now find, unexpectedly, almost against our better judgment, that we are seeking the Eternal again. Distanced from the modern Zionist dream, we turn to dreams even older.

To suggest that many Jews in Britain are experiencing a rekindled interest in religion because there is now a gap ready to be filled may seem a tendentious statement. The connection between a disidentification with the state of Israel and a growth in religious life in Britain is ambiguous. The evidence is contradictory and, on the surface, points in the opposite direction. Israel's vital place in Jewish life can be seen to go hand-in-hand with many diverse forms of religious commitment, be it that of Progressive Judaism's Pro-Zion organisation, the Martin Buber-style religious humanism of the dovish Peace Now group, the Orthodox Jew's support for the religious Zionists of the *Oz V'Shalom* ('Strength and Peace') movement, or the fundamentalist Biblical literalism and mystical messianism of the right-wing *Gush Emmunim* ('Bloc of the Faithful') faction in Israel.

Religion can be hijacked for evil as well as for good, for repressive aims as well as holy living. In Israel part of the expansionist drive has been fuelled by religious slogans, with Biblical notions of a 'Greater Israel' providing a powerful rationale for the annexation of Judaea and Samaria. Yet some religious figures in Israel – in a view echoed by Anglo-Jewry's Chief Rabbi Jakobovits – have cautioned against justifying on religious grounds the continued occupation of conquered territories. The saving of human life is seen as preeminent within the hierarchy of Jewish values. With increasing consistency – and in tandem with Israeli military leaders such as Generals Yehoshafat Harkabi and Aharon Yariv – many religious Zionists in Israel and the diaspora have advocated surrendering land for peace-with-security. As well as reinforcing nationalistic sentiments, Judaism can offer a prophetic critique of the consequences of an unbridled nationalism.

In July 1967, when Ben Gurion emerged from retirement on his desert kibbutz to address the Israeli Labour Party, he insisted that for Israel's inner health all the captured territories (with the exception of Jerusalem) should be given back quickly. Holding onto them would distort – and might even, ultimately, destroy – the Jewish state. As so often in Jewish history the prophetic voice went unheeded. The irony of it coming from a supposedly 'secular' Jew should not go unremarked. The warnings of Israel's first prime minister 'were read in Israel as only another one of the angry outbursts of the founding father, who had now become a public scold'.[2]

The unabated enthusiasm after 1967 led tens of thousands of British Jews to visit Israel for the first time. Its magnetism was compelling: the Western Wall and the beaches for the tourists, working on kibbutz for the youthful in body and spirit, students learning Hebrew at an *ulpan* ... And a new phenomenon arose. The post-war generation of Anglo-Jewry experienced at first hand, and often for the first time, traditional Eastern European-style religious life as marketed in one of the newly-opened *yeshivot*. These single-sex, predominantly diaspora-financed seminaries were purpose-built for the searching young Jew, alienated from his or her secular or Reform or nominally Orthodox Jewish background.

Eastern European Jewry may have been destroyed, but its religious vitality was resurrected. Learning in a *yeshivah* was not only a living contact with a lost world of piety. Its attraction was not only that it was part of a rejection of parental values and hypocrisies. At its best it seemed to offer a life of intellectual coherence and spiritual sustenance, the emotional comradeship of a shared exploration of Jewish purpose, and the reassuring security of answers: through total immersion in the tradition the inquirer could be shielded against the pervasive confusion and fragmentation of Western values and any disquieting sense of the underlying hopelessness and meaninglessness of contemporary urban life.

The sixties' flight from Judaism was matched by the seventies' and eighties' flight into Judaism. No longer were the gurus in the East. The searching Jew no longer needed to turn to the Maharishi or Rajneesh for religious enlightenment when he or she could sit at the feet of the Lubavitcher Rebbe or one of the dozens of other religious luminaries, Hassidic or neo-Orthodox, who had built up networks of dedicated followers in New York or Jerusalem.

Israeli-inspired *ba'alei teshuvah* – 'those who have returned' (to the path of Jewish life) – infiltrated back into Anglo-Jewish life with their 'Torah-true' Judaism. The moribund establishment Judaism, with its English compromises, seemed a pale shadow of the revitalised Jewish religious life in Israel. Having 'returned', those who returned home now knew that something else was possible.

The conflicts began: children who would no longer eat in their parents' homes; the frustrations with old-style lackadaisical Reform or United Synagogue Judaism; the dissatisfactions with a previous generation's lack of Jewish commitment and self-assertion. The Israeli cocktail of renewed Jewish pride and old-time religion proved to be a potent brew – and the Anglo-Jewish religious revival was underway.

So the 'revival' – if that is what it is – may appear to have been catalysed in the wake of that renewed sense of Jewish destiny that emerged after '67, when God's covenant with His people seemed to have been re-established. Yet here a contradiction surfaces. Although Israel may have inspired a renaissance in religiosity, Anglo-Jewry has seen a protracted decline in synagogue membership. It is estimated that at least one in three British Jews are unaffiliated to any synagogue.

Clearly, the motives of those who do pay synagogue subscriptions are manifold; and not the least is to provide an insurance policy, so to speak, for the guarantee of a Jewish burial in a Jewish cemetery. But even when alive, the majority of British Jews are not overly committed to practising the Judaism that their synagogue represents – and this phenomenon is shared across the religious spectrum. If we take, for example, synagogue attendance (rather than membership) as a measure of Jewish observance, most of the members of Anglo-Jewish congregations have priorities other than regular prayer.[3]

The overwhelming disaffection of Anglo-Jewry for synagogue Judaism seems clear. Chief Rabbi-elect Jonathan Sacks, with clear-sighted honesty, acknowledges this reality: 'We must recognise that for many people, the synagogue service is at best meaningless and at worst, positively alienating.'[4]

Whatever the traditional indices of Jewish observance might be – Sabbath observance, *kashrut*, festival and life-cycle celebrations, laws of family purity – alongside our demographic decline there has been a decline in Anglo-Jewry's committed adherence to the practices of the past. Only the ultra-Orthodox fringe groups have resisted this dual decline, although the cost in terms of social and health problems – from poverty to depression and the emotional deprivations of some large families – is usually hidden from the eyes of outsiders, even in the Jewish world.

In the third era of Jewish history, synagogue membership can no longer be used as a reliable guide to a Jew's sense of his or her Jewishness. When statistician Dr Stephen Miller reports that 'the operational definition of a Jew is somebody who will eventually be buried in a Jewish cemetery' we can see the narrowness of so-called 'affiliation by Jewish burial' as the criterion for Jewish identity.[5] The inadequacy of this for our self-understanding as a community is painfully obvious. One trenchant commentator on the Anglo-Jewish scene remarks on the 'remarkable stamina and loyalty' of British Jews:

They marry one another, they create Jewish families. This is all done without fuss and often outside the ambit of organised (and enumerated) Jewish life. Ways of being Jewish change, but transformation is not the same as decline ... Synagogue attendance, observation of festivals, trips to Israel, extent of Jewish education, Jewish marriages, births and deaths are archaic ways of 'measuring' Jewishness and premissed upon quaint notions of Jewishness that are defined in terms of denomination and placed in the context of a society that dissolved years ago.[6]

The transformation described here is part of Anglo-Jewry's exodus. The quest for a revitalised Jewish identity has burst through the traditional contexts for Jewish self-expression. The energy of Jews in Britain is no longer confined within the straitjacket of the old rabbinic world. Nevertheless, certain needs – the natural human religious impulse, the rejection of a solely material existence and the urge to find and express a spiritual dimension to life – seem irrepressible. This is not only a reaction to doubts about Israel: in a world increasingly insecure, distracted by trivia, consumed by materialism, Jews are reacting to the loss of collective meaning and social coherence by returning to the apparent security of religious ways.

There is a marked contrast between the older provincial centres of Jewish life struggling for survival, and the plethora of new, small, independent congregations in the traditional London suburbs of Golders Green and Hendon. We have seen the rapid growth of numerous outer London 'greenbelt' Jewish communities (M25 Judaism); and as Jews move from the metropolis, burgeoning congregations sprawl across into the West Country (M4 Judaism).

Religion is a growth industry. There are the increasingly successful *minyanim* inspired by Project Seed; the expansive outreach of Lubavitch; the vibrant intimacy of unaffiliated Orthodox *shtiblach*; the spread of the Masorti movement; the alternative New Age-style Jewish approach of the *Ruach Chavurah* groupings; and progressive Judaism's network of new communities created wherever ten Jews can gather – in Hampshire, Sussex,

Norfolk, Kent, Yorkshire – no longer expecting Jews to congregate only in the larger cities, but taking Judaism to where Jews now live. Finally, there's a new congregation for the marginal Jew who may feel disaffected or alienated by normative synagogue Judaism: those 'who are, for one reason or another, on their own ... Jewish women and men who may not think of themselves as formally religious ... lesbian Jews, and gay Jews ...'[7]

The outsider – Jew or non-Jew – may feel baffled by this mosaic. But Anglo-Jewish life has never had such a variety of religious choices on offer. Whether it is a return to the tried and tested ways of old or an exploration of new pathways in Jewish spiritual life; whether it is through the inspiration of traditional *davenning* in an informal and relaxed setting, or the excitement of workshops on Jewish dreams; whether it is Kabbalah groups impregnated with modern psychological notions, or shared meals and communal singing after services in a synagogue; when we look around us at the multifarious and thriving manifestations of contemporary Anglo-Jewish religious life it does not seem too bold to suggest that the Spirit is alive in manifold ways, and sometimes in the most unlikely places.

In recent years Jewish feminists, first of all in Israel and America, decided to try and reclaim Rosh Hodesh *(the time of the new moon), particularly for women ... getting women to come together and celebrate, and find a way of establishing ritual which was separate from the men, and not in any way trying to ape mainstream religious practice but rather a special women's way of doing it. It was in this spirit that our group was founded ...*

We meet almost every Rosh Hodesh. *We represent a reasonably broad spectrum ... I think that's quite new for women within the traditional Jewish community: to find a way of being Jewish which acknowledges the richness and depth of our heritage, and of the role that the* halachah, *Jewish law, has played within that – but also to find a way of expressing everything which the contemporary women's movement has struggled for and is still struggling for ...*

I lived all my life in Israel and I never was Jewish. I was an Israeli. I couldn't care less about Judaism. I had no interest whatsoever. I've now spent almost five years here and I realised I was Jewish, not because I started suddenly having an interest in religion. As a matter of fact, the difficulty I found was that Jewish life in the UK does concentrate round the synagogue, because this is the only place that people identify with each other as being Jewish. I found I was Jewish when my son decided he wanted to have a barmitzvah. I was absolutely surprised. I even tried to tempt him to go on safari to Africa instead of having a barmitzvah. But he insisted. He said, 'Look, I'm a Jew and I'd like to have a barmitzvah' ...

---

*

The average synagogue always struck one as a sort of pub without beer. It was a place where people met, but if one actually tried to experience something or concentrate on feeling during the service, no doubt someone would touch you on the shoulder and ask you if you were feeling all right! So there was an attempt to create something which one felt was sincere and genuine ... for those who wanted a religious community where one wouldn't fool oneself that one could read Hebrew at a quicker pace than one was reading English; where one would be encouraged that Jewish prayer should be something experiential ...

What is characteristic of many of these expressions of Jewish religious revival is that they appeal to – and are often led by – that younger generation in their thirties and forties who have moved away from the post-war accommodations with Englishness that their parents adopted. It is not that British identity is being discarded, rather that exodus is about self-assertion of Jewish identity; and the move from 'exile' to 'exodus' is manifest in a growing self-confidence in overtly religious or spiritual manifestations of Jewish identity.

It is true that across the religious spectrum one can find status-conscious Jews adopting religious practices as part of a particular modern life-style: shopping in Marks and Spencer, and Selfridge's kosher food hall; holidays in Marbella and Disneyland; at least one charity committee; the right golf/health/sports club; and, alongside these, membership of one's local *shul*, a little light learning and a display of *mitzvot* is naturally *de rigueur*.

Yet something less ephemeral is happening too. Often the renewed interest in ritual observance, roots, tradition, spirituality, is developing in tension with mainstream Anglo-Jewish synagogue Judaism. It is a kind of 'do-it-yourself' Judaism, which resists bureaucracy and centralisation in favour of a more personal and intimate relationship to Jewish tradition.

The inspiration behind this revival seems to come from several sources.

Israel and Gateshead[8] have provided *yeshivah*-based Judaism combining, in various degrees, the intellectual rigours of Talmud study with the spiritual joy of devotion in prayer. Hassidic exuberance caters for the more mystically inclined. Lionel Blue's idiosyncratic version of 'holiness at the kitchen sink' or in the local bar has brought the Lord of Hosts to suburbia with humour and humaneness.

The feminist revolution has enabled women, Orthodox and non-Orthodox, to reclaim their Jewishness through prayer and study and political action, not only in the home or through the family. Here, the United States has provided the Jewish role-models. From America too has come a holistic 'Jewish Catalog' – Judaism with its anti-establishment ethos combining traditionalism with innovation and experimentation.

Many of these forms and sources of religious self-expression operate quite independently of any commitment to Israel. Some are a reaction to an Israel-centred Judaism. Almost in unconscious defiance of Israel's narcissistic claims for the devoted attention and continuous selfless dedication of diaspora Jewry, Jews in Britain are resisting this denigration of our intrinsic worth and, seeking each other out, are gathering together for the time-honoured rituals and markers of Jewish life.

Rejecting our role of obedient children to self-centred parents, we have grown recalcitrant. We argue back. We even dare to criticise. And while we still are sure to show our love, we get on with our own lives. We no longer seem to be prepared to have our Jewish identity so dependent on our distant but always-present parent, Israel. We no longer deny the inherent value of our own religious ways and truths. 'Exodus' means that Anglo-Jewry is growing up. We let our overbearing, disputatious parent continue its quarrelsome ways. Meanwhile we flourish – with some guilt, but not a little pride in our own achievements.

Sometimes it even feels that we in the diaspora are the parents who are having to cope with a needy and unruly child. The child wants to go its own way and leave us behind. All it needs is our money – and our unqualified support for whatever it does. Then it gets angry when we say no. Pulled between wanting to be treated like all the other kids and wanting to be special, Israel will make sure we never get it right. But Anglo-Jewry's collusion with this game seems to be coming to an end.

In the third era of Jewish history Israel may stand at the centre of our loving attention but we are also learning that that does not place us on the periphery. Indeed, we are realising that in terms of our spiritual needs and our religious lives, for most of the time we are actually at the centre of the stage – and wish to be so. A vicarious Judaism, where Israel is supposed to fulfil our sense of Jewish belonging, no longer works for us.

'I will deliver you . . .' In the first cycle of Jewish history God was to be found in the Temple. In the second stage God was met in the synagogue. In this third period of Jewish history God has moved outside the confines of the religious establishments, to be encountered here where we stand: in the relationships between us, in the spirit within us, in the bodies we inhabit, in the holiness of the small gestures of everyday life. The third era of Jewish history requires a quantum leap in our understanding of where God can be found: a move as cataclysmic for the old ways and as momentous in opening up new directions as that which took place when the Temple was destroyed and the synagogue took its place.

And just as there were Temple authorities then who anathematised Rabbi Jochanan ben Zakkai as a quisling when he abandoned Jerusalem and made an accommodation with the Romans to build up a new and more egalitarian Judaism outside the Holy City, so the protectors of the still-existing institution of the synagogue continue now to defend their patch of holy ground.[9] But the Spirit has moved Anglo-Jewry beyond the walls of the synagogue.

The religious polarisation of Anglo-Jewry is the death-rattle of the old cycle. Divisions in the community between right and left, ultra- and centrist Orthodoxy, Orthodox and Progressive, and all the other tedious internecine quarrels are the detritus of an age gone by. The new scriptures of our times – taking their place alongside the old and to be listened to with as much attention – are the revelatory texts of our own lives, where God speaks in our triumphs and in our despair, in our pain and in our longings, in our doubts and in our questions. The Eternal One teaches Torah to us, through us.

Perhaps British Jews are unaccustomed to that generosity of human spirit which recognises in something unfamiliar or strange or threatening the workings of a larger Spirit. And yet it seems that this is what the third era of Jewish history may require of Anglo-Jewry – the recognition of the divine at work not only where we think it ought to be, but where we least expect it.

―――――――――――――――* ―――――――――――――――

One thing that was always missing from my Judaism was any feeling of direct experience of the spiritual world. Being in a synagogue was nice but I didn't feel moved by it. Recently I've been involved in a group – a chavurah *– and all that's changed for me. We meet in each other's homes. We have no leader – we do it for ourselves. We endeavour to reach some form of spiritual experience, and that means reinterpreting the tradition for ourselves.*

The chavurah *is a community in which we are all equal and we can bring our own experience to it. We're not going through a pre-set format. We're going for direct spiritual experience, not mediated by a rabbi or a* chazan *who's going to do all that for us. Some of the things that we're tapping into now were available in the past, but they were available to the men. And it's very important to us that women are there as equal and full participants. The women's insight is challenging the tradition. What they bring is different from what the men bring . . . I have to start challenging what I grew up with – the emotional feeling in a virtually all-male community. What I'm trying to get to is what I perceive as the heart of the religion – but that heart was a male heart.*

The people that are coming to Ruach Chavurah *are people who have found it very hard to be part of a Jewish community. They felt there was no room for them in it. And there's also something inside them that was stopping them being Jewish, something from the past. Perhaps it's the Holocaust – to be Jewish meant pain . . . The* chavurah *is a safe place. It's a place to be Jewish and say, 'Well, there are bits that I don't like about being Jewish.' You can't do that in* shul. *You can't do that within traditional communities. Being in the* chavurah *they can explore all their Jewishness – including their pain and their ambivalence: it is a safe and caring community, and supportive. So for many people it's been a healing experience.*

11

'I Will Redeem You . . .'
The Blossoming of
Secularism

---
*

I was taught in both my religious education and my Zionist education that the last two thousand years were years of unmitigated misery, of persecution, purges and pogroms. More recently I've learnt much more about modern Jewish history – which I've realised now was completely cut out of my Jewish education. I now play Yiddish music and I'm interested in the Yiddish language and Yiddish culture and I see it as a result of understanding my own history and the history of other European Jews. It feels authentic to me. It's something that derives from my background that is familiar and comforting.

That my grandparents were Yiddish speakers, my parents were Yiddish speakers – even though they were born here – has given me a sense that Jewish diaspora communities were vibrant and lively, culturally progressive communities that saw themselves as having a future. And can still see themselves as having a future because it's that diaspora culture which has been portable, which has been adaptable, which has been pluralistic, which has been mutually supportive between different communities, and which has enabled Jews to survive.

---
*

I was in a women's group meeting, minding my own business. Someone came up to me and said, 'Aha, you're the Jewish one.' And I thought, 'Oh, here we go again.' I just got up and walked out because I didn't see why I had to take this. I went down to where the Union of Jewish Students have their headquarters and asked to speak to the women's officer, thinking that there's got to be more to being Jewish than being attacked the whole time. But that year none had been appointed . . .

The next week I went back to my women's group and I told them that I was now the women's officer for the Union of Jewish Students. At this point I became the token Jewish woman for everything that I have ever done since ... At student meetings I would stand up and say, 'I'm from the Union of Jewish Students,' and every single person in that room would start hissing before I'd begun. That type of thing used to annoy me – and saddened me probably more than anything else ...

At the end of 1988, in a radio broadcast on 'Jewishness and Judaism', Rabbi Jonathan Sacks described how 'whether in Israel or the diaspora, for the first time in centuries, Jews feel they *belong*'.[1] The subsequent rise of nationalism in Europe notwithstanding, we recognise the truth of this – at least for ourselves here in Britain. We may have our bouts of paranoia and our periodic retreat into an atavistic defensiveness – not eased by cemetery desecrations, or attacks on Jews in Stamford Hill – but on the whole we know that twofold sense of belonging: to our host country and culture, and to our own people with its wondrous and unenviable history.

Rabbi Sacks voiced his regrets about the continuing religious decline, but acknowledged the overwhelmingly secular nature of contemporary Jewish identity:

And so, a most curious phenomenon has emerged. Jewishness without Judaism, or at least Judaism as traditionally conceived. For perhaps the first time in two hundred years, since the process of emancipation began, Jewish identity is no longer regarded as a burden but a natural fact. Jews no longer seek to escape by a conscious strategy of assimilation. At the same time, and equally unprecedented, Jewish identity has little identifiable content. The secular Jews of the diaspora are happy to be Jews, but not quite sure what that means.[2]

In this chapter we will be suggesting that it is not the flourishing and self-assertive secularists who are 'not quite sure what it means' to be Jewish. Rather it is the embattled religious establishments who remain confused about forms of Jewish self-expression that may lie outside their control or chosen frame of reference.

If we use the traditional yardstick of formal religious observance as the criterion by which we measure the vitality of contemporary Jewish life, then we see Jewish identity on the decline. Yet extensive American research[3] into the patterns of Jewish continuity and change has illustrated that, at least in the United States, Jewish group identity is maintained in other ways.

Jews end up living in the same areas, shopping in the same shops, attending the same schools and institutions of higher education, entering the same professions. A sense of cohesion occurs too through their friendships, their attitudes, the causes they support and the beliefs they uphold. This complex set of group interactions seems to perpetuate a distinctive Jewish identity, though looser and more informal than in previous generations. Perhaps surprisingly, intermarriage does not significantly alter this amorphous sense of Jewish group identity. Yet as impoverished as these self-definitions may at first appear – and sometimes, undoubtedly, secular Jewish identity can be as emotionally and spiritually empty as crasser forms of religious behaviourism – this phenomenon of non-religious Jewish continuity is recognisable in Britain too.

The estimated 90,000–95,000 unaffiliated British Jews form a substantive though variegated constituency. David Cesarani, a Jewish academic long concerned with the experiences of 'ordinary Jews', has described the ethos of this 'alternative Jewish community' who are looking towards:

... the creation of a pluralistic, heterogeneous, decentralised society in which all religious and ethnic groups will have the space to flourish ... Jews in various political parties, social movements and cultural activities have established associations predicated on a common, Jewish ethnic identity but built around issues and cultural concerns common to diverse ethnic groups. Jewish ethnicity and a particular cause then become dual axes by which to articulate Jews into society on equal terms to other citizens.[4]

One of the earliest 'causes' to which Anglo-Jewry rallied in this new wave of self-assertiveness was the campaign on behalf of Soviet Jewry. Again, 1967 was the key year. The Six-Day War had given new impetus to Jews in Russia to reassert – or discover for the first time – their Jewish identities. With the upswing in demand for human rights within the Soviet Union, including the right to emigrate, the 'refusenik' phenomenon began to receive increased attention in the West. With background memories of the world's passivity in the 1930s in regard to German Jews, Jewish activists found their feet.

———————————————*———————————————

The first time I was asked to go on a demonstration I walked down Piccadilly and I saw the demonstrators standing on the edge of the pavement holding placards. They were mostly young people and I thought, 'No, that's not me, I couldn't do that.' So I walked past them and bought a birthday card for a friend and I thought, 'Well, it's not going to kill me to stand on the pavement.' So I went back and I took a placard and I started talking to the other people in the demonstration and I realised that it was something that was very possible to do because the others were so pleasant and supportive. From that moment onwards I joined in demonstrations and eventually I went to the Soviet Union in 1978 . . .

Our scale of values changed and has remained changed over the years. I found that I had less and less time for the social life that I was leading. We certainly no longer do the formal entertaining and the time-consuming things that I had done in the past . . . It has made us very aware of what is important in our lives and what is of less importance. I would say that it has made us better Jews and I hope better human beings.

———————————————✳———————————————

I was meant to be a very quiet ladylike Jewish girl. When I first got married many years ago I wouldn't have said boo to a goose. We weren't brought up to shout or complain. We learnt to do it. I think we felt there was a need. Once Israel was there, there was something behind us. If anything happened we had somewhere we could go. I felt the need to shout out for Soviet Jews and to shout out for myself. I found my feet working for Soviet Jews. Maybe without that I would still be the nice quiet housewife that my mother wanted me to be, with three children. But I found something here: that I was needed.

In the 1960s Jews in Britain had campaigned for CND, anti-Vietnam War, anti-apartheid . . . every cause and group in the world but their own. Primarily this was the Jew acting not out of his or her Jewishness but as a morally and socially concerned human being. However, in the seventies, when women and blacks and Asian groups campaigned to assert their own identities, Jewish self-assertion also emerged.

Cutting across the religious/secular divide, the National Council for Soviet Jewry coordinated groups as diverse as students, women ('the 35s'), ex-servicemen, MPs and the Reform movement.[5] Israel's successes gave Anglo-Jewry added confidence, though the defence of Soviet Jewish rights was, in a way, a safe cause. We had the moral advantage and could use it to test ourselves as Jews. The cause was just, and it was altruistic – we were not defending our own rights as Jews, but the rights of other Jews in a distant land. Like support for Israel it could be a vicarious – though crucial – expression of Jewish identity.

Towards the end of the 1970s another cause around which Jews could congregate began to define itself: the need for a progressive Zionism which could be both critical of Israel yet supportive of the idealism inherent in the Zionist vision. There were disillusioned Zionists searching to maintain their Jewish integrity. Some found solace within the idealism of Jewish socialism. And then there were many marginal and outsider Jews who, having given up on Judaism, were encountering in their political, social or working lives an increasingly strong anti-Jewish feeling, often masked as anti-Zionism.

✳

A row broke out between Spare Rib, *the 'orthodox' publication of the feminist movement, and Jewish feminists who'd established themselves as a group in the late seventies. It published an article which had as its subheading something like, 'Any woman who calls herself a feminist must also call herself an anti-Zionist.' A lot of Jewish feminists wrote to* Spare Rib *and none of them had their letters published, which was perceived as silencing – which it was.*

One of the most important things that came out of that debate for me was a sudden realisation that there were only two ways you were allowed to identify as Jewish: religious or Zionist. And I was neither. I was a secularist. I was a socialist, which did seem to me to have quite a lot to do with being Jewish, and I was an anti-racist.

That was when I met somebody in the Jewish Socialists Group, which was quite clearly active in anti-racist politics but had organised meetings between Jews and Palestinians, and this didn't seem to threaten people's Jewish identity. Here were people expressing themselves as Jews, standing up and acting politically as Jews, but they didn't fit any of the criteria that seemed to be offered by the establishment of the community. And that was very liberating for me. It meant that suddenly all sorts of bits of my politics could come together: that I could be a socialist and a Jew and a feminist.

The *Spare Rib* conflict forced many into a re-evaluation of their own identities and beliefs as Jews. In re-examining Jewish history and culture they found rooted values which could stand up to the barrage of criticism and propaganda coming from extremes of right and left. Women, and men, ideologically on the left but under pressure, experienced a sense of shared concern with those doubting Zionists who also felt under pressure. One of the first meeting places, from the early eighties onwards, was the British branch of the Israeli peace movement.[6] But progressive Zionism was by no means the only avenue to be explored by those re-evaluating the inner dynamics of their Jewish identity – or seeking it out for the first time.

Other socially- or politically-orientated groups were born, or were revitalised. The Jewish Socialists Group predominated, but we have also seen Jews Against Apartheid; the Jewish Cultural and Anti-Racist Project; JONAH (a Jewish anti-nuclear group); the Jewish Lesbian and Gay group; and Jewish feminist groups. Single-issue based Jewish groups continually emerge: Jews Against Clause 28; the Jewish Campaign for the Homeless; Jews concerned with environmental and ecological issues . . .

Some of these groups come and go. Some survive. Membership can overlap and membership is often small. But the youthfulness and energy of these groups is a growing aspect of Anglo-Jewry's exodus from the self-negating habits of the past. This celebratory exploration of personal Jewish identity outside the establishment structures may be a minority phenom-enon – and one which religious and lay leaders sometimes may wish to dismiss as of negligible significance – but it points to the richness of the Ango-Jewish revival that is now taking place.

But for Jews in Britain the process of self-discovery can lead in other directions than the political-cum-social. Growing numbers, as we have seen, have found themselves drawn to the religious heritage. Often this can mean Judaism in its more traditional forms; for others it entails attempts to renew the tradition and liturgy by restoring their personal meaning and relevance: spiritually, psychologically or politically.

✳

I had been on anti-apartheid marches and was always shocked to find the Christian churches represented and Muslim and Hindu organisations, but the only Jewish organisation on such marches was the Jewish Socialists and sometimes a group from the Jewish Feminists. I was always annoyed at the fact that the Church leaders were speaking about how the Bible recommended that all people were equal and there should be no racism and they always quoted from what I called the Jewish prophets – from Isaiah, Amos and Micah. If that was what the teaching of the prophets was, then this is what I agreed with and I thought it was time for the Jews to stand up and say, 'Yes, this is our heritage. We want to reclaim it. This is our Bible, these are our prophets and this is our issue.'

In February 1987 when we at Jews Against Apartheid were thinking about what we would be doing for Pesach, we decided that we would continue having a seder *outside South Africa House, calling for freedom in South Africa, until such time as South Africa was free and democratic and non-racial . . .*

---
*
---

*What seems to me a natural extension of a holistic attitude, of religion being
part of one's personality, is still not acceptable. Yet it's the authentic expression
of Jewish tradition – a God who's concerned with social justice, with a just
society. So I find it very difficult to understand how one can be a committed
Jew and remain insular ...*

*I don't think it's particularly radical to have the world of contentious issues
within an Orthodox context. To say that Judaism is concerned with these
issues – it's natural ... When Yakar invited Archbishop Desmond Tutu that
was seen as something which was totally out of the ordinary. I believe that one
should encourage dialogue. One tends to be frightened of what one doesn't know,
but if one knows one's roots and is reasonably self-confident, why should one
be so frightened of bringing one's tradition to bear on the outside world?*

If the progression from *cheder* to marriage, parenthood and *shul* membership has been seen as the normative route for the post-war British Jew,
those who reject this conventional middle-class journey to Jewish self-
expression have had to fight for alternative modes of personal Jewish
fulfilment. The vigour of the recent cultural manifestations of Jewish
identity testifies to the urgency of this need.

The cultural rejuvenation of the community embraces the remarkable
revival in interest in Yiddish as a language and culture; the regular Jewish
film and music festivals; the emergence of various forms of Jewish theatre;
exhibitions by Jewish artists; new museums for local Jewish history; and
the growth of Holocaust studies and Jewish history projects as a source of
values and the inspiration for a renewed sense of Jewish identity.

These acts of ethnic identification constitute a trend which parallels that
of the religious *ba'alei teshuvah* phenomenon, 'except that the criteria for
the return are not religious or racial'.[7] Whereas the traditional religious
criteria for Jewish belonging were of necessity narrowly-defined – above
all, birth from a halachically-acceptable Jewish mother, and then the
observance of *mitzvot* – the pluralism of this secular 'community' involves
a self-defined and inclusive latitudarianism.[8] A sense of belonging cannot
be defined by others from outside. There is a growing recognition of the
value – and the necessity – of an autonomous approach to Jewish identity:
it is not only to be defined collectively, but personally. Exodus is about the
freedom to explore expressions of Jewish identity which are self-chosen.
Those who persecute us do not discriminate between us. It is up to us to
resist the homogenising impulse – whether it comes from outside the

Jewish world or inside it – which seeks to deny the rich heterogeneity of Jewish life as lived by individual Jewish men and women.

Clearly, self-defined expressions of Jewish identity pose a challenge to Judaism as traditionally conceived. Doom-laden scenarios have been sketched out of 'an imminent split within the Jewish world that will parallel the Jewish–Christian schism nineteen centuries ago'.[9] This is a serious and substantive issue. In the third era of Jewish history proud affirmations of self-ascribed Jewishness do not always coincide with the Judaism of the past. One of the central challenges of this new era is to reconcile the integrity of modern secular Jewish attitudes with agreed criteria for personal Jewish status. Is a consensus possible that will satisfy the needs of both religious and secular Jews? Who has the authority to define 'who is a Jew'?

Meanwhile the cultural and political activities go on, defiantly secular and as integral to Anglo-Jewry's psychological health as the religious and educational manifestations of the community's exodus. All are part of that redemptive process by which we are freed from the shadows of exile.

The secular Jew may well baulk at being included within a spiritual perspective. It is precisely in contradistinction to traditional religious Judaism that they may wish to define themselves. They can point – with pride, and sometimes with defiance – to the longstanding tradition of Jewish diaspora secularism: 'all those millions of Yiddish-speaking Jews who belonged to secular Jewish institutions, sent their children to secular Jewish, non-Zionist schools, who went to the Jewish theatre and read secular Jewish books, who sang Jewish songs and fought the Nazis in Jewish partisan units . . . many of them were Bundists – Jewish socialists – or Jewish anarchists or Jewish communists'.[10]

But redemption – like oppression and annihilation – embraces religious and secular Jews. In truth, the bringing of redemption is not the exclusive provenance of one section of the Jewish people alone. It cannot be treated like largesse to be bestowed – beneficently or condescendingly – on others. All Jews are both authors and subjects in the drama of redemption.

With their pronounced scepticism about religion, Jews who choose an involvement with Jewish life that is actively secular often seem to see themselves – and are seen by the religious community – as if they were the 'wicked child' (the *rasha*) described by the Passover *haggadah*. This child represents the person who defiantly distances himself or herself from participation in the collective religious re-enactment of the exodus at *seder* night. But the irony is that the *rasha*, scornful of such expressions of communal solidarity, is still actively participating through his or her defiance.

The *rasha* is still at the table, questioning, still a vital critical voice without whom the unfolding drama of Jewish history cannot be enacted.

Judaism without the contribution of Jewish political, cultural, social and artistic dissent is like bread without the yeast: dry, flat and tasteless. And we need eat *matzah* for only one week out of the year.

If we are honest, we can recognise that the *rasha* also represents an internal aspect of ourselves. We each contain that critical, argumentative voice that wants to pull away from others (yet stay connected too), that may be angry, cynical, sceptical, bloodyminded, that wants the answers yet refuses to be satisfied, that cannot rest content, that cannot stay still, that cannot find peace, that questions everything – and that keeps us alive.

Just as the healthy individual learns to hold the tension between the different aspects of the personality, so too a community can learn to value its constituent parts. The blossoming of Jewish secularism alongside the religious renewal testifies to the growing richness of Anglo-Jewish life. It is sometimes hard for a community caught up in a form of sibling rivalry to see itself as the lively and life-affirming family it actually is. For the tensions between religious and secular are always with us. The forms of secular Anglo-Jewish self-expression are legion, and are often united only in opposition to the Jewish religious establishment, or what is perceived as the archaic Judaism of the past. And yet, as Hyam Maccoby has wisely commented: 'There is no such thing as complete emancipation from a religious tradition. What actually happens is a transition from conscious to unconscious membershp of that tradition . . . To fight for Judaism without knowing it has been the usual fate of modern Jewish secularism.'[11]

The latter sentence can fall hard upon the ears of secular and religious alike – especially when the secular Jew wishes to stand at a distance from Judaism as traditionally understood, and the religious Jew in turn wishes to defend the boundaries of what it means to be 'religious'. The spiritual evolution of the Jewish people continually breaks through the boundaries we seek to impose upon it, unmasking our poverty-stricken attempts to confine it within structures of thought with which we feel secure. The Spirit defies our carefully-constructed parameters and elides the distinctions between religious and secular spheres. It is simpler to cling to the belief that religion and secularism are mutually exclusive categories, and quite distinct world-views, than to face the shaking of our certainties which occurs when we recognise their essential interchangeability. For beneath the conflicts, something deeper is shared.

There is an irrepressible Jewish messianic urge which drives us on, which refuses to be defeated by the vicissitudes of time and history or the absurdity of the defiantly hopeful claim that humanity can be transformed. Jews are the mad adventurers of history, unable to accept the mundaneity and mediocrity of human fate. This is our gift, our blessing, our burden. We carry hope to a world we are not sure deserves our hopefulness. But in spite of our doubts, maybe because of our doubts, we persist in our impossible, yet impossible-to-relinquish, task.

Whether consciously or not, many of the social, cultural and political groupings we have mentioned are involved in sparking that messianic process. Exodus implies gaining freedom from the constraints of being Jewish in private but British in public. We do that for the sake of our own souls, and for the sake of the wider Jewish and non-Jewish world in which we struggle to survive.

Our personal liberation is inextricably interwoven with our collective obligations. As Jews who are now free, but have known slavery, our exodus requires of us – whether we like it or not – a continuing sensitivity to the needs of others. This ethical demand is the rationale for our exodus and the justification for our continued existence as a people. Whatever the language used to describe it, the prerequisite of Jewish continuity – for secular and religious alike – is this commitment to holy living.

This daily and mundane sacramental work was given the name of *Tikkun Olam*: the restoring (or repairing) of the world. *Tikkun Olam* is, in origin, a mystical doctrine emphasising human responsibility for the transformation and perfecting of our world. Its mythic imagery, drawn from the *Kabbalah*, is somewhat provocative for our contemporary consciousness. For the doctrine states that in order to make room for the creation of the world, God withdrew into Himself, as it were. Into the 'empty space' thus created, God projected divine light, but this light was so powerful that a catastrophe followed: the 'vessels' designed to contain the energy of the light shattered, and the divine light was trapped as sparks in the broken shards which now littered creation.

Every human action partakes in the subsequent cosmic drama and can hasten or delay the restoration of cosmic harmony. The 'raising of the sparks' (*tikkun*) is the task of humankind and is achieved through the performance of *mitzvot* (ethical and ritual actions). Even those living outside the tradition, yet whose actions conform to the tradition's ethical demands, are contributing, perhaps unbeknownst to themselves, to the redemptive process and the restoration of cosmic harmony. When the process is complete, the messianic age will dawn.[12]

Although the anthropomorphism of the imagery of *Tikkun Olam* may seem strange to our modern sensibilities, its impact on Jewish self-perception is undoubted. All areas of human activity – and indeed every individual action – were seen as potential opportunities for his immense restorative work. This summons to a personal commitment to collective transformation reverberates still within the consciousness of both religious and secular Jew, for the religious and secular Jewish endeavours share a single commitment to that tantalising myth of redemption.

Tikkun Olam is a collective journey dependent on each individual. *Tikkun Olam* is divine work dependent on human beings. *Tikkun Olam* is a 'religious' imperative enacted in the 'secular' world. *Tikkun Olam* is messianic work beyond our power and control, dependent on the ways we find to activate the spark of the Messiah in our souls.

The Messiah will come only when he is no longer necessary; he will come only on the day after his arrival; he will come not on the last day, but on the very last. (Franz Kafka)[13]

————————————————————————*—————————————————————————

One of the biggest events was the Molesworth Seder, a symbolic, third seder. We went to the Cruise missile base at Molesworth, at Easter: there were tens of thousands there. It was wet and muddy and absolutely packed. We gathered around the outside of the base, the barbed wire — the police inside, us outside. And we had a seder *service. We took our own* haggadah *book with us. We'd rewritten it to apply to nuclear weapons and to the potential nuclear holocaust. We gave out* matzah *and bitter herbs to people who were passing by and we gave them a leaflet explaining why. We gave them wine. And it felt good to be with Jews doing that.*

It felt strong to be out there publicly doing something Jewish. We were taking our particular tradition and making it applicable. And it wasn't forced. The matzah *represented freedom and the bitter herbs represented the slavery of nuclear weapons ... The crowd grew, and more and more people came, and people started saying, 'I thought* seder *was last week', and, 'Have you asked the* Ma Nishtanah *yet?' And people started joining in the singing and I realised that we were collecting around us a larger groups of Jews. They were on the demonstration anyway and they had no idea that you could be there and Jewish. And it meant something to them as well, to see a group who was publicly Jewish doing something Jewish and obviously proud of it ...*

12
'I Will Take You to Me as a People ...' The Renaissance of Jewish Learning

---
✳

My mother's generation had no Jewish learning at all. I very much doubt that many women of that generation were allowed to learn. I think we have recreated something. We've found a need for it. There is an obligation on us to learn.

✳

The initiative was to try to create an adult educational centre which would be open to everybody, where somebody who knew absolutely nothing – couldn't distinguish between an aleph and a swastika as it were – would feel unthreatened and not embarrassed, and would mingle naturally with somebody who was quite intense about their Jewish life ... The classes had a characteristic of their own, which was an atmosphere of thrust and argument, where there's an attempt not to be apologetic and to give the standard answers, and to acknowledge that one didn't know necessarily what the answers were.

✳

There was lots of discussion and debate about the issues of peace. We wrote out some position papers and put the text in the middle of the page and passed the paper around and people put commentaries on the outside. So it was actually using the model of the Talmud ... There weren't any right or wrong answers – there were different opinions, and if we collected all the opinions together then as a body we would have something. It didn't really matter what the solution was – the debate was important, the argument was important. It felt alive to

something Jewish. I started to learn that I had the right to argue it out as well as anybody else ...

Something I'm still grappling with is to what extent you can deviate away from the tradition as passed down to me, that's familiar and might disappear. But then if it doesn't mean anything, what's the point of keeping it except to make it my own? And the more I've done that, the more strong I feel – that I'm not being a Jew because of the legacy of this century, the Holocaust, but I'm being a Jew for myself.

And it's a different sort of Judaism. It's a Judaism that excites me a lot more, that is about joy and being positive – and it's fun! It's not always serious – and I didn't know that was possible. It's like breaking out of my own personal ghetto that I'd put myself in because I had all this guilt. Well, guilt's the wrong word. I felt all this weight of responsibility.

Jewish belonging is no substitute for Jewish living. And Jewish living is predicated upon Jewish learning. During the last decade and a half there has been a flowering of Jewish learning within the community. Anglo-Jewry seems to have begun to rediscover what it means for Jews to be 'the people of the Book'.

We knew already that the ultra-Orthodox communities of the Hassidic and yeshivah worlds had taken it upon themselves to be the saving remnant of Anglo-Jewry: the Nazi destruction of East European religious life catalysed an unprecedented commitment to renewed Jewish learning. In a remarkably short time and, initially, with few material resources, a lost world was recreated. In north London, in Manchester, in Gateshead, prodigious feats of learning were recorded.

Up until the 1960s, their single-minded dedication to the task in hand – Jewish survival and renewal – left behind the rest of Anglo-Jewry. The uncertainties of the majority of British Jews, struggling to find a place and rationale for Jewish education within a secular society, were irrelevant to those traditionalists whose programmes and institutions made no compromises with *goyische* culture. '*Goyische* culture' was itself a contradiction in terms.

The demographic decline of Anglo-Jewry – which reflects its socio-economic position and the numerical diminishment of the urban middle classes throughout Europe – did not touch these ultra-Orthodox enclaves. Numerically and educationally they continued to expand. Yet we seem to have entered a boom time for Jewish education in the community as a whole.

145

The ancient Biblical affirmation of Jewish faith, the *shema*, repeated twice daily through the generations, instructs us: 'and you shall teach them diligently to your children . . .' At the centre of Jewish continuity was this injunction to pass on the words, doctrines and lessons of the Torah to the next generation. As with all other aspects of Jewish life, the *shoah* cast its huge shadow of doubt on the wisdom of this traditional imperative: too many Jewish children had been diligently destroyed for us to remain wholehearted in our pursuit of Jewish learning. In the post-war assimilationist years Anglo-Jewry placed its faith in the 1944 Education Act and secular British education.

Jewish education took place at a minimal level. The traditional *cheder* system of irate and unqualified teachers attempting to indoctrinate quarrelsome and bored pupils with seemingly irrelevant information, left its mark on more than one generation. The spiritual inwardness of Judaism was ignored, and the complex integrity of the texts and the traditions reduced to meaningless rote learning and religious behaviourism. The soul of the tradition shrivelled almost to nothing.

Jews in Britain were faced with a dispiriting choice between gradually drifting away into total assimilation or a grudging acceptance of a Judaism imposed from outside and cut off from everyday life. We joined synagogues when the children were old enough to receive that modicum of Judaism that was largely irrelevant for us as adults but which we nevertheless thought necessary for Jewish continuity. We dutifully sent them along on Sunday mornings so that others could teach them how to be Jewish. Understandably, children grew up alienated and frustrated. When later they felt the residual urge to maintain some continuity for their kids, the charade was played out once more.

As the failure of the system became painfully apparent, alternatives began to be sought: the era of the Jewish day school had arrived.

———————————————————✳———————————————————

I didn't have a Jewish education. I'm sadly lacking in many areas and don't have the same sense of identity that I think my children have got. I've got older children now at Jewish secondary schools and they have a tremendous awareness of their Jewishness and a confidence. They're able to talk to other people about their religion in an informed way that I never could.

In spite of parental anxieties about the separation from the rest of British society which could result from sending one's child to a Jewish school, the proportion of Jewish school-age children attending such schools continued, and continues, to rise. Twenty years ago it was 5 per cent. It is now between 35 and 40 per cent.[1] This may suggest a growing self-confidence in expressions of Jewish ethnicity rather than a sign of religious renewal.[2] However, the optimism engendered by the expanding phenomenon of the Jewish day school has been tempered by recent research into the effectiveness of this education in retaining Jewish commitment into adult life.

A passion for Jewish living cannot be taught as if it were a mathematical theorem. Parental example and a primary Jewish education seem to be determining factors in an individual's continuing commitment to Jewishness. Research has suggested that when these factors are removed, 'the effect of Jewish secondary education on attitudes to Jewish observance was virtually non-existent' and, with regard to belief in God, 'actually induced a negative association'.[3]

This should come as no surprise. It is an old maxim that 'religion cannot be taught, it has to be caught'. If Jewish secondary schooling reinforces the mechanical performance of prayers and rituals at the expense of the intellectual and spiritual dimensions of Judaism, it cannot but be doomed to failure.[4] Another white (Jewish) elephant bites the dust.

Of course it is possible that the spiritual and intellectual dimensions of Jewish life can be introduced to Jewish youngsters in exciting and imaginative ways. But here parental cooperation is crucial. As Clive Lawton, head teacher of the King David High School in Liverpool, has written:

It is not so much a matter of educating parents – or of educating children – but rather more of persuading parents to feel that they own the religious ethos of the school sufficiently to enable it to move forward in its attempt to raise the Jewish consciousness of its young people until they are unable to resist the Jewish implications of every momentary experience and choice that they take throughout their lives.[5]

This idealism is invigorating, but the sad truth is that often the confusions and uncertainties of many parents prevent the necessary working alliance being made between parent and child, family and school. So particularly for those with young children, the recent and remarkable growth spurt in adult education is an investment for the future, not only an enhancement of personal Jewish living.

———————————————*———————————————

Somehow we as women have to understand why we relate to our tradition as we do, and where we think we're going, because I do think we owe it to our

147

daughters. And daughters who start asking questions and making demands and wanting to be involved are very precious to us, and in order not to fail them we have to get on with the process really. I don't think it's good enough to say our daughters will carry this on for us and take it further. I think we have to offer them something that they can relate to and respect.

Yet with 20–25 per cent of Jewish children now receiving no Jewish education at all,[6] the future intellectual and spiritual health of Anglo-Jewry will require a radical revisioning of how Jewish education is best effected. Anglo-Jewry is a deeply conservative community and changes to the structure of part-time synagogue-based education will be resisted to the death. Yet there are some encouraging signs. Chief Rabbi-elect Jonathan Sacks has recognised that:

Learning-through-doing, informal education, youth groups, residential retreats, adult education and 'outreach' programmes are all likely to figure more prominently in the future as the limits of formal education, particularly for children from non-observant homes, are recognised. Increasingly Jewish education will be seen in its traditional role – if in modern forms – as the transmission of a total culture to total social entities, rather than as the imparting of information to children in isolation from their family context.[7]

If this transformation in the education of children is to happen, the key will be the renaissance of Jewish adult learning. Jewish identity depends upon Jewish learning. Self-confidence is born of familiarity with the sources of one's own tradition. Our texts, our traditions, our history, our philosophy, our stories, our spirituality – the accumulated wisdom of our millennial wanderings – all this is being sought out with new enthusiasm. A brief review of some recent developments in Jewish learning suggests that our Anglo-Jewish exodus from the self-denying habits of the past is well under way. Self-deprecation is born of ignorance, and a fear of having that ignorance exposed. Assertion of our Jewish identity emerges out of our renewed curiosity about who we are and where we have come from.

So we see the unprecedented success in London and the provinces of the Spiro Institute, which aims to bring a knowledge and understanding of Jewish history and culture to both Jews and non-Jews. And the rejuvenated Jews' College, bursting at the seams with a Rabbinics programme, and post-graduate and part-time and teacher-training courses. And the growth of the Leo Baeck College, now offering part-time Jewish learning as well as BA, MA and Ph.D. degree courses in Jewish Studies, alongside its rabbinic courses and its pioneering extra-mural study programmes. And the imaginative development of the Sternberg Centre for Judaism containing a day school, educational resource centre, synagogue, bookshop and museum as well as cultural activities and exhibitions, student chaplaincy and coun-selling programmes. And the innovative and dynamic work at Yakar, offered in a spirit of open inquiry and combining intellectual integrity with honest religiosity.

These are the institutions which have placed themselves at the forefront of Anglo-Jewry's educational renaissance. Yet we also have the personalised one-to-one religious learning of the ever-expanding countrywide Project Seed; the London Board Family weeks; the communal excitement engen-dered by the Traditional Alternatives symposia; the omnipresent liveliness of Lubavitch; the Limmud conferences for Jewish educationalists, models of intra-religious tolerance, commonsense and purposefulness; the aca-demic gatherings in Oxford at the Centre for Postgraduate Hebrew Studies; the sensitive and scholarly work of the Centre for the Study of Judaism and Jewish/Christian Relations, in Birmingham. The list seems endless. And most of these projects have emerged only within the last decade or so.

Then there is the proliferation of regular and one-off lectures, *shiurim*, seminars and workshops on everything from kashrut to kabbalah, and Hebrew to Holocaust. Open the pages of the *Jewish Chronicle*, week in, week out, and one finds there a veritable smorgasbord of opportunities for Jewish study: business or medical ethics, psychoanalysis, feminism, socialism, Jewish theology, Israeli politics, Talmud ...

Jewish education implies Jewish books. Yet Anglo-Jewry does not seem very keen on Jewish books. One publisher turned down this present book because, he said, 'Jews in Britain don't buy books of Jewish interest, books about themselves.' We might buy Saul Bellow or Philip Roth or Bernard Malamud – or Maureen Lipman – but *Jewish* books? Perhaps Lionel Blue's success has broken down this resistance, though it still seems that it is necessary for the gentile world to accept us before British Jews can learn to love their own.

But there are indications that things are changing. The *Jewish Quarterly* can now be bought over the counter at W. H. Smith, rather than being a secret in-house journal for a few select devotees. The newer journals emerging from Jews' College and the Manor House, *L'Eylah* and *Manna*, continue to reach and enliven an ever-wider Jewish reading public: with their studied discussion and debate on contemporary issues of Jewish concern, mixed with the usual self-serving polemics, they exemplify Anglo-Jewry's growing confidence and self-promotion.

Tentatively, with a caution necessary whenever one tries to decipher the

picture at the end of a kaleidoscope, we might say that our exodus is leading us – as in days of old – towards Sinai. Just as the political liberation
of the Hebrew people from Egyptian slavery led inexorably to their
collective commitment to a new way of life embodied in the Torah, so
too Anglo-Jewry has been experiencing its own distant echo of that mythic
experience.

Part of the new mood of Jewish self-assertion involves making new
connections with Torah. This is 'Torah' both in its narrower senses – the
Five Books of Moses, the whole of the Biblical canon, the oral traditions
stemming from the written texts and embodied in the Talmud and the
legal codes – and in its widest sense of the totality of Jewish learning.
Within this grandly inclusive latter understanding, Torah is conceived of
as 'a great dynamic idea stimulating Jewish minds and inspiring Jewish
hearts to search for religious and moral truth and in finding that truth add
to the totality of Torah. The Torah is both creative in the lives of Jews
and in turn created by the Jews.'[8]

'I will take you to Me as a people ...' This promise meant that Exodus
was connected, indissolubly, to Sinai; the creation of a people to the
revelation to the people. The Israelites interpreted their experiences as the
irruption of the divine into human history. The covenant with one man,
Abraham, was transformed into the covenant with the whole people, Israel.

In the third era of Jewish history there has begun to be a reaffirmation
of that sense of covenant, in spite of the belief of many that that covenant
had been broken by its author. Anglo-Jewry's reapplication to the world
of Jewish learning is one manifestation of this renewed commitment to the
fractured covenant. The trauma of the *shoah* numbed a generation or more.
Who could put their hearts into Jewish learning when hearts were still
broken? Slowly the soul-deadening experience of oppression and exile is
giving way to the new energy of exodus. Perhaps, as Robin Spiro says, it
is 'the energy of the six million coming through'.

---

*

---

*I was not particularly Orthodox and I was not particularly Zionistic. Not
finding myself in either of these two obvious strands of Jewishness I was a little
lost, unable to become involved. Then I was given this unique opportunity to
study Jewish history at the age of thirty-seven, at Oxford. At the end of the
time, I knew where I was. I knew that I was the result of Jewish history and
I knew that I had a future as a Jew.*

*There's no profit in education, apart from the soul, but I felt a sense of
responsibility ... We have to a very great extent provided a bridge to a great*

many people to return to religion. But that is not our object. Our object is merely to create an identification which will not make a mockery of this extraordinary, magical subject called Jewish history.

---*—————————————————*✳*—————————————————*---

I think that people are seeking a sense of belonging and once they have achieved that sense of belonging in society I think everyone is looking for something which is true and where he or she really belongs. Through the programmes that we are offering we are giving people a way in which they can identify, which is not alien to them. It doesn't require the discipline of fulfilling mitzvot, *religious ritual. It's something which is appealing to the intellect and to the soul at the same time. I feel that through the different alleyways that we are opening, people are finding their path towards themselves. And I feel they find something within their soul that they feel at peace with ... (Nitza Spiro)*

The increased willingness of Jews in this country to inquire again of the texts of old has been happening in such a fragmented way – in so many different contexts, and with such different motivations and degrees of commitment – that it has been hard to appreciate the quiet revolution going on in our midst. But this largely unconscious process of re-establishing the centrality of Jewish learning within the life of the community is now becoming increasingly clear.

This openness to Torah, in its broadest sense, embraces formal and informal education. It involves the religiously committed, the searchers and the unaffiliated. It involves all ages from toddlers at Jewish kindergartens, to university students, to city businessmen and women, to retired pensioners. And it undermines the worn-out dichotomy between 'religious' and 'secular' Jewish learning.

We are coming to realise the extent to which the multifarious texts of our tradition have both formed us as a people and enabled us to survive as a people. The fabric of Jewish life is woven out of a myriad of texts, and their interpretation and application through the ages is 'at the heart of Jewish identity'. This is, as George Steiner says, the 'open secret of the Jewish genius and of its survival. The text is home; each commentary a return.'[9]

But which are the texts which have formed us, and which are the texts to which the Jew today looks for self-understanding? These are deceptively simple questions, yet they evoke impassioned argument. There are the fundamental disagreements, well-documented, between Orthodoxy and non-Orthodoxy over the divine nature of the original texts of Torah. There are disputes within Orthodoxy over the status of the 'Torah' taught by the Hassidic rebbes and their successors. And there are key questions about what actually constitutes the corpus of Jewish texts of relevance for Jewish identity and survival.

Religious authorities such as Rabbi Jonathan Sacks argue for the necessary particularity of those Jewish texts which, from the earliest rabbinic times through to the nineteenth century, 'were themselves, in form or substance, commentaries to one particular text, the Torah, whether as exegesis, law or philosophy'.[10] What counts are the original Biblical texts together with each generation's responses to those central texts, which are 'capable of infinite interpretation'.[11]

In our contemporary setting, it is not that the so-called 'secular' voice denies the centrality of the traditional texts. On the contrary. As Steiner asserts:

The Torah is the pivot of the weave and cross-weave of reference, elucidation [and] debate which organize ... the daily and the historical life of the community. The community can be defined as a concentric tradition of reading ... neither Israel's physical scattering, nor the passage of millennia, can abrogate the authority ... in the holy books, so long as these are read and surrounded by a constancy of secondary, satellite texts ... Via magisterial commentary, the given passage will, in times and places yet unknown, yield existential applications and illuminations of spirit yet unperceived.[12]

Here Steiner illustrates his fidelity to the tradition, providing his own 'magisterial commentary' to the ever-expanding corpus of Jewish texts. For Steiner, as for Sacks, the Torah and its commentaries stand at the centre of Jewish learning. Their study renders them timeless, enabling the past to inform the present. And yet for the Professor, it seems, the 'concentric tradition of reading' moves ever outwards in wider and wider circles, embracing 'the "bookish" genius of Marx and of Freud, of Wittgenstein and of Lévi-Strauss ... a secular deployment of the long schooling in abstract, speculative commentary'.[13]

It is here that the Rabbi smells heresy. The 'secular' Professor is judged to be guilty of a dangerous eclecticism of interest in wishing to enlarge the scope and range of seminal Jewish texts to include new sources of contemporary revelation: 'We stand in awe at the straight-facedness with which he makes the transition from *the* text, Torah, to an abstract textuality; from the Divine word to words-in-general; from sacred reading to reading as such.'[14]

This is an ancient debate. In Biblical times the iconoclasm of the prophet was always a challenge to the conservatism of the priest. Both were needed to maintain the spiritual continuity of the people. Yet at times both considered themselves to be the true guardians of the 'Word'.

Indeed, the supposedly 'secular' voice *is* profoundly subversive of the normative religious tradition, guardian of the sources of revelation. The notion of progressive revelation is built into the tradition itself. As Steiner says: 'every Jew, when he is wholly present to God's word, to the living summons of the Torah, is in a condition of prophecy and prevision'.[15] This will always be a challenge to religious authority. And this dialogue itself – on-going and impassioned – is, at its best, a vital life-giving addition to the spiritual and intellectual health of a community.

We have dwelt on the debate between these two preeminent Jewish scholars because the issues they raise are central to Anglo-Jewry's current educational renaissance. For the unarticulated question underlying this revival is, 'Where can we find revelation *for our own times?*'

Some might answer that we already have the Bible, the Talmud, the countless legal, homiletical, philosophical and mystical texts that have sustained us thus far in our heroic pilgrimage through time. These constitute our spiritual and intellectual resources, our heritage. Taken together they have created us, revealed their truths to us, and they will lead us to redemption.

Others may feel that 'at a time when revelation is not immediately apparent, then at least we can try to go for an honest evaluation of our situation today.' So it may be necessary to attend to those contemporary teachers who speak the truth to us in words we understand: 'If a Kafka, a Freud, a Karl Kraus tell us the truth about ourselves, then theirs are the voices *that should be added to a contemporary religious consciousness*' (emphasis added).[16] This goes beyond Sacks and Steiner.

Whether we search out revelation within the context of traditional *Talmud Torah* or seek out the insights of the latest novelist, poet, dramatist or artist; whether we choose to learn about our Jewish identity through the Biblical Levites or Primo Levi, we know that we do not have to make either/or choices. We can have Abraham Joshua Heschel, Isaac Bashevis Singer and Jacob Epstein as well as our patriarchs Abraham, Isaac and Jacob. And from Hannah's Biblical psalm of thanksgiving, 'He guards the steps of His faithful; but the wicked perish in darkness – for not by strength shall man prevail'[17] it is not a million light years to the poetry of Hannah Senesh:

There are stars whose light reaches the earth only after they themselves have disintegrated and are no more.

And there are those whose shining memory lights the world after they have passed from it.

These lights which shine in the darkest night are those which illuminate for us the path.[18]

Whenever we stand in a relationship to our sources of revelation we are engaged in Jewish learning, in learning what it means to be a Jew. And it is a new kind of learning. Anglo-Jewry's renewed willingness to re-approach Torah – sometimes eagerly and with a thirst for knowledge, sometimes tentatively and full of doubts and questions – is happening in the spirit of one of our century's greatest Jewish teachers, Franz Rosenzweig, who was the first to recognise that in our times a 'new learning' is being born: 'It is a learning in reverse order. A learning that no longer starts from the Torah and leads into life, but the other way round: from life ... back to the Torah.'

Rosenzweig's crucial realisation was that in our times nobody starts solely from within the mythic tradition: 'There is no one today who is not alienated, or who does not contain within themselves some small fraction of alienation.' Since the Enlightenment, our religious or ethnic or cultural identity as Jews is in constant dialogue with the values and thought of the secular cultures in which we live. As a result, we must approach our Judaism by bringing everything that we are to it. To feel a sense of Jewish belonging means that we must not deny any part of ourselves and who we are: 'in being Jews we must not give up anything, not renounce anything, but lead everything back to Judaism. From the periphery back to the centre; from the outside, in.'[19]

The ways in which we combine our adherence to Jewish culture with our commitment to modernity will define our Jewish identity. Our sources of revelation are the wisdom of the past and the inspired insights of the present. Their cross-fertilisation is at the heart of Jewish learning. The fruit they bear enriches our lives. And this becomes the third source of revelation: not only the texts of the past, and not only the modern discoveries of the human spirit, but our own lives.

To learn the art of reading the texts of our own lives is also a part of Jewish education. We know that our own personal stories can be just as fragmented and confused, their meaning hidden from view, as any ancient mythological tale. And yet that complex art of reading, interpreting, deciphering, translating that chaotic, mysterious text which is the story of *our* lives – this is of the essence. To understand who we are – each one of us –

is the hidden agenda of Jewish learning. 'From the outside, in.' Our sense of belonging depends upon what sense we make of our own lives. The fourth section of the book is an exploration of this theme – the personal journey.

Part 4
OUT OF THE WILDERNESS

13
Buried Treasure

---- ✳ ----

On the night of 18–19 March 1944 I dreamt that we were taken in lorries to a place where I used to do target shooting. From where the driver sat a man with a swastika, in uniform, stepped out. He was blond and I can even see him today as he looked in the dream. He stood us in lines and as he walked by, he hypnotised everyone to step into a grave. It was a long grave and at the end of it there was a guillotine. Each time the guillotine fell somebody died; and I stood there facing this man, who looked into my eyes.

I was moving towards the grave and I said to myself, 'No, not that. If I have to die, you bastard, you will die with me,' and I picked up a shovel, the shovel with which they had to actually dig their graves. I ran against him and I wanted to hit him, but I was interrupted and what I saw next second was a burnt-out figure of clay. And I didn't know when I woke up whether I killed him or he killed me. Who won? Who lost? I didn't know and I had to live with that feeling and fear throughout the war, not knowing what this dream has meant.

In the back of my mind there was the feeling I probably had killed him, because if the last image I had was a burnt-out figure then I must at least have survived him in some way, and that kept me going. It was in a sense a prophetic dream because without us knowing yet, it was at that particular moment of time, about 3.30 in the morning on the 19th of March, that the German Nazi armies had crossed the border into Hungary. And that was the most unforgettable event in my life ...

When I got to Auschwitz I thought that I recognised the SS doctor – he was the man who got out of the lorry, selecting people for life and death by hypnotising them. Then I left one barrack and went into another barrack, and during the night every other barrack was taken to the gas and I wasn't. So that dream somehow forewarned me to be in a particular kind of, I like to call it, psychic state. And that carried me through the whole camp and even after for a while.

That psychic state was about a dimension of existence which we don't take into consideration very often, which is there and which becomes operative in very dangerous or difficult situations ... These irrational forces have directed me under very strange circumstances and here and there later on I had a glimpse of these powers still. Now, where they come from, and what they mean, and why me, I don't know.

There is a story which tells of a man who was full of worries. His name was Eizik, son of Yekel, of Cracow. After many years of poverty he had a dream. In it a voice told him that in Prague, under the bridge which led to the king's palace, a treasure was buried. He dismissed the dream: he had problems enough; and the journey was long and exhausting. But the dream returned, and when it recurred a third time Eizik set out for Prague.

When he reached the city he recognised the bridge, but it was guarded day and night and he did not dare to start digging. Every morning he went to the bridge and waited indecisively until evening. Finally the captain of the guards, who had been watching him and thought him a spy, asked what he was doing. Too frightened to invent a story, Eizik told the truth: a dream of buried treasure had brought him here from a distant land.

The captain smiled: 'You're such a fool, paying attention to a dream and wearing yourself out like this! Listen, if I'd had faith in dreams, I would have travelled to Cracow long ago, for I used to dream of a treasure buried there under the stove of a Jew – Eizik son of Yekel, that was his name. But can you imagine me going from house to house searching for the right man and an imaginary dream treasure?' Eizik thanked him, travelled home, and dug under his stove – where he found the treasure.

This is an old story, found in the folk literature of many cultures. An individual makes a journey, following a dream, a vision, an intuition. The seeker is looking for a treasure; and a journey is necessary; and there are hardships on the way; and something unexpected is discovered; and the traveller returns; and all is the same; and everything is different.

This is also the poet's understanding:

> We shall not cease from exploration
> And the end of all our exploring

Will be to arrive where we started
And know the place for the first time.[1]

In our Hassidic version there is a certain ambiguity in the tale. Its author-
ship is disputed, and each *zaddik* (spiritual teacher) to whom it is attributed
draws out of it a different lesson. Martin Buber tells it in the name of
Rabbi Simcha-Bunam of Pshiskhe, who adds at the story's conclusion:
'Take this story to heart and make what it says your own: There is
something you cannot find anywhere in the world, not even at the *zaddik's*,
and there is, nevertheless, a place where you can find it.'

Buber himself goes on to elucidate the parable's 'true meaning': 'There
is something that can only be found in one place. It is a great treasure,
which may be called the fulfilment of existence. The place where this
treasure can be found is the place on which one stands.'[2]

In Buber's spiritual-existentialist reading of the story, gurus and teachers
and rabbis and spiritual guides cannot help the individual find the meaning
and fulfilment of their lives. There is no external authority. Truth is to be
found within each person. Paradoxically, this does not invalidate the outer
search for the answers to life's questions. On the contrary, as the story
makes clear, it is essential to follow where the inner voice leads, perhaps
to the other side of the world.

To find the treasure, Eizik needs to make the journey away from home.
Only when he's moved away from the familiar does he come to find the
direction he needs to take. This leads him back to where he started, but
with new understanding. And the new knowledge enables him to find the
treasure that was there all along but which he'd never realised was available
for him, and him alone. The 'treasure' we each possess is to be claimed
wherever we happen to be, and in whatever situation we happen to find
ourselves.

Rabbi Nahman of Bratslav's version of the story leads us, however, in
the opposite direction. Having found the treasure under his stove, the
seeker says: 'Now I know that the treasure is always with you, but to find
out about it you have to journey far away.' And the final message reads:
'So it is with one's spiritual life, Rabbi Nahman concluded. Each one
possesses the treasure himself, but to find out about the treasure he must
journey to a spiritual guide.'[3] What is emphasised here is the importance
of the journey to find the teacher who will point the seeker in the right
direction.

Of course there is no 'correct' reading of the story. Its beauty lies partly
in its ambiguity. As with our own lives, so with these stories: infinitely
analysable, no unequivocal interpretation is given with them. They remain
elusive. We struggle towards the meanings they hold. And today's meaning

may be gone tomorrow. Our personal temperaments will determine what meaning we draw from this paradigmatic parable about the necessity of the individual's journey of self-discovery.

To talk about the 'necessity' of this journey may seem strange to our modern sensibilities. We are so used to thinking in collective terms about 'the Jewish people', *Klal Yisrael*, 'the Jewish community', that we can all but drown out this sense of the uniqueness of the individual. Conformity to the communal norms is advocated by both secular and religious authorities; not stepping out of line or dissenting in public or deviating from the group's mores is the received wisdom.[4]

Nevertheless the vibrancy of the community in the end depends on the individual who has found his or her own way through the morass of collective pressures and expectations. This can be a lonely and frightening journey. Yet the movement from joy to pain and back, from hope to despair and back, this insecurity and fragility of the journey is of the essence. The psychological health of the whole community depends upon those individuals brave enough to risk this journey. We still need each other but it can be argued, following Jung, that nothing shields us better against the solitude of the divine experience than community. It is the best and safest substitute for individual responsibility.[5]

The necessity for individual Jews to take personal responsibility for their own thoughts and actions is an integral part of our heritage. Long ago, the security of the Jewish people was seen to depend upon the integrity of the High Priest on Yom Kippur as he entered the Holy of Holies in the Temple to utter the secret name of God. On this special day of the year the fate of the community was in the hands of one man. But since the Temple was destroyed and the diaspora was established, there has been no High Priest. The democratisation of Judaism has meant that the holy work continues only through the people: 'each spot where a person raises their eyes to heaven is a Holy of Holies; every individual, having been created by God in His own image and likeness, is a High Priest; every day of a person's life is a Day for Atonement; and every word that a person speaks with sincerity is the name of God.'[6]

Each one of us is now enjoined to be a priest in a kingdom of priests. Whether we know it or not we still live within the myth: mortal and fallible, we mediate a grace and glory beyond our understanding.

This section of the book contains the testimony of some of those members of Anglo-Jewry who are attempting to follow their own inner truth, as Jews. These individual journeys can take place within a traditional religious setting; alongside or in tension with religious traditions and practices; or in opposition to established Jewish ways. These journeys may involve a connection to a synagogue – or leaving the synagogue. They may involve a commitment to work in the Jewish community – or outside it. These journeys may include an active identification with the Jewish world – or a wish to maintain a distance from it. Sometimes – to return to our opening parable's imagery – there is an emphasis on the discovery of an inner treasure; sometimes it is the vagaries of the journey which preoccupy; and sometimes there is a fascination with the signposts and guides met along the way. What is shared, however, is the integrity of the search.

I became the top boy in the Hebrew classes. I was a regular shul *goer. I sang the solos in the choir. I was enthusiastic and enjoyed it very much, but as I became older the other interest in my life was sport, and I had to make a choice between playing football on a Saturday morning or going to* shul. *And this was a very difficult decision for me. I thought about it and made the decision I wanted to play football.*

Then the rabbi asked me if I would stay on after Hebrew classes, he wanted to speak to me. And he said to me, 'Leslie, tell me it's not true that you're playing football on Shabbas.' *I'll never forget this. And I said, 'Yes, it's true.' And he said to me, 'I think you're not doing this voluntarily, you're under pressure. Surely you're under pressure. It must be the case.' So I said, 'No, I've made this decision of my own accord.' He said, 'Let me speak to the school.' And I said I didn't want him to do that and I had made my decision. And that started a new phase in my life.*

In the last couple of years of my legal career I went into therapy groups: I seemed to be living very much on a level, with no highs and no lows; I very seldom got angry, very seldom felt any elation or joy ... In the groups I started quite soon giving voice to something which I'd always known but never really voiced and that was: I wasn't really happy at law. But what else could I do?

That question stopped being important during that group time – it was quite possible to take a plunge into doing nothing. I remember the discovery that all I had to do in order to leave law was do it. And once I'd given myself that permission I left. I gave notice to my partners within a few days. It's something about taking responsibility for myself and not having to get permission and refer back to my parents. It's not their life, it's my life ... I was doing what good Jewish parents wanted a good Jewish boy to do.

————————✳————————

When I was a child I'd ask several times, 'Where does God live?' and I was always told he lives up in the sky, or he's like light, or something like that. It was difficult to imagine ... At night I always used to look across from the roof where we slept in summer and see this huge garden and this factory which had so many, many windows. The greatest number I knew at the time was a hundred. If something was a hundred it meant that it was beyond counting, beyond number, beyond imagination. And I used to think that God lived in that place: having been told that God can see everything, it made sense that he had so many windows that he can look out of and see everything that went on ...

When I looked up from the roof at night there was this magnificent dome which was so huge and so black and the stars shone like drops of water; and against it stood this date palm, with this green bough so serene, and its trunk so powerful, and the fruit which hung from it and it was like the Garden of Eden. And the house of a hundred windows made God very close, made him very real as well. He dwelt in a house as well, and yet he lived in the house of a hundred windows so he was beyond anything else that I could imagine.

Judaism contains a mythological framework which many Jews have abandoned as irrelevant to their lives: what has crossing the Red Sea or wandering in the wilderness to do with my life in the suburbs? For others, the old stories and traditions are not so much irrelevant as incomprehensible: the exodus from Egyptian slavery, a people's escape to freedom, celebrating *seder* nights, revelation at Sinai, the restless years of desert wandering towards a distant promised land, building those strange booths which blow down when the wind blows, yes we feel we are somehow connected to all this – but what does it really mean?

For still others these are the pieties of old we acknowledge as our own and their meaning is not questioned: this is what Jews believe in, these are the practices that Jews have always followed, there is nothing else to say or ask. For a few, the myth is still alive – the truth is secure and there is an unbroken chain of tradition from Sinai to Stamford Hill.

However we define ourselves in relation to the myth, its imagery is part of our psychic life. Whether we believe in God or not; whether we follow Jewish traditions or not; whether we feel inside the Jewish community, or marginal to it, or divorced from it; however thoroughly secular and British we feel, however cynical and dismissive our actions or thoughts, the power of the myth still lives on to penetrate our defences and to pierce our pretensions. Sometimes it illuminates our own life questions. At other times it offers clues, but not solutions. Always it points us back to our selves. The treasure is within. But the treasure is hidden.

We have always known this, and yet we have to discover it for ourselves. On the second floor of the Workmen's Accident Insurance Institution in Prague, Franz Kafka is in conversation with a young visitor. It is 1920:

'I am still in Egyptian bondage. I have not yet crossed the Red Sea.'
I laughed: 'The first thing after the Red Sea is the desert.'
Kafka nodded: 'Yes, in the Bible and everywhere else.'
He pushed his hands against the edge of the desk, leaned back in his chair, and, his body relaxed, stared up at the ceiling.
'The false illusion of a freedom achieved by external means is an error, a confusion, a desert in which nothing flourishes except the two herbs of fear and despair. That is inevitable, because anything which has a real and lasting value is always a gift from within. Man doesn't grow from below upwards but from within outwards. That is the fundamental condition of all freedom in life. It is not an artificially constructed social environment but an attitude to oneself and to the world which it is a perpetual struggle to maintain. It is the condition of man's freedom.'[7]

———————————————————*———————————————————

I got involved in drug smuggling and spent a year in Israeli prisons ... Years previously I'd had a dream. I woke up in the middle of the night with this very strong dream of pillars and barbed wire. It was just so beyond my experience. I tried to relate it to being Jewish: maybe it's some concentration camp or something. I kind of pushed it to the back of my mind, as you do with very strong dreams, nightmares ... So we were being walked through this prison, and suddenly this guard opened the door — and there was this dream I'd had two years before. And I thought, I'm just meant to be here ...

My dreams have always been really important to me, especially now as a painter ... We all put masks on and what I said to myself was: when I get out of here I'm not going to live a lie. I'm going to be me, no matter what it is. I didn't know who 'me' was but I felt I'm not going to be what my mother wants or what my father wants, or what society expects of me, but I'm going to be me. And what is that? Who am I? And I started to read in there. So prison became quite an exciting experience ...

14
The Gift from Within

I tried lots of different philosophies, lots of different ideas, lots of different countries . . . I went to the Metropolitan Museum in New York. I was walking through and I suddenly came into 'Twentieth-Century Painting' – and that was it! I really at that point knew: this is who I am. I'm a painter. All the dreams, all the realisations, all the experiences were in this room.

Much later I painted a painting called 'A Step Into the Burning Bush'.
Stepping into the burning bush inside is when you ask the question 'Who am
I?' and then you burn ... 'I'm not Jewish, that's something I left behind. I
don't want anything to do with this' – 'But you're Jewish ...' That kind of
dialogue takes place. And I can remember thinking: 'I'm going to have to go
back into the synagogue.'

It was one Yom Kippur and everybody's fasting. And I always had fasted –
but not with much commitment. The rabbi was walking around with the Torah
and everybody's standing up and they were all kissing the Torah and I was
thinking: 'This is ridiculous, there's no way I'm going to get involved with
this.' The rabbi is getting closer and closer and closer, and I feel out of respect,
okay, I'll stand up, because everyone else is standing up. And he's getting closer
and I thought, Okay, I'll touch the Torah with my tallis. *And it was 'thud' –*
literally just this: a thud on my heart. And I just kissed my tallis *and sat*
down.

And I thought, well, it's not about up here (in my head). It's here (in my
heart) and I can't explain that. It's no big deal. It's just part of me. I painted
that, and it was the first painting that I got an award for. It's now hanging
in Exeter Synagogue.

How do the myths, the metaphors and the symbols of the Biblical and
Judaic traditions illustrate, in Kafka's words, human growth 'from within
outwards'? An exploration of some aspects of the Jewish liturgical year
may provide some pointers to our own 'gift from within'.

The symbolism of the Jewish liturgical year can be said to revolve around
three major themes: creation, revelation and redemption. This theological
language may seem rather daunting but, as we shall see, these terms are a
kind of quasi-religious shorthand. They have a personal dimension that
touches the lives of Jew and gentile alike.

One of the most important aspects of the development of Jewish tradition
was the way in which events in the agricultural cycle became overlaid with
historical associations. So Passover (*Pesach*), originally a spring festival,
became a celebration of the exodus from Egypt; Pentecost (*Shavuot*), an
old midsummer harvest festival at the end of the wheat harvest, became the
celebration of the day on which Torah was given at Sinai; and Tabernacles
(*Sukkot*), an old autumn festival of vintage, came to commemorate the
dwelling of the Israelites in booths during their wanderings in the wilderness.

Eventually these festive days became part of the spiritual cycle of the people, with each festival embodying one overriding symbolic theme. We journey from Pesach in the first Hebrew month of the year, when the people are created, through seven weeks to Shavuot when the people have Torah revealed to them; until, as autumn gathers, we explore the ambiguities of redemption in historical time through the festival of impermanence, the Festival of Sukkot.

But we do not come to these holy-day themes free of our own thoughts, memories and feelings about them. For the Jew there is an inevitable emotional response: affectionate recognition, an irritated wish to argue, an embarrassed lack of knowledge, an uncomfortable upsurge of buried memories, an interested desire for more, an angry urge to dismiss, a curiosity reawakened, a spasm of guilt, an unexpected pain, a moment of sadness, a welcome renewal as in meeting an old friend . . . The mythological events of the tradition already have a psychic resonance within us. The images may alienate us – or help us feel a sense of belonging.

———————————————————✳———————————————————

When I came to live in Glasgow I stayed with an aunt and uncle in a very warm Jewish household and the experience was incredible. Apart from falling in love, I'm sure one of the reasons I was married so young was to have the chance of my own home, to be able to keep it as a Jewish home and have separate dishes and so on. I thought I was living the complete absolute perfect Jewish life. I realise today there was more to strive for than I was aware of then. But I was perfectly happy that I had arrived as a practising Jew. I felt I was part of a cultural group. Up until then I hadn't belonged.

I felt that by observing the festivals I was being Jewish. I don't know that I felt anything deeply spiritual, the way I feel now about the festivals, but I felt very much that my fate was tied up with Jewish people. I would think, when it was Pesach, that Jewish people all over the world were celebrating the festival. There was a strong feeling of being part of something, part of a tradition that was thousands of years old.

The Jewish liturgical celebration of Pesach takes the form of a kind of religious psychodrama. The *seder* night is centred around the recitation in the home of the story of the exodus of the Hebrew people from Egypt. But on this night liturgy is aided by additional symbols, so that the event is not just recalled, it is almost literally re-enacted.

So the bitter herbs allow the participants to taste the bitterness of their ancestors' experience. They are eaten with the brown paste called *charoset* which recalls the clay of the bricks of the Israelite slavery. The unleavened bread, the *matzah*, transports us back in time to the legendary departure of the people in such haste that even the bread had no time to rise. And the roasted shankbone held aloft during the narration of the events reminds us of the pascal lamb sacrificed before that departure – which thereby points back beyond the historical overlay to the agricultural origin of the celebration.

One can see that the whole liturgical thrust of the evening is to recall these events not just through thought but through experience: taste and touch and sight and smell combine in order for the past to live again for us now, in the present. One of the key passages of the evening reads:

In every generation each individual should regard themselves as if they personally had come out of Egypt, as it is said: You shall tell your child on that day, 'This is on account of what the Eternal One did for *me*, when I went out of Egypt.'

For the Holy one, blessed be He, redeemed not only our ancestors but us along with them, as it is said: He led *us* out from there, so as to bring us into the land he had promised our ancestors, and give it to us.[1]

Here the humbling arrogant claim on our own lives is spelt out: what devolves upon us is an act of identification with the collective history of our people – 'This is what God did for me.' This is a daring liturgical statement, defying us to disagree, taunting us with its contemptous disregard for the conventional logic of chronological history. In retelling our history, our creation as a people, we not only bind ourselves to that history of degradation and grandeur, but we are invited to consider that our own coming-into-being as Jews in our generation is contingent upon that distant event.

To enter into the mythic dimension of our history through the multi-layered event of the *seder* can be a very powerful experience. Each year the symbolism of the evening draws in those who may remain uninvolved for the rest of the year. Perhaps this is just nostalgia. Perhaps it is the vestiges of a faith long dissolved. Yet it is the one evening in the year when the extended family still gathers, often with protest, boredom or embarrassed frivolity, often with that uncomfortableness which is born out of a subliminal awareness of the very power and drama and significance of those distant events retold once more.

That embarrassed guilty jokiness is often around at Jewish religious occasions. It seems to arise out of a vague sense of something having been lost, be it a lack of belief, the lack of secure identity, the loss of familiarity with the rituals or the Hebrew, or the realisation that the inner feeling for the symbol or the myth seems to have died – but that there is nothing to replace it.

So on *seder* night we still gather: for grandparents to get *nachas* (vicarious pleasure) from the precocious grandchildren; for a meal which the woman of the house may have cooked under conditions she likens – with barely-disguised irritation – to the original Egyptian slavery; and to compete to see whose family tunes should be sung.

Our problem is that when we read that passage from the Passover liturgy which says that God redeemed not only our ancestors, but us along with them, our modern consciousness rebels from the literalism of it all. There is a secularised voice inside all but the most fundamentalist of modern Jews. We are all outside the myth now and it seems as though there is no going back to the straightforward and undivided consciousness of earlier times. And yet, there is a symbolic dimension to this liturgy which, perhaps, may still allow us to keep hold of these themes from inside ourselves – from 'within outwards'.

For Passover is not just an agricultural festival; it is not just the celebration of the creation of my historical identity; it is not only the celebration of God's delivering power in the history of my people; and it is not only the reminder that I personally stand as a link in that chain of tradition stretching back into that mythic past of my ancestors. Alongside nature and theology there is an inner existential and psychological dimension with which we have to struggle.

The key, as so often, is in language, in the Hebrew word for Egypt: *Mitzrayim*. The root of the word is connected with the Hebrew *tzr* which means 'narrow/constrained'. 'To come out of Egypt' is to come out of what confines me, traps me, shuts me in. If one wants to take the Passover liturgy as seriously as it asks us to take it, then we must work at it in a personal way – which means in a psychological way.

When we read that 'In every generation each individual should regard themselves as if they had come out of Egypt,' the reader is forced to ask: 'Have I come out of Egypt yet?' Have I come out of my narrowness: my narrowness of perception, my narrowness of feeling, the constraints I'm conditioned to bear, the constraints I impose on myself? When Passover comes round, again, the Jew who is still open to the possibility that the old myth has not quite died, wrestles with some basic questions: What am I still a slave to? How is that exodus from my own inner Egypt going to take place this year? It is not just a once-and-for-all, completed event. Emotionally, intellectually, spiritually I am still in the process of being created. Can I ever leave Egypt, my own narrowness, behind?

There is in us a deep regressive urge. The desire to stay in Egypt is very great: it is familiar and safe. It is the womb. It is home. It requires some kind of special energy to break through the waters, in that symbolic birth into the new, the unexplored, the uncharted terrifying territory ahead.

Many of the people we talked to for this book began their journey by leaving their parents. Some rebelled, others were sent away, others walked away. Leaving is a *sine qua non* of an individual's forging their own path through life. Often it can take years to discover that the path chosen has been defined in opposition to parental wishes or expectations, and that this reaction is itself a constraint.

'Creation', the first of our three symbolic themes, is not just a historical or theological category. We glimpse its personal relevance in our own struggles to be delivered from what holds each of us back, what constrains us in the safety of the routine and the familiar and the unconsciousness of daily events. The creation of our 'Self' requires a psychic birth, an exodus, as awesome as the delivery of a whole people from slavery. Perhaps we recognise in the complexity and pain of our own struggles that this is not presumptuousness on our part, but a reflection of the sacred nature of our own spiritual journey.

I remember wanting to paint all the dreams and fears I had as a child. I can remember this goat that used to be outside my window, and I wanted to paint this goat. All this world was going on inside myself and I thought everyone was seeing the same world – but they weren't ...

My painting changed: it was no longer the landscape outside. It was the landscape inside – a lot of memories and dreams. A lot of Jewish memories. I can remember wanting to paint a seder *– the first* seder *I ever went to, when I was five. It was in the East End and the Elijah's cup was put on the table and my uncle said, 'If this cup gets drunk the Messiah will come.' And I can remember that the next time I looked the cup was empty. For years I used to walk around thinking, 'The Messiah's here, it's okay.' And it wasn't until I painted it that I realised well, maybe this Messiah hasn't come!*

It's so hard to explain because it's about things I don't understand really. It's about something that doesn't feel past, something that doesn't feel present and something that doesn't feel future ...

We walked till our soles cracked open
and the sand rubbed in our wounds.
The hammer of the sun

beat the anvils of our skulls,
turned our flesh into
a pulp.
We thirsted for water
till our tongues were dry bricks,
our nostrils were made of mud.
At night we huddled together,
man and beast
yearning for comfort
searching for solace,
finding none.
We thought of straws and slavery.
We hoped for milk and honey.
But our dreams were of cucumbers,
Cool, fresh, green cucumbers.
We dreamed of the sweet juice
of a ripe melon.
We dreamed of home.

We walked till our eyelids glued together
and the sand baked in our lashes.
At noon our shadows shrank.
We thought we were melting
melting into the sand,
vanishing for ever.
At night the gaping mouth of darkness
swallowed us alive.
The black beast of the desert
howled in the hollows of our ears,
We shuddered in our fears.
We thought of 'strangers in a land'
We hoped for the help of a 'mighty hand'
But our dreams were of golden gods.
We dreamed of their glowing warmth,
of their protecting powers,
of their human reality!
We dreamed of home.

We walked till our stomachs shrivelled
and the sand settled in its wrinkles.
At dusk, we crouched in pain
our tattered rags covering our shame
we were

a miserable multitude of malnourishment
maintained on 'manna'
– a handful of coriander seeds
crushed to an oily pulp.
We thought of mud and mortar,
We hoped for priests and princes.
But our dreams were of quails.
We dreamed of fish
of silvery streams, of turquoise and aquamarine.
We dreamed of home.

And for this,
and for all these,
You punished us,
forgave us not.
For being weak,
You chastised us with plagues.
For being frightened,
You lashed us with fire.
For being hungry,
You murdered us with flesh.
For this
and for all these,
You punished us,
granted us Your wrath –
Till in our torn breath
we cried out:
Enough! Enough!
Now hear us
Hear us!
. . .

In whose image were we made?
By whose hands were we shaped?
From whom came our flesh and bone?
Did we choose to be born?
Do we not suffer if you wound us?
Do we not mourn if you forsake us?
Do we not bleed if your wrench our
children from us?
By whose choice was the seal broken?
Did we *choose* to be your chosen?
Enough! Enough!

And that night,
standing at the foot of the mountain
we had no thoughts
we had no hopes.
That night
we stood, each man alone,
a wilderness within wilderness.
But that night
standing alone
sometime at dawn
A quiet quilted cloud covered us,
A throbbing thunder gently rocked us,
A voice hummed us a lullaby,
And we dreamed a single dream.
That dream became
our memory, our hope, our home.
We dreamed of the promised land:
The land of the landless
The land of the hopeless
The land of the Beloved.
That night *I* dreamed of *You*.
For who makes the trees to shade for me?
who makes the birds to sing for me?
who makes the stars to shine for me?
You, my Beloved.
It is Your image in my eyes,
Your milk in my breast
It is your dew on my lips.
My Beautiful Beloved,
It is Your seal
upon my soul.
. . .

Mehri Niknam

From creation we move to revelation. Pesach is followed by the festival of Shavuot, the Feast of Weeks. The rabbis gave it another name: *Z'man Matan Toratenu* – 'the time of the giving of our Torah'. So the festival in memory of the creation of the people gives way to the festival in memory of a revelation to the people. It is a celebration of the word. The word of God was not made flesh, but the word was incarnated nevertheless. The word of God was made present in the midst of the community through

175

Torah, through this document to which we continually turn and return, for, as the rabbis said, everything is within it.

Traditionally the eve and night of the festival is spent awake, in study, in preparation for the revelation of the word. The Biblical text read in the synagogue on the morning of Shavuot contains a description of the events leading up to the revelation of the Ten Commandments. It begins: 'In the third month after the children of Israel were gone forth from the land of Egypt, on this day they came into the wilderness of Sinai' (Exodus 19: 1).

This seems at first reading simple enough: the people's liberation from Egypt is the necessary prelude to the revelation they will receive at Sinai. But there is a puzzle in the text. Why does the Hebrew say that 'on *this* day' they came to the wilderness of Sinai? Surely it should say 'on *that* day' – after all, it is a description of a past event.

To the rabbinic imagination the phrase 'on this day' can only point to one thing: that the day of the giving of the Torah was never to become only a past event. Revelation could never be relegated to history alone. The text draws us into the eternal present of the giving which happens on *this* day, which is every day.

Martin Buber has recorded a perspicacious Hassidic saying on this theme: 'Everyone ... is told to think of themselves as standing at Mount Sinai to receive the Torah. For us there are past and future events, but not so for God: day in, day out He gives the Torah.'[2]

Or, as another mystically-inclined thinker puts it:

> Time past and time future
> What might have been and what has been
> Point to one end, which is always present ...
> And all is always now.[3]

And how does revelation begin? Exodus 20 begins: 'And God spoke all these words saying: "I am the Eternal One, your God ..."' God's words begin with 'I'. Revelation begins when what is Eternal speaks that most personal of all words. Revelation begins when that which is radically transcendent, completely other, is also experienced as immediate, as immanent, as intimate as that whispered 'I am ...' The Hebrew word used in the text for this 'I' of the Eternal One is the word *anochi*, and that word begins with the first letter of the Hebrew alphabet, the silent letter *aleph*. Revelation begins with ... silence. The beginning of revelation *is* silence.

When we can hear that soundless first letter of the first word of the first commandment at Sinai, on *this* day, then we have penetrated to the heart of the liturgy. Or perhaps it would be better to say that it has penetrated to the heart of us. For throughout the liturgy 'the word' dominates the scene. Jewish prayers contain hundreds of thousands of words, so many words repeated so often that they can lose all meaning. But all the words spoken are only the prelude. For the aim of the liturgy is to initiate us into the silence, to the spaces between the words.

When we hear the silence at the heart of the liturgical year then we are, momentarily, freed from our narrowness of perception, our reliance on words to provide meaning, and we experience as much of redemption as it is granted to us to receive before we die. This moment, of the revelation in silence, the revelation of silence, is eternal life.

---------------------------------*---------------------------------

At the end of the eighteen months I spent four or five days in a retreat with this therapy group. We were in a hotel in Devon, all in separate rooms with blindfolds and earplugs faced with the question: who am I? And I spent most of that time being extremely bored; and then on the third or fourth day I suddenly had an absolute certainty that I was part of God. And I remember, still wearing my blindfold, writing down 'I am part of God'; and writing down the Hebrew letters Yod Hay Vav Hay, *which spell the name of God which isn't sounded; and also in English the words 'I am that I am'. I didn't understand the connection between all those three but somehow they felt very important.*

And it was one of those times of certainty which didn't remain. The flash of certainty didn't remain over the coming years but somehow the knowledge that I was part of God remained. I told virtually no one because it felt – in terms of the kind of God I was brought up to believe in, the God that's 'out there' and we're just down here – it felt like a very arrogant statement. So I didn't share it: 'I'm part of God, we're all part of God.' But it was a certainty I sort of put away in a drawer, and it wasn't until much later I found myself among people who believed the same thing.

_____

There is a medieval mystical text which presents the alarmingly subversive idea that the Torah is actually the white spaces between the letters on the parchment scroll, not the black of the letters inscribed in ink.[4] A new *gestalt* reveals what is hidden: the silence between the words.

It may be that the spiritual dis-ease of Anglo-Jewry – our insecurities and bickering and fragmentation – is rooted in our personal and collective inability to value silence. Not the empty or embarrassed or defensive silence we know so well; but the full, rich silence which comes from the cessation of busyness, the open-hearted silence which emerges when we finally lay aside the endless preoccupation with the things that do not matter.

We talk so much. We have so many opinions and ideas and points of view. We have such a *penchant* and predilection for argument. Words are our life, speech is our gift, language is our passion. And we are so uncomfortable with silence. If we have nothing to say, then who are we?

It is nearly two millennia since Shimon son of Rabban Gamliel distilled a lifetime's experience into his statement: 'All my life I grew up among the wise and found nothing better for anyone than silence'.[5] Silence frightens us; yet without the capacity to be silent, how can we learn to hear the still small voice within? Perhaps it is that which frightens us. Who knows what it might ask of us?

The poet, the artist, the visionary, the dreamer points the way: 'You know all the rules. You know all the transgressions. But do you know about dreams? Do you know about the glory of the imagination? ... You dwell in the sole and banal dimension of logic. You have no visions, for your eyes are not open. You read the Law, but you do not divine the space between the words.'[6]

On Shavuot Sinai is made present once more. Struggling to experience revelation we wrestle with eternity and the Eternal One. In the silence Torah is revealed. Torah – which means 'teaching'. How does the contemporary Jew relate to these 'teachings'?

Every Jew is in some relationship to Torah. It can be a relationship of defiance or acceptance, of submission or rebellion, of curiosity or coldness. We may feel inside the tradition, on the margins, or outside. During the course of a lifetime we may move back and forth along this spectrum. We may dabble with the rituals, or immerse ourselves in them, or assemble our own private anthology of practices which make sense to us. We may turn our back on them, with discomfort or relief. For some the Torah will be primarily a repository of moral and ethical norms. For others it will provide a creative well of stories and legends to sustain in dark times. Yet whatever our conscious inclinations, this tree of life has roots hidden in our hearts, and hidden routes into our souls.

The Hebrew word *Torah* is from the root *y'r'h*: to point in a direction. It's used of an archer shooting arrows. Torah is not only 'the Law', forbiddingly revealed for all time, static and unchanging. Torah is about the direction in which we are called upon to move. It is the lightning flash of insight when we see the way ahead. It is the moment of knowing what we have to do, or not do. To be open to receive from life what is constantly given to us, is to stand in the presence of the Torah which is revealed 'on *this* day'.

These moments of personal revelation are aspects of eternity mediated through time and human consciousness. The Eternal silently speaks and we hear the inner meaning of Torah as 'teaching'. On this fleeting midsummer festival, 'the time we are given our Torah', we are invited to ponder on the symbolic significance of Sinai: our own openness to receive what is given to us all moment by moment.

It is not necessary that you leave the house. Remain at your table and listen. Do not even listen, only wait. Do not even wait, be wholly still and alone. The world will present itself to you for its unmasking, it can do no other, in ecstasy it will writhe at your feet.' (Franz Kafka)[7]

We have moved from creation to revelation. And from there – where do we go? We go into the desert; we go into a long period of wandering, of confusion, of moving towards a 'promised land' we've never seen and may not even believe in. We journey on, trying to recapture the vision, relive the moment, following the fire or the cloud[8] or whatever signs we think might guide us in our uncertainty. It is during this long and painful period that we recognise the impossibility of this journey we are on – and its inevitability.

———————————————*———————————————

I finally left social work to go into the Cancer Help Centre. There was a growing awareness of a world that wasn't rational and I no longer insisted that only what is evidenced by the senses is true. I found myself wanting to believe in something beyond – spiritual or divine or supernatural . . .

I came first of all as a patient, but knowing from the very start that I wanted to work there and within a few months I was. That felt like a really big turning point: I had the sense that I'd come home. It was like discovering, in working with patients, the voice of intuition, discovering a universal spiritual way of being: it was about God being within as well as without. It was during that time that I realised that saying that I was part of God wasn't such a ridiculous statement after all . . .

After I left the Centre and I was working as a psychotherapist I went up to the Centre one day for a meditation with a group of patients and the person leading it asked us to find a healing symbol, or allow a healing symbol to come. And the one that came to me immediately was a little silver Sefer Torah, *like a little model of the scrolls of the Torah, and I knew that that meant something to do with my heritage. It was the first pointer that my own heritage was something important I was missing out on.*

That afternoon I made a phone call to a cousin who had himself been a patient at the Centre. In fact he had died that morning. He had a great love of Judaism, though not in a strictly observant way . . . I loved him a lot.

Then there was a third event that same day. A colleague of mine had asked me to be a godfather for his son, to hold the baby for the circumcision. I had said no, I'm just too horrified by the idea, and I felt bad about letting him down. But he rang me again that day and I said immediately yes, I would. It became something about Jewishness and something about the cycle of death and birth and life — and that remains the significant day. I never dreamed I'd start to become a practising Jew or go back to the synagogue.

15
Wandering in the Wilderness

———————————*———————————

First of all, a desert is not what most people in the West imagine it to be. It is not a place where Lawrence of Arabia comes riding a white steed. Desert is a wilderness. It is vast. A desert is so hot – and I should know that because for so many years I lived on the edge of it. When the sun rises to its peak in the desert it is so boiling hot that you feel it tightening your skin as it wrinkles it. And then when it is cold it isn't a pleasant coldness. It is so cold that it curdles the blood. And then you have the sand, which normally you think of as going to the seashore and paddling. Which it isn't. This sand is the grit that you feel under your teeth and it's so dry, so without moisture, without relief, that you feel your whole mouth is tightening, tightening, tightening, as if you can't breathe any more because it is so dry.

And yet when it rains, it isn't the pitter-patter of the rain: it's a deluge. It's like Noah's flood. You think, 'Oh my God, I'm going to die because of this, this gush of water that is coming, there is nothing to hang on to. The water's going to take me with it.' And so the feeling of life and death, of extremes, is very, very real, of this constant struggle to make some sort of balance and to be able to get on.

And the other thing of course is that the desert is a very, very lonely place. It is lonely because it is so empty. It is empty except the shadow in the day and the shade in the night. There is nothing else that one can see or touch. And yet because of this emptiness it becomes so full because the sense is that although all is vastness, in there is just me – a tiny, tiny me in the middle, and yet this vastness is filled with me. So you get these two opposing feelings: that I am everything and yet I am nothing ...

You wander and you see things and you go on day after day – and now I am talking not just about the desert outside but the wilderness inside really. Like a camel I go on day after day after day and always a little bit further and always a day nearer and a day nearer and eventually you reach a point where you really cannot go any further and you have no more strength: the legs become the sand and the sand becomes the body and everything goes. The mind goes and the body goes and the spirit reaches the level of the sand. So everything becomes the sand and you just lie down and you say, 'Oh God, I can't, I cannot go any further. It is enough. I want to die. I want to lie down and die and that's the end of it. I want no more. I don't want to search for anything or see anything. It's enough.'

And either you dream it or it actually happens, but it is there. I don't know, but somehow an oasis does appear. And an oasis is not a plush carpet and a great refrigerator with drinks, and an abundance of food. If you are in the desert what is comfort is that you realise how much comfort is offered in so little. There is a little place where one can rest and then maybe set off again. And there are wells in the wilderness. They have water and so of course they are life-giving and you come to them and you draw the water. If you have never heard the sound of the water being drawn from a well in the heat of the day, you don't know the sound of the river that runs through paradise.

But there are also dry wells in the desert and those are horrible ones. Those are the wells which are so dark and so black, so empty. There is not even a stink in them. There is nothing to breathe, not even a foul smell. There is no moisture. They are hard and dry and empty and black and when you fall into them they are also bottomless. You can fall and fall and there is nothing to stop you, nothing to hang on to. They are total hopelessness. It was a dry well that Joseph was dropped into. So they exist, they're real.

So the desert was real on the outside but also real inside. It meant a lot to wander and always, always be just behind. Now I know why the children of Israel went from mountain to mountain to mountain to mountain: because just beyond it of course is what you are looking for. And sometimes you do find a little bit of what you're looking for.

The Bible elaborates upon the collective history of Israel through stories which resonate with personal metaphors that reach out, across the generations, to us as individuals. Remembering the past is not an escape from the present. Memory is different from nostalgia. But even as the past is recalled, there is no lack of ambiguity. As the nation's stories are told, their meaning and purpose are far from clear. Indeed, the stories from the past often illustrate precisely this point: the indeterminacy of human actions, and the daily uncertainties with which we all live.

The Bible's eternal truthfulness lies in its refusal to allow us to evade the necessity of facing uncertainty. As the novelist and critic Gabriel

Josipovici makes clear in his penetrating analysis of Biblical story-telling: 'We all long in our daily lives for an end to uncertainty, to the need for decisions and choices ... Yet we also know that life will not provide such an end, that we will always be enmeshed in uncertainty. What is extraordinary is that a sacred book should dramatise this, rather than be the one place where we are given what we desire. But that is precisely what the Hebrew Bible does.'[1]

Within the symbolic framework we are following, creation and revelation are followed by redemption. But the journey from revelation to redemption is a journey of wandering, of desert, and of facing up to the inevitability of death. There are no short cuts. There is no other way out. There is nothing else.

On the first day of the second month, in the second year following the exodus from Egypt, God spoke to Moses in the wilderness of Sinai, saying: Take a census of the whole Israelite community, listing the names, person by person ...

So we begin the book of Numbers, a little over a year after the children of Israel have left Egypt. In the course of this book, the rest of the years of their wandering will be described: the restless years, the waiting years, the years of hope and bitterness as the journey towards the Promised Land goes on and on and on ...

A census is taken at the beginning of the long march, and the book of Numbers ends – thirty-nine years later – with another census, this time just before the people enter the land promised to them. There are a lot of numbers in this book: figures and lists and genealogies threaded through the story as it slowly unfolds. Lists of the tribes, their leaders, their offerings, their marching orders, their numbers: facts and figures to hold on to as the confusion of the journey grows, the years pass, the generation born in slavery and freed with such high hopes slowly ages and dies, without reaching its goal.

Is this farce or tragedy – or both? The narrative is unsparing in its portrait of the people, disillusioned, rebellious, frightened, at war with themselves and with those they encounter around them, continually complaining amongst themselves and to their leader Moses. Amidst the rational, logical, calm, soothing details we hear the opposite: anger and despair, where nothing is fixed and understood, nothing is certain.

This book is well named. In English (which follows the Latin and the Greek) it is called 'numbers' because of the census in the first chapter. And the rabbis in the Mishnah gave it a similar name: *Chumash HaPekkudim* – 'that part of the Torah that deals with the counted'. Numbers convey order. Yet we can see that under the ordered surface of the book of Numbers there is a people, lost, confused, wandering. Beneath the order we see chaos. And this leads us to the other name for the book. In Hebrew this book is called *Bemidbar*: 'in the wilderness'.[2]

Of course all the events recorded in the book do take place in the desert, so the title is on one level merely descriptive. And yet *Bemidbar*/'in the wilderness' is also a state of mind. Indeed, it is a state of soul. To be in the wilderness means to feel the confusion, the disappointment, the disillusionment, the anxiety, the hopelessness of a journey where meaning is hidden, where we do not even know if there is a meaning. To be in the wilderness means facing the bleakness and the harshness of our destinies.

To be in the wilderness means acknowledging the despair we feel when we realise that we are on a journey without end, to a future we cannot control. We are caught up in something larger than we know, more powerful than we understand. The manna comes every day. And it is still not enough. We do not crave food, we crave certainty. That is the one gift that God does not – and cannot – give.

Beneath the surface, beneath the obsessional counting, numbering, ordering of life, there is the heartbreak. The pain of life has to be faced. The people who left the security of Egyptian slavery with expectations of a quick march across the desert to the security of a new and better life were doomed. Stubborn, rebellious, sullen, the hopes die, they die. All that is left is the next generation, to carry the hope: 'You will do what we have not done; you will succeed where we failed; you will do it for us.' A blessing and a curse, that burden of hope.

A new generation is born: in the wilderness. Carrying the hopes of their parents, carrying their own hopes. Where will it end? When will it end? The fear of the journey, and the loneliness at the heart of it all. Where are we going? No one seems to know. Everyone was counted, everyone had their place, their tribe, their job, a tabernacle in which to worship, everyone was bound up in the ordered fabric of the group moving through the wilderness to that promised land. All the numbers gave a kind of security, an illusion of being held inside the group, the mass, the 'community of Israel': it's supposed to be safe, to be part of a people, with a destiny and a future.

But when it came down to it you had to wake up each morning and face the desert, the unknown wilderness, ahead and around and here and now. How terrifying for the soul not to know where the day's journey will end, let alone the journey of a lifetime. Beneath the surface order, a generation is lost and confused and very frightened. 'Lead us back,' they demand: the past was safer. 'Lead us forward,' they cry, 'away from here, away from here...' But the wilderness is where they have to be. The wilderness is where they learn that uncertainty is also built into the fabric of life. The wilderness is where we learn that not knowing, and not understanding, has a value too. Life is not all quick marches to what is promised and hoped for. Life is more often than not about wandering, and waiting, and wondering.

The *midrash* says that when God chose to speak to the people He chose not to speak in the land of Israel, when they had finished their journey. God spoke at Sinai, in the heart of the wilderness, in territory that belonged to nobody – or everybody.[3] It is in the wilderness that revelation comes: something new breaking through, something new which speaks to us in a voice we understand: there is hope, there is purpose, there is a direction to the journey.

The new understanding we are given may last only a moment. A flash of lightning. A voice within. Perhaps only a whisper, a wisp of understanding, a sigh. But we know that the soundless voice of the Eternal One has spoken: we are in the wilderness; we have to face our wilderness; there is meaning within what appears sometimes without meaning; there is meaning in the dying of one generation and the survival of the next; the journey through the desert has a direction, a purpose, and it is bigger than we are.

---------------------------------*---------------------------------

There's no end to the journey. There is no arrival. It's the way I felt for a long time. I don't know where the future is. I don't have a kind of certainty. If I was asked now, do I believe in God?, I would have to say, well it depends what I mean by the word. Each time someone asks me that, I define it differently, and I think fairly consistently I do believe in something divine. I don't know in what form...

Once I was involved in Judaism again I came to think that there was something I'd been missing in that previous period, that there was a kind of dried-up aspect – not in terms of my emotional life, but spiritually there was something missing. I realised that if I didn't go to synagogue for maybe four, five, six weeks, it was like I had a thirst and coming back again was finding an oasis. The desert wilderness has been there for me: when I was in it I wasn't aware of it. I was living the only life I could lead at the time. I certainly don't feel any regrets about having been wandering – and coming back.

There's a certain kind of joy that I now sometimes find that I didn't before. Belonging to a continuity allows me to feel part of something, when before I was just wandering alone. I mean, being part of the universe was all very well, but it's very big. A continuity of one people with a miraculous story – miraculous simply that it still exists, this Jewish people – that somehow gives more meaning to me.

As British Jews we belong to a people for whom 'wandering' has historical, psychological and spiritual resonances. To celebrate our wandering as a vital constituent of the personal journey means to forgo the consolations of Zion. Redemption is not determined by geography. Our homeland is in time rather than in space.[4]

There are many contours to our wanderings, and they rarely are what they seem to be at the time. It is hard to get a perspective on the shape of our lives. As our quest renders itself invisible, the present can seem omnipresent. If we are fortunate we may come to feel that we shape our lives in partnership with others, and with the world around us, and that the mystery and blessing of this partnership is what we call God. And that the evil we have experienced happens when that partnership is sundered or denied, so that either we or the world around us feels omnipotent.

It is a peculiarly Jewish characteristic to want to imbue the small and large events of daily life with a sense of the divine and not to want to separate God into another sphere, celestial and unattainable, and against which we find ourselves wanting. At its best, this sense of the everyday mysticism of materiality is part of what we carry as a blessing to the world. This is also our homeland.

Because the prevailing culture emphasises the split between mind and body, spirit and matter, and because Anglo-Judaism has absorbed much of this message, we are brought up with a lot of confusion about where to look for spirituality in our Jewish lives. The moments which we experience as being most meaningful to us aren't necessarily consonant with our sense of what a 'religious experience' is meant to be: in the bath; in the countryside; watching a cat move; doing a satisfying and creative piece of work; in close conversation with good friends; observing an act of unexpected generosity; hitting a great shot at tennis; striking up a conversation with someone you don't usually talk to; moments of close contact with children; feeling part of a community in synagogue; feeling at one with ourselves and others in ritual or prayer. These are all moments when we feel the connectedness between ourselves and others, or ourselves and the world, where we lose consciousness of the boundaries of time and space, and just 'are' for a short while. We don't have to fight for our sense of self in these moments; it is somehow a given.

Perhaps this wished-for meaning seems too easily spoken of. For most of the time, and for most of us, the shape of our wanderings is glimpsed only in fragments. And sometimes we hate what we see, the harshness of the outlines, the suffering at the centre. Our own experience of life is our most precious possession – nobody else can tell us it has a meaning we do not feel for ourselves.

But something was shared by all those whose experiences are recorded in this section of the book. Each had at some time in their lives been faced with deep despair, loss, tragedy or evil. They had experienced the harshness of the desert and the unremitting emptiness of the dry well. They have had their love of life and zest for living most deeply challenged. And this challenge has provided them, in the end, with the inspiration and motivation to plumb the depths of themselves and find richness.

The fact that my fourth child was born profoundly handicapped had a tremendous impact on me spiritually. I remember that I did speak to the rabbi at the time and we were told that only people who can cope with such troubles are given them and I almost felt it was a privilege to have Richard. As I became more religious in fact I saw such a spirituality in him. There was something very special about him and perhaps having Richard – he lived to be twenty-two – helped awaken a spirituality that had been dormant, just waiting for something to fan the flame...

I decided to learn with one of the local ministers, Dr Jeffrey Cohen, and he sat down with me and taught me basic Hebrew. We sat down with the chumash, *the text of our Bible, and through that he opened doors for me and my life has been changed, really changed, since then. I began to start to keep more things. I can remember the last time I drove to synagogue to go to a barmitzvah saying to myself, 'This is the last time I'm going to drive on a* Shabbat' *and I stopped driving on* Shabbat. *Then I decided I wouldn't cook on* Shabbat: *I remember consciously working through everything and each step I took I struggled with...*

You suddenly come through a tunnel and you're blinded by the light and you're never the same again. It was quite a dramatic experience. I can remember lighting my candles and actually feeling a presence, feeling the change from the ordinary week to the beginning of the Sabbath and it was something I could touch. Something had changed. Because I was putting something into it and I was observing it the whole quality of Shabbat *changed for me. And my experiences continue to be like this, that the more I put in, the more I get out of it. And I do feel the spirituality, I do feel that I can communicate with God. He doesn't always say yes, but I do feel He listens and my life has been changed since then...*

On the historical level, the third holiday of the agricultural year, the autumn harvest festival of Sukkot, is linked by the Bible to the portable homes the Israelites made for themselves as they progressed on their forty years of wandering through the desert towards Canaan, their promised land. Sinai gives way to more desert and the long journey ahead. Moments of revelation are replaced by ages of waiting and wandering and wondering.

For one week in the year the traditional Jew moves from his or her familiar home into a makeshift booth, a hut constructed by the side of one's more permanent dwelling. This *sukkah* symbolises fragility and impermanence in the midst of life. It 'serves to remind the people that no matter how solid the house of today may seem, no matter how temptingly it beckons to rest and unimperilled living, it is but a tent which permits only a pause in the long wanderings through the wilderness of centuries'.[5]

And this, one may ask, is redemption? There is a disconcerting paradox here: the Festival of Booths celebrates both wandering and rest. During their journey through the wilderness, the Israelites stopped every so often and set up temporary homes – sometimes for months, sometimes for years – to rest, recover their strength, reflect on where they had come from, fight a local war: whatever the next day brought.

So too for us there are moments of rest, of respite in our struggling for direction. There are times when we pause to look back on where we have come from, recognising the mistakes and the achievements, the victories and defeats. We stop to look back to where we began, reflecting on the frustrations and the satisfactions of the journey so far.

—————————————————*—————————————————

Sometimes I feel angry when I think back on those first few years. It is the feeling of being a child. In the tradition it says you are like a newborn child when you convert. And you really are – but you're not. You're an adult as well and there's a real sense of insecurity, of being vulnerable, of learning something new: a new language, new rituals, new prayers, new cultural background.

There were personal expectations of being able to do that, and the expectations from outside; and the fact that one doesn't talk about it and people are not really taking part in one's journey or its problems and questions means that you're very much left to your own devices. Looking back it sometimes seems a very black period of a lot of tears, a lot of unhappiness and struggling – and I only know that now, when I feel happier and more integrated and more adult in being a Jew.

—————————————————————————————————————

The moments when we do stop and rest and celebrate the stages of our own pilgrimage perhaps only highlight the context of wandering in which our journeying takes place. How permanent is what we have achieved? If we are honest then perhaps we do recognise how fragile things really are, how temporary the structures we build around us and within us, how easily fragmented our lives can become.

Sukkot sensitises us to our transience, yet at the same time it opens up for us the awareness that we are part of something larger. We are participants in a human drama, a collective drama of redemption in which our individuality is both impossibly insignificant and yet absolutely of the essence.

This week-long festival of wandering and rest, this festival of redemption, comes as the finale to the liturgical year. It follows almost immediately on the end of those ten days of inwardness and self-reflection – from the New Year to the Day of Atonement – which offer an unmediated experience of soul-searching and re-evaluation for each individual. At Sukkot redemption is not present in this intimate and personal way but is set in the context of the collective, the community. It is the Jewish people who are wandering, with redemption only and ever in the future. The promised land has been decreed – this is a hope and a certainty. Redemption from exile will evolve out of the suffering and chaos and impermanence of daily living.

As Rosenzweig says: 'In this festival of redemption there is no present redemption'.[6] At the moment of resting, of respite from the wanderings, there is a recognition of what has been achieved: it is solid, it is here, we have done it. And it is transient, it is ephemeral. The cloud will move on, as it did in the desert, and the journey will have to resume. We rest and we wander, and on the festival of Sukkot we hold this tension between the opposites.

Just as redemption is glimpsed at the end of the Sabbath as a yearning and a certainty before the new week commences, so at the very end of the liturgical year there is a paradoxical moment of yearning and certainty. There is a yearning for rest from the never-ending wanderings – and a certainty that the promised land is just over the horizon, only a chapter away. There is the yearning to keep moving, to begin again, to repeat the cycle but this time with our newfound insights – and the certainty that if we stop we die, and that if we claim the 'promised land' has been achieved this is a spiritual defeat, a lie.

To be a Jew is to live with paradox. The spiritual journey does not fear paradox, does not try to resolve the innate tensions of human existence. The Jew embraces paradox. The Jew celebrates paradox. To be a Jew is to live holding the tension 'generated out of the friction between two contradictory, equally commanding truths: annihilation is certain and therefore all human endeavour is futile – annihilation is certain and therefore all human endeavour is victorious'.[7] Through paradox we make our lives into works of art, susceptible to many readings and interpretations. Through paradox we glimpse the mystery of our humanity, made in the divine image; and the mystery of the divine, made in our own image.

At the very end of this festival of paradox we celebrate an additional day which encapsulates this theme of the spiritual year which is 'not permitted to . . . close but must flow back to the beginning'.[8] The day is called *Simchat Torah*: the Rejoicing in the Torah.

The slow, regular, week-by-week progression of the liturgical year based on the cycle of weekly readings from the Torah comes to an end on this day. We read the last verses of the Torah where Moses, 120 years old, goes up the mountain and, before he dies, is allowed to look at the promised land: a glimpse of what the whole journey has been leading to, but a place which he himself cannot enter. It is the next generation who will inherit the land. We join with Moses in glimpsing where we too cannot tread.

But the momentary sadness and the pain of unfilfilled longing give way to the new beginning. The opening verses of the book of Genesis follow on immediately and the holy drama begins again. 'In the beginning God created the heavens and the earth . . .' Moses has died, but creation is renewed. The journey is over, we have failed to reach our destination. And the journey is beginning again, and all lies before us, waiting . . . 'In my end is my beginning.'[9]

When we dance with the Torah on the festival of *Simchat Torah*, we are celebrating the return to the beginning, we are celebrating the renewal of the quest for understanding, we are rejoicing in the unending journey which links our personal destiny with that of all creation. This *chutzpah* staggers the imagination. And the question remains: does a mythic and metaphorical understanding of Jewish tradition move us any closer to it? Part of the paradox of the contemporary Jewish search for a spiritual dimension to life is the realisation that there is probably no longer the possibility of living with an undivided consciousness. There may not be the desire to, either.

The most that any of us can do is form a personal bridge towards that collective wisdom the myth offers. To know that there is still a framework in which we can ask some of our questions may be all that is left to us. As one of Arthur Miller's characters says, we Jews have learned to be acrobats.[10] With luck, or skill, or maybe years of anguished practice, Jews learn that delicate balancing exercise where we stand with one foot inside the tradition, the Bible, the mysticism and the midrash, the liturgical year . . . and yet accept – with gratitude, rather than grudgingly – that our other foot is firmly rooted outside of it: in the Enlightenment, in T. S. Eliot and Kafka, Woody Allen and Freud, Karl Marx and Groucho Marx, in the great dizzying splendid secular world which is also our home.

We may not find this a very comfortable way to stand in the world. Sometimes we may despair of the possibility of finding a synthesis between our Jewish and secular selves – too many irreconcilables and frustrations may lie in the way. And sometimes we may rejoice in the unfinished, unfinishable nature of our journeys.

In the end, the spiritual journeys we make are for ourselves alone. No one else can fully understand what we ask of ourselves. No one else can hear what summons us. We may be in a situation where those around us do not even hear any call to journey. We cannot even prepare for what we are to encounter on the way. Before we begin, we teeter on the brink of defeat: the journey is impossible. And yet it is, fortunately, a truly immense journey.[11]

We may find the journey through the liturgical year very hard. As the Jewish holidays come and go so much of ourselves seems to get left out in the ritual procession through the year. Yet for some the religious motifs are attractive precisely because we can leave the daily grind behind us when we engage with them. They open us up to another reality, help us to see life from a different and larger – or deeper – perspective. They can allow the individual a space to reflect, to recharge exhausted batteries, to gain some respite from the problems of the world. The chaos outside us or within us is stilled for a while. Our souls drink deep from the living well of myth. The words and melodies vibrate inside us in harmony with the ancient rhythms of the liturgical year.

However, the call to continually encounter the past in the present, when the past can feel such a dead weight, an alien and alienating territory, can often feel suffocating. There is in many Jews now the feeling that they are 'getting it wrong', or 'not doing enough' – an undefined yet invidious sense of failure. Sometimes we do feel very distant from that mythic world of the ancestors, or very lost with it. But we may also feel very lost without it. The inner core of the year, its symbolic level where it touches *us*, can remain unresponsive, impenetrable. We get very moody with it, or irritated about it. We may end up defiantly or abjectly rejecting it. And yet . . .

And yet it's also like a lover, whose embrace we cannot bear to be distant from; in whose gaze we cannot bear not to see ourselves; whose touch we crave and whom we crave to touch. We know there is healing in this touch, and wholeness. And so we cannot keep away from this passionate engagement, the often desperate struggle to break inside this tradition to which we are an heir and in which we long to rest; and yet in which we so often feel a stranger, a wanderer.

Sometimes all we have left are stories. Stories allow our paradoxes to breathe. They refuse us the consolations of certainty; but they allow us the freedom to explore. They are our waking dreams. Our stories are aspects of our searching; and our searching is reflected in our stories. We are far from the centre of our millennial traditions; and yet we are still within a hair's breadth of their inner core.

When the great Rabbi Israel Baal Shem Tov saw misfortune threatening the Jews it was his custom to go into a certain part of the forest to meditate. There he would light a fire, say a special prayer, and the miracle would be accomplished and the misfortune averted.

Later, when his disciple, the celebrated Maggid of Mezeritch, had occasion, for the same reason, to intercede with heaven, he would go to the same place in the forest and say: 'Master of the Universe, listen! I do not know how to light the fire, but I am still able to say the prayer,' and again the miracle would be accomplished.

Still later, Rabbi Moshe-Leib of Sasov, in order to save his people once more, would go into the forest and say: 'I do not know how to light the fire, I do not know the prayer, but I know the place and this must be sufficient.' It was sufficient and the miracle was accomplished.

Then it fell to Rabbi Israel of Rizhyn to overcome misfortune. Sitting in his armchair, his head in his hands, he spoke to God: 'I am unable to light the fire and I do not know the prayer, I cannot even find the place in the forest. All I can do is to tell the story, and this must be sufficient.' And it was sufficient.[12]

16
Creating Our Selves

---✳---

I remember the first evening: we really entered into a discussion, an exchange, about how we felt vis-à-vis our religion. And I was very quickly moving towards, or excited by, his way of being a Jew, and being Jewish, and being religious. And in a way he introduced me then to Jews, not only through the religion but also through literature and theatre and music. It felt as if I had come home ...

I think what excited me first was the service: there was a structure, a rhythm one could be part of and feel safe in, which also left enough time for personal reflection and prayer. But there was no sense of being manipulated, as I often had in the services of my childhood, of having to confess, or speak out, or having to speak prayers which I didn't feel. I felt so at home in those services and such a relief at being able to be part of a community without pressure over me to do the right thing, say the right thing ... There was a sense of freedom and joy in it, which I'd missed.

The roots of human culture and creativity lie in our attempts to make sense of our own experiences. Religion, art, literature, philosophy, drama, music, poetry, science, psychotherapy, storytelling, myth – we constantly create forms to express our questions, give shape to our intuitions, provide structure in our quest for understanding and a framework for the expression of our knowledge and our desires.

Towards the end of his life the psychoanalyst and essayist Bruno Bettelheim responded to the question of the meaning of human life in this way: 'We are entirely the chance by-products of evolutionary accident. There is no purpose whatsoever in our existence, but we must proceed as if there were ...'[1] We can cherish the wisdom and warmth of that last phrase, which balances the harsh suggestion of our meaninglessness. For indeed we do seem to proceed as if there were a purpose. We do seem to experience the very incompleteness of our knowing as a kind of challenge. We learn to live with the question, respond to it, play with it, confront it indirectly over and over again.

These questions are part of our shared humanity. As Vaclav Havel wrote from his prison cell, our questions about the meaning of life provide us with a beginning, not an end; they enable us to experience life more deeply. We have to learn to live with as much light as our questioning yields, a light which is a reflection from an unknown source. Sometimes we take pleasure from the illumination we receive like a gift; at other times the absence of understanding casts its shadow over us and causes us much suffering. But either way, our ever-renewed contact with this mysterious process 'is what makes us genuinely human'.[2]

Often when we are in crisis and chaos threatens to overwhelm us, our questioning becomes intensified: when we are faced with illness or separation or bereavement, the loss of work or a home or a homeland; or if we are victims of attack or persecution. It is at times like these that we may experience an emotional emptiness, a spiritual vacuum; our cries go unheard, our prayers unanswered, and we wonder, 'What's the point?' And there are times when there may seem no apparent cause for our emotional unrest, our feelings of emptiness or disillusionment or lack of meaning.

————————————————————*————————————————————

When my marriage broke down it felt like my whole life literally fell to pieces. I lost almost all my sense of identity: everything was chaotic, everything that I had, had been either destroyed or blown apart by some force or other; and I was left wandering and not knowing what or who I was. It was as if I was in this wilderness and I saw coming towards me this terrifying — more than terrifying — this awe-inspiring whirlwind. As a child I remember that sort of wind ...

But whereas as a child I only accepted it as a phenomenon that comes and passes and goes, this time it actually posed the question: why? And eventually it grew and this question 'why?' grew and I decided — or it was decided more by the whirlwind than me — that I wanted to make a commitment to myself, not to anyone else any more, not to human beings but to myself for myself and for what was inside me. And so the question of the batmitzvah came into being ... So I set off to learn Hebrew, which I couldn't read at the time; but not only that, to really find out why I wanted to be batmitzvah, what it meant to me.

Through the poetry of legend, the mystery of myth, the vision of religion, humankind has struggled for millennia with the question of meaning. The Hebrew Bible is one great attempt to rescue and create meaning from the chaos of human existence. It is the dream of the Jewish people, a great bringing-to-our-attention of our collective experience: we turn it and turn it and find ourselves within it. Like us as individuals, it has its own internal logic, its own laws of cause and effect, its own hidden correspondences and connections. Our scriptures attempt to give us a history in which *our* lives are contained, and given meaning, purpose, direction, yet without predetermining how we actually construct our own individual meanings and connect ourselves to what has gone before. They help us create meaning for ourselves – and at the same time, like all great art, they deny us the consolation of having 'the answers'. As with the often disjointed aspects of our own lives – sometimes emotionally-laden, sometimes emotionless; sometimes soaring in our imaginations, sometimes lost in the details and the trivia – we wait and we listen, and we listen again, hoping for some understanding to form out of the fragments.

The ancient Hebrew writers conveyed the complex moral and psychological realism of their ideas through storytelling. The importance of this cannot be overstated: to convey mythology through narrative necessitates that the *meaning of events is not fixed*. In fact one could even say that the narrator's aim was to produce a certain indeterminacy of meaning, particularly in regard to the motives of characters, and their moral and psychological makeup: 'Meaning was conceived of as a *process* which required continual revision – both in the ordinary sense and in the etymological sense of seeing again.'[3]

Within the Jewish myth 'God appears, to order, guide, promise, and argue – but never to explain, to make everything clear'.[4] This is the blessing with which we struggle. As opposed to a reading of our central texts that would stress the clarity of the divine dictat, we have an alternative tradition which subverts our desire to stop thinking for ourselves and have someone else tell us what to do. We do not forsake the burden of consciousness for the sake of an infantile wish to be consoled by simple-minded truths.

A rabbinic maxim states that 'there are seventy faces to the Torah.' In other words, there are many different ways of understanding and interpreting the same Biblical stories and images. And this is true too of our personal narratives. We may feel we know the storyline of our own lives and how it all fits together, but often the attempt to make sense of what happens to us is not at all straightforward, and sometimes we have to admit that we just don't understand what is going on. The spiritual journey often consists of learning to 'read' the constantly unfolding story of our life.

In the television drama *The Singing Detective* the playwright Dennis

Potter captured just this sense of life as a mystery story, the meaning of which unfolds in its telling, with clues scattered through time and in our memories. He shows the way in which the meaning of our lives is revealed slowly, surprisingly, painfully, fragmentarily, with reality as a multi-layered, atemporal, alogical, contradictory compilation of experiences superimposed on one another. In an interview Potter said:

What I was trying to do in *The Singing Detective* was to make a detective story about how you find yourself: so that you've got this superfluity of clues – which is what we all have – and very few solutions (maybe no solutions). But that the very art of garnering the clues and the very act of remembering not merely an event but how that event has lodged in you and how that event has affected the way you see things begins to assemble a system of values. And only when that system – no matter how tenuous it might be – is assembled, was Marlow [the 'hero'] able to get up out of his bed.

The past and the present weren't in strict sequence – because they aren't; they are in one sense obviously, the calendar sense, but they're not in your head in that sequence and neither are they in terms of the way you discover things about yourself, where an event twenty years ago ... can *follow* yesterday instead of precede it. And out of this morass of evidence, of clues and searchings and strivings – which is the metaphor for the way we live – we can start to put up the structure called 'Self' within which we can say at least I know, you know, better than before what it is we are.

The illness is the crisis ... the Job-part if you like ... that starting point of extreme crisis and no belief, nothing, except pain and a cry and a hate out of which were assembled the fantasies, and the fantasies became facts, and the facts were memories and the memories became fantasies and the fantasies became realities – and all of them became him and all of them allowed him to walk.[5]

Perhaps we can recognise in this artist's description of his own creative process, just how we do create ourselves – that montage of fantasy, fact, memory, reality which combine to become us and 'allow us to walk'; or which combine to form the Biblical texts, which in turn help us to see ourselves more fully.

When I arrived in Auschwitz and the orchestra played music and it was a hot summer day and we were in what appeared to be pyjamas, I thought I was in a holiday camp. Now of course this was after three or four days' journey when you didn't eat and didn't drink, but I thought it was some kind of holiday – because the associated processes of the mind hooked this on to similar events in the past.

And I remember that having been given water and hearing the music, I went over to one of them – a Kapo or whoever it was – and asked where one could shave. And he answered me: 'In the crematorium.' And I didn't even know what the crematorium was, but it gives you an idea of one aspect of irreality or irrationality or something bizarre which you can't put your finger on. What my camp experience really taught me was that the horror is not just the physical degradation and torture and hunger, but also about what goes on inside you as a result of all these things.

I regained my senses after I got away from Auschwitz but this is the kind of dimension I'm talking about, with the memories mingling and meeting and separating. You live in another dimension where time sometimes is mixed up with past time, and past time is future time: it's all mixed up.

For example, I saw myself in the third person singular. 'Here he goes; he does this; he does that.' Perhaps it was easier to tolerate what was going on if I could project myself 'out there' and yet in this extraordinary state, I don't know, by the grace of God, I managed to do the thing which saved my life always: stand in one line instead of the other, say one thing instead of the other ... Survival was pure luck – if it was luck. It seems to me that when the dimensions of normality have been removed then something else came into operation. I can't give a name to it, but there it was.

In our generation it is often to the creative artists in our midst that we need to turn in order to learn the insights that religious traditions have offered in the past. Sometimes those who are marginal to a religious tradition, or outside of one, or even antipathetical to one, are closer to the essence of spiritual or religious teachings than more traditional religious teachers, who may be constrained by that very tradition from a full exploration of how the spirit now moves within the human psyche.

Secularism is not an enemy. The spiritually sensitive secular voice – be it Jewish or not – is an ally of the Jew seeking his or her own way into, or back to, the soul of Judaism. There is no simple route to find a living connection with our largely lost mythological world. To approach the buried treasure may require a gruelling journey far from the smooth highways. And a single journey may not suffice.

While it may be true that secular Jews are re-engaging with Judaism and finding within it contemporary meaning, what is not so readily acknowledged is that often it is the insights which emerge from the supposedly secular world that are the keys with which Jews today are finding new access to the Jewish treasures. Whether these insights come from psychology or literature, science or the arts, there is a growing awareness that Judaism can be renewed and enriched by this creative engagement with secular knowledge and understanding. Far from abandoning secular thought, or distancing themselves from it, Jews have much to gain from re-consecrating it.

It is only a religion on the defensive, a religion in retreat, a religion scared of the truth, that turns away from the divine spirit at work in the world at large. In the past the greatest Jewish thinkers were those who attempted to synthesise their Jewish heritage with the dominant philosophical ideas of the 'secular' world around them: Philo of Alexandria, Saadia Gaon, Judah HaLevi, Maimonides ... the creative geniuses of our tradition were always open to the disconcerting realisation that not all truth lies within the received Jewish wisdom. They always returned to the centrality of the Jewish texts, but integrated into them the new understandings they had learnt beyond the confines of their own faith community. The challenge in our time is no different.

Perhaps we have grown frightened of asking questions. As a community, Anglo-Jewry tends to play it safe. We have grown accustomed to mediocrity. We prefer the security of old answers to the insecurity of questions which open us to the deeper uncertainties of existence.

Many of us have learnt now to talk about relationships and sex and death and how much we earn – the old taboos. And yet there is still a conspiracy of silence about our spiritual life and our religious questions and doubts. What do we really believe? What does God mean for us after Auschwitz? Where do we go to ask the questions we long to ask, the secret questions in our souls? With whom do we share our hidden doubts, our uncertainties about what it is all about?

The malaise of Anglo-Jewry is at heart a spiritual problem. Immersed in the irrelevant, enamoured of the superficial, our collective psychic health is imperilled by our refusal to challenge the prevailing pieties, the polite conventions, the preoccupation with the impression we are making. The dis-ease of our community can only be healed by an honest engagement with the spiritual questions buried within our consciousness. The courage to ask questions is embedded in our heritage, but we have lost our capacity to live creatively with the ultimate questions of Jewish life, of human life.

———————————————————∗———————————————————

I went to a workshop run by two therapists, one a rabbi and one a colleague of mine. And the theme of the workshop was 'Wrestling with our angel' – the story of Jacob. It was really about wrestling with the whole issue of spirituality and Judaism and I thought maybe I'd come away with some answers but I didn't get any answers; but I did get a really strong feeling of being a Jew.

When I drove back home afterwards, I wrote in my mind a letter to my father: 'Dear Dad, I'm a Jew again.' That was the beginning of a new relationship with him, the beginning of wanting him to share the joy of me being Jewish, but not under his instruction. So I did eventually join a synagogue . . . but it isn't the belonging to a community that's been important. It's belonging to a continuity over thousands of years that's felt very important.

I realised that when I'm in synagogue, quite often it isn't to do with the spiritual connection with God. It's to do with 'being Jewish'. Singing and taking part in the rituals seemed to have a lot of meaning for me, just because it was part of this continuity. But slowly, spiritual meaning came as well. At first I had great difficulty with the notion of a God that's out there and a God that you can speak to in prayers, and praise, or ask things of. That was very odd. But gradually I came to discover that the words and the prayers could be translated into another meaning, into an understanding of the divine within, that we're part of.

17
Living with the Questions

---*---

The search never really stopped. It wasn't a Jewish search but it was a search which started with the sky which was unreachable and developed from there. The Jewish roots were always in it of course ... I wanted to be able to ask questions and participate, know why I was there and know what it was I was reading. The first time that I came across Reform Judaism, I was accepted for what I was. I didn't have to be like someone else. I didn't have to do as others did. I was there because of what I was and because of what I could as an individual contribute, which meant so much to me. It also meant that I could go to the rabbi and actually ask questions and say 'Why do we do it?' or 'What does it mean?' ...

I have now given up work and gone back to learn. The learning is to give me the tools so that I can excavate for myself. I don't want someone to come and say, 'Look, here it is, isn't it beautiful, we just came upon it, it's a great antique piece, you can have it.' But give me the tools and I'll go and dig myself. It's very exciting and I suppose all these efforts are bound up really and honestly with the question: 'When I am gone, what will remain?' Am I just going to go and that's the end of it, or will something remain? And I don't know.

A story:

A man was going from village to village, everywhere asking the same question, 'Where can I find God?' He journeyed from rabbi to rabbi, and nowhere was he satisfied with the answers he received, so quickly he would pack his bags, and hurry on to the next village. Some of the rabbis replied, 'Pray, my son, and you shall find Him.' But the man had tried to pray, and knew that he could not. And some replied 'Study, my child, and you shall find Him.' But the more he read, the more confused he became, and

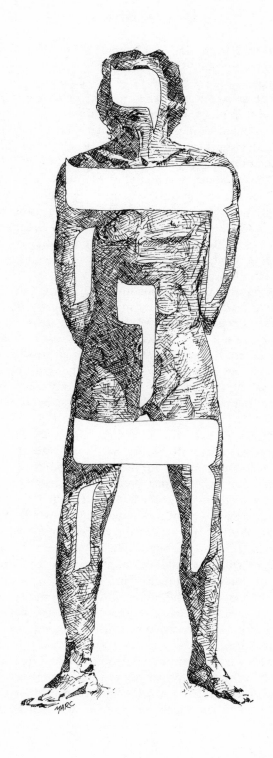

the further he seemed from God. And some replied 'Forget your quest, my child, God is within you.' But the man had tried to find God within himself, and failed.

One day the man arrived wearily at a very small village set in the middle of a forest. He went up to a woman who was minding some chickens, and she asked whom he could be looking for in such a small place, but she did not seem surprised when he told her that he was looking for God. She showed him to the rabbi's house.

When he went in, the rabbi was studying. He waited a moment, but he was impatient to be off to the next village, if he could not be satisfied. Then he interrupted, 'Rabbi – how do I find God?' The rabbi paused, and the man wondered which of the many answers he had already received he would be told this time. But the rabbi simply said, 'You have come to the right place, my child, God is in this village. Why don't you stay a few days; you might meet Him.'

The man was puzzled. He did not understand what the rabbi could mean. But the answer was unusual, and so he stayed. For two or three days he strode round and round, asking all the villagers where God was that morning, but they would only smile, and ask him to have a meal with them. Gradually he got to know them, and even helped with some of the village work. Every now and then he would see the rabbi by chance, and the rabbi would ask him, 'Have you met God yet, my son?' And the man would smile, and sometimes he understood and sometimes he did not understand.

For months he stayed in the village, and then for years. He became part of the village and shared in all its life. He went with the men to the synagogue on Friday and prayed with the rest of them, and sometimes he knew why he prayed, and sometimes he didn't. And sometimes he really said prayers, and sometimes only words. And then he would return with one of the men for a Friday night meal, and when they talked about God, he was always assured that God was in the village, though he wasn't quite sure where or when He could be found. Gradually, too, he began to believe that God was in the village, though he wasn't quite sure where. He knew, however, that sometimes he had met Him.

One day, for the first time, the rabbi came to him and said, 'You have met God now, have you not!' And the man said, 'Thank you, Rabbi, I think that I have. But I am not sure why I met Him, or how or when. And why is He in this village only?'

So the rabbi replied, 'God is not a person, my child, nor a thing. You cannot meet Him in that way. When you came to our village, you were so worried by your question that you could not recognise an answer when you heard it. Nor could you recognise God when you met Him, because

you were not really looking for Him. Now that you have stopped persecuting God, you have found Him, and now you can return to your town
if you wish.'

So the man went back to his town, and God went with him. And the
man enjoyed studying and praying, and he knew that God was within
himself and within other people. And other people knew it too, and
sometimes they would ask him, 'Where can we find God?' And the man
would always answer, 'You have come to the right spot. God is in this
place.' (Jeffrey Newman)

This contemporary parable is part of the long-standing Jewish tradition
of storytelling. It belongs to those Jewish teachings known as *aggadah* (lore
and legend), which are themselves a central medium for the individual to
come to understand about God: 'If you wish to know He-who-spoke-and-
the-world-came-into-being, learn *aggadah*; for through that you will come
to know the Holy One blessed be He and cleave to His ways.'[1]

Stories like these usually raise as many questions as they answer. They
help us realise that the search for understanding is open-ended, and that
the truths we learn are not definitive solutions to life's problems but
touchstones on our journey. The spiritual search may lead us to continue
the traditional ways; it may lead us back to observances we thought we
were too modern to tolerate; it may lead us away from the conventions of
the past; it may lead us straight into the wilderness. But wherever the search
may lead in relation to Jewish law (*halachah*), its defining characteristic will
be the value we place on asking religious and spiritual questions. And these
questions will necessarily be personal ones.

What unites the voices in this section of the book is the recognition that
whatever is meant by 'religious experience', in the end it has to be made
personal. For until it becomes a personal experience, religion remains
meaningless. All the laws and traditions, the teachings and prayers, the
liturgies and the literature, the words and the music – all of these are only
pointers, introductions, hints, suggestions: signposts for the journey. But
how do we make Judaism into a personal experience?

Anglo-Jewry could not exactly be described as a community searching
to know God. Yet at the heart of our tradition is the call to search. What
remains the stumbling-block is . . . God. Often we shy away from this. The
word itself causes a slight embarrassment. We can avoid the uncomfortable
feelings it raises by jumping to the security of a simple credo: 'I believe in
God'; 'I don't believe in God'. Both of these are an avoidance because, as
the story says, 'God is not a person . . . nor a thing.' Belief in God can
never be like believing that this book you have in your hands started its
life as a tree; or that the earth is round.

Yet the question of God refuses to go away. This book has been written with the assumption that its readers will represent a whole spectrum of religious belief and practice, from commitment to marginality and beyond, and that non-Jews as well as Jews will have an interest in an exploration of how Jewish identity is experienced in Britain today. Our sense of belonging will remain flawed unless we engage with the central and sustaining enigma of the Jewish myth – our sense of God.

The question of God inevitably impinges on a Jew's sense of belonging: whether we define ourselves as an ethnic or racial group, a cultural or social or religious community, the Jew's self-definition requires, at some stage, a wrestling with the core dilemma of Jewish existence: what do we, as individuals, think, feel, believe, know about God? Avoiding the question is, of course, one response to it.

We may well come to a comfortable sense of Jewish belonging without feeling any need for a personal spirituality, or any form of religious commitment. But to do so without facing up to the question of God seems to verge on a failure of integrity. The freedom to respond honestly to the questions of belief, and allow the questions to take us where they will, is the hallmark of a contemporary Jewish spirituality which values the search and the journey as much as the homecoming.

So what is it that Jews are asked to believe, or believe in?

The central statement of our monotheistic tradition is the Biblical text, now a prayer, an invocation: 'Hear [*Shema*], O Israel, the Eternal [*YHWH*] is our God, the Eternal [*YHWH*] is One' (Deuteronomy 6: 4). These are the words drummed into us as children and endlessly repeated, or repudiated, until the day we die. Indeed they are the words with which the Jew, traditionally (does it still happen?), is to end his or her life: like the river rejoining the sea, one's dying breath forms the syllables of God's Oneness as we surrender our souls to the soul of the universe.

But what are we talking *about* when we invoke the name of the divine? Cautiously, anxiously, provisionally, like Moses enjoined to take off his shoes on holy ground, we allow ourselves to explore the key word of Jewish tradition – the untranslatable four-letter name of God: *YHWH*.

Yod, Hay, Vav, Hay: the four Hebrew letters at the heart of the mystery. The divine name: *YHWH* (Yahweh). Most of our translations render this as 'Lord'. The inadequacy of this is starkly obvious. Instead of opening us up to the mystery of life, it impoverishes our imaginations. Our minds move to the human associations of the word 'Lord' and although we know that the Hebrew word signifies something beyond itself, we become trapped by the anthropomorphism. We betray the essence of the divine when we translate *YHWH* as 'Lord'.

YHWH is a Hebrew neologism: it is an amalgam of the past, present and future tenses of the verb 'to be'. So the term *YHWH* can be rendered as 'being', 'is-ness', 'the eternal (One)' – we grasp after a way of expressing the inexpressible. The central statement of Jewish faith demands of the community: 'Hear, O Israel, That-which-was-and-is-and-will-be [*YHWH*] is our God, Being-and-becoming [*YHWH*] is One.' Formless and genderless is our God. 'That-which-is' is our God.

It proved difficult for humanity to stay in a personal relationship with the nameless Eternal One. That which is without name and form and sex acquired a thousand names, a diversity of identities and descriptions and designations. Many of these involved gender: father and king were two of the most common, one expressing intimacy, the other distance. Sometimes the words projected onto the divine One who resisted being named carried a feminine resonance, like the attribute *rachamim* ('mercy/compassion') which comes from the Hebrew word for womb: here God was seen as having the capacity to hold us and contain us and nurture us as we grow in our being, just as a mother carries a child.

Jewish tradition always recognised that the Eternal One contained duality, indeed multiplicity. God was a transcendent, dominating, all-powerful, angry and loving 'masculine' force. God was an immanent, playful, strong, angry and loving 'feminine' force. Just as our human 'being' contained multiplicity, the constant interaction of contradictory creative energies and impulses, so too did (the) divine 'Being'.

Here we press up against the inadequacies of our language. C. G. Jung hypothesised two 'intuitive concepts' in each one of us. 'Logos' – active; penetrative; objective interest. And 'Eros' – emotional; receptive; implying psychic relatedness. He suggested that both principles ('masculine' and 'feminine') exist within us all, men and women. Their interrelationship – harmonious or otherwise – constitutes the drama of our lives. Here Jung is using *symbolic* terms for psychological factors that are independent of anatomical sex.[2] And so it has to be when we talk of 'masculine' and 'feminine' in the divine.

To name the nameless energy that animates all of life will always betray its essence. A necessary betrayal perhaps, an inevitable betrayal – but a betrayal nevertheless. Once we confuse the symbols and metaphors which have evolved to describe the divine, with the reality to which they point – we are lost, hopelessly.

———————————————*———————————————

I don't really know what spirituality means: sometimes something touches me and touches something at a depth. But when I then try to recapture it, it's not there – except it was there. Sometimes prayers speak to me, or just a sentence, or a word: it can carry me along so that in a way, I'm free to stay with something that speaks to me at that particular moment ... Sometimes it's just walking in a beautiful park, even seeing the colours in the autumn, or the sun, or the clouds, or going on holiday in Yorkshire! And then it has nothing to do with a particularly religious context.

Also sometimes it can happen when I'm working with someone through the body and we just happen to work very intensely or quietly, there's some energy or flow. It's something quite spiritual or religious in a way, setting in process a healing – or a connecting – element, that allows somebody to have a better quality of life.

──────────────────────────────*──────────────────────────────

I created God for myself in a bakery when I was a little boy. There was this beautiful-smelling bread everywhere and there were angels. In the middle of the angels was a figure and that figure for me was God. So whenever I smell any kind of bread or bakery I have an almost religious experience. But I can't accept how when we say that God is unimaginable, unthinkable, unspeakable we then give Him a voice: that He's speaking here and speaking there, and ordering this and ordering that – and tolerating this catastrophe. So God is alive in me, but the God I was taught about isn't, not that much.

In the camps I was not so concerned about God. The whole idea became really almost ridiculous. Yet the notion of God as it was thought to be gave way to something else, and that was that I tried to make contact emotionally with my mother. And through her of course with something else, or Someone else. The Someone does not make me happy, because if it's one thinking Being who allowed these things to happen, then I cannot reconcile myself to that. But if there really are forces which are in operation, whose existence I became aware of in the camp and often afterwards, that is what God really is according to the Jewish religion: unspeakable, unknowable, unmentionable.

We well understand how we all, in the face of personal or collective insecurities, desire more than anything else the reassuring warmth of certainty. Fundamentalism in religion and politics and economics caters for that deep human need. Away with uncertainties! Abolish ambivalence! Give us clear answers to hold on to. We can recognise in ourselves the temptation to beat a horrified retreat from the suffering and disorder of our times – or our lives – to the comfort of traditional values and answers.

The comfort is illusory, but superficially gratifying nevertheless. The certitudes of one dogmatic faith or another are always present, the safety of '-isms' and a world ordered according to a revelation that has already been handed down.

We can sense how the germ of violence and repression which is latent in all dogma attacks us unawares, and we find ourselves reacting with that same intolerance we so quickly identify and condemn in the other. Ironically, much of this is done in the name of God. Religion so easily descends into idolatry. When the divine becomes a tool in a power struggle, we have made God into an idol. When the name, or the word, of God becomes an instrument of oppression or coercion or manipulation or repression, we have succumbed to idolatry. This heresy we readily see in others, never in ourselves.

There are many temptations on the spiritual journey. Within the Biblical story we hear how, after a forty-day absence of their leader Moses, the people turned to Aaron and asked him to make them a tangible god, something familiar and secure to relieve them of their anxiety in the face of the unknown. The Golden Calf represents whatever we give ultimate value to in the absence of certainty about the future. Towards the beginning of this century Franz Rosenzweig taught about it:

Names change but polytheism continues. Culture, civilisation, people, state, nation, race, art, science, economy and class – here you have what is certainly an abbreviated and incomplete list of the pantheon of our contemporary gods. Who will deny their existence?

No 'idolator' has ever worshipped his idols with greater devotion and faith than that displayed by modern man towards his gods ... a continual battle has been going on to this very day in the mind of man between the worship of the One and the many. Its outcome is never certain.[3]

At the other end of the century another Jewish teacher acknowledges that the battle against idolatory is still part of the human condition:

No one of my generation can be understood without reference to his relation to Marxism as 'the God that failed', but I have come to think the phrase is wrong. It was an idol and no God. An idol tells people exactly what to believe, God presents them with choices they have to make for themselves. The difference is far from insignificant: before the idol men remain dependent children, before God they are burdened and at the same time liberated to participate in the decisions of endless creation. The dilemma has many surfaces and is no closer to being disposed of now than it was in the early thirties, nor will it be while Western society continues to leave so many of its people spiritually alienated, so empty of the joys of life and culture that they long for a superior will to direct their lives.[4]

Here Arthur Miller recognises that our spiritual alienation leads to the desire for certainty, answers, external direction for our impoverished lives. And we know how easy it is to abandon our awareness that uncertainty is built into the fabric of life, and collapse back into defensive, polarised attitudes. We then maintain with some passion opinions or beliefs which we do not hold with the degree of conviction, or moral certainty, that we feel forced to express.

The therapist knows about this kind of regression, how often our adult feelings are a re-enactment of our earliest years. Either mummy is here feeding me, holding me, and I love her and I feel secure and I am in heaven; or she has gone and I am all alone and I am in distress and I hate and I am in hell.

Crudely expressed as it is, this primitive dichotomy of experience is in us all. How we deal with these conflicting emotions may determine our psychological health. The need for definitive answers or rigid divisions is a manifestation in adult life of the failure to move emotionally beyond our infantile dependence. We cannot tolerate the absence of security. So we continually split the world into good and bad, right and wrong, us and them, black and white, religious and secular, Jew and non-Jew, Orthodox and Progressive, masculine and feminine, emotion and intellect, capitalism and socialism, my way or else ... a whole series of polarities which keep stable the dynamics of our world. All our good feelings stay with us and our group – all the bad feelings we put into 'them'. We feel we would be lost without these clear and simple 'truths'.

Yet the security involved in allowing ourselves to be consoled in this way involves a spiritual collapse. It is the triumph of death over life, the defeat of the question by the answer. For to ask a true question is a great spiritual act, a drama of personal responsibility which devolves on each of us alone. To question is to resist the totalitarianism of certainty. For an individual to question is to maintain the stance of ambivalence in the face of the world's pull towards the security of the familiar, the safety of the known.

Often religion seems to offer this consolation of certainty. And yet there are religious teachers, like the late Rav Shmuel Sperber, whose adherence to traditional forms was combined with a playful yet profound awareness of the significance, and indeed the necessity, of spiritual questioning: 'Religion offers answers without obliterating the questions. They become blunted and will not attack you with the same ferocity. But without them the answer would dry up and wither away. The question is a great religious act; it helps you live great religious truth.[5]

The ability to ask questions, and the ability to see questions as religious acts which enable us to live religious truths, is deeply rooted in the Jewish heritage. The Russian-Jewish poet and essayist Joseph Brodsky has written that 'the psychology of any minority is overtly one of nuance and ambivalence'.[6] The rabbis of the Talmud were masters of the question, geniuses of nuance and ambivalence. Their questioning spirit is part of the fabric too of our modern Western consciousness. The Jewish compulsion to question flowed from its traditional sources into some strange, but compelling, quarters: through Freud and Kafka, Einstein and Chomsky, Trotsky and Schoenberg and Chagall, Emma Goldman and Rosa Luxemburg ... the almost endless roll-call of our century's revolutionary thinkers.

And of course we know that this openness, this questioning spirit inveighing against the darkness and the dead weight of outworn formulae and past answers, is not a Jewish prerogative. Havel's pellucid evocation of 'the mystery which makes us genuinely human' follows close on John Keats' 'Negative Capability': 'when a man is capable of being in uncertainties, mysteries, doubts, without any irritable reaching after fact and reason ...'[7]

During his years in prison the Czech playwright-cum-president wrote a series of memorable letters to his wife Olga. In them Havel bears witness, with unimpaired sensitivity, to the necessity of 'living with the question'. Unfortunately we have been refused permission to quote from these letters – which are nevertheless some of the central spiritual documents of our times. In one key passage Havel contrasts systems of knowledge which attempt all-inclusive explanations with various open-ended attempts at grappling with the ever-elusive questions of meaning. The latter category includes religious texts. The challenge we all face – as he perceives it – is not to foreclose on our deepest human questioning, but to find ways of 'living with the question'; that is, to search out ways throughout our lives of encountering it over and over again, if only elliptically or indirectly.[8] Like Jacob, alone and wrestling for a blessing with an unknown force (Genesis 32: 25–32), Havel struggles towards a secular spirituality adequate for our times.

Yet a voice in us is still entitled to ask: what value is the individual spiritual journey in the face of the sheer unacceptibility of the world? In the face of the increasing gaps between rich and poor in Britain and around the world; in the face of totalitarianism and dictatorship; in the face of the still invidious presence of all-too-easily-imagined, unimaginable nuclear annihilation; in the face of the day-to-day invisible encroachment of ecological suicide; in the face of the whole bloody, tortured, undernourished, overpopulated world where only collective action can appear to effect change – what on earth is the point of emphasising the centrality, for Jewish survival-with-purpose, of the individual's own spiritual journey?

Again, we must turn for clues to the artists in our midst. For example, to Salman Rushdie: 'That the Czech revolution began in the theatres and is led by a writer is proof that people's spiritual needs, more than their material needs, have driven the commissars from power'.[9] In Anglo-Jewry our spiritual needs have been too long neglected. Religious dogma and hierarchy, communal disputes, gala fundraising events for charity, striking postures in relation to Israel, endless moral exhortations from rabbis and lay leaders – none of this is enough, none of this touches the soul.

Outsiders can see that this impoverishment of the soul spells the end of Anglo-Jewry. In a somewhat polemical conclusion to his review of three recently-published works concerning contemporary British Jewry, the distinguished historian David Cannadine wrote: 'The best that can be said about these admirable books [on the social politics of Anglo Jewry; anti-Semitism during World War Two; and *The Club: The Jews of Modern Britain*] is that they exactly mirror the contemporary state of British Jewry itself. They are more a requiem for a dying culture than the products of a living, vibrant and central historical tradition.'[10]

If we are in a 'dying culture', it is because our souls lack sustenance, and the individual spiritual journey is not taken seriously. In the face of all the collective forces around us, personal spirituality is not a luxury. It is a necessity. For Anglo-Jewry to re-emerge from its moribund and ossified condition and become a 'living, vibrant ... historical tradition' it will need to rediscover the soul.

We live with our stories and the fragments of understanding we gain along the way. And we look for help wherever we can find it. So we pay attention to teachers such as Joseph Brodsky: 'The comprehension of the metaphysics of personal drama betters one's chances of weathering the drama of history.'[11]

A generation and more after Auschwitz, Jews in this country will inevitably feel compelled to evoke 'the drama of history' in any debate about how to evaluate the individual's personal spiritual journey. Comprehending 'the metaphysics of personal drama' may feel laughable in the face of the collective forces around us. There are those who will dismiss this as sheer self-indulgence when set alongside political and social realities.

We Jews have indeed learnt that 'the drama of history' can destroy our finest endeavours like a petulant child tearing apart a butterfly's wings. Yet what hope there is we may sense in the beautifully measured tone, the dispassionate conviction, of Brodsky's words. This is also Torah, in its widest sense: teaching for our times. He addresses the ambivalence of the conflict that we all feel at times between the idiosyncrasy of our own lives, the uniqueness of how we experience the world – our 'personal drama' – and the 'drama of history' in which we are also swept up every day of our lives, where we know just how powerless we are individually as the historical juggernaut crushes all in its path.

And yet, as we saw at the opening of this book, personal and family dramas are the substance of our history. Each of us, part of a family, enduring exile, liberating ourselves from what traps us, wandering towards our own promised land, renewing our days – this is the story of our lives, our history, our belonging.

Our sense of belonging is nurtured by this awareness that Brodsky illumines. The self-knowledge we gain on the spiritual journey *is* significant: it 'betters one's chances'. But only 'betters' them, for there is no certainty of success. And what we as Jews in Britain are engaged with – trying to live out the destiny of our people, carriers of the blessing of Abraham – has only a 'chance' of fulfilment. Perhaps we will fail on the way or, like Moses, at the very end. And whatever we succeed in doing is only 'weathering' those impersonal forces of history the Jew hears beating at the door. The hope we are offered – which is also our prayer – is that perhaps, after all, we will survive the storm.

---

*

There was a search – don't misunderstand these words – for some kind of integrity or honesty, a search for the truth in the sense that I did not want, and I don't want, to be deluded. I don't choose a faith in order to free myself from problems. I want to know what is true to me at least.

It's very important that there is a guiding force, call it God, call it what you like, and I know that several times in my life it has been active. These visions and dreams and whatever, they didn't just come from my imagination. And perhaps the search was for values which I could hand over to other people, again not in a grandiose way, but to my clients, to my patients, to my friends, to my children and whoever comes after that. It's not a compulsive journey. It's not that I have got to observe certain rules and certain laws and certain whatever in order to arrive. I don't think I ever arrive in a sense, not in this life anyway . . .

Glossary

The following definitions relate to the context in which the words appear
in this book

Aleph: first letter of the Hebrew alphabet

Aliyah: emigration to Israel (lit. 'going up')

Bimah: platform in the synagogue from which the Torah scroll is read, or the
service is led

Broigus: Jewish anger

Challah: plaited bread for the Sabbath

Chazan: cantor

Cheder: part-time Hebrew and religion classes for children

Chumash: the contents of the Torah scroll in book form, i.e. the first five books
of the Bible, the Pentateuch

Chutzpah: a cheekiness which verges on arrogance – as in the man who kills his
parents and then throws himself on the mercy of the courts because he is an
orphan (from Leo Rosten)

Davenning: praying

Galut: exile from the promised land (Israel); the diaspora

Goyim/goyische: gentiles/gentile

Haggadah: the book which contains the liturgy for the Passover *seder*

Halachah: the ritual and behavioural aspects of Jewish teaching; Jewish law (lit.
'the way'/'the path')

Heimische: the relaxed emotional warmth of a happy home

Kabbalah: the Jewish mystical tradition

Kapple: see 'kippa'

Kashrut: Jewish dietary laws

Kaynaynhora: time-honoured phrase used to ward off the evil eye, the authentic
voice of Jewish superstition (lit. 'let there be no evil eye')

Kiddush: sanctification over wine during Sabbath and festivals

Kippa: traditional (male) headcovering

Klal Yisrael: 'the community of Israel', i.e. the Jewish people

Kol Nidrei: the service on the eve of the Day of Atonement, named after its
opening prayer

Ma Nishtanah: one of the opening passages of the Passover *seder,* inquiring into the symbols of the evening

Matzah: unleavened bread, the staple diet of Passover

Mensch: a decent human being

Midrash: the genre of homiletical amplification of Biblical texts; one example of this art

Mikveh: ritual bath used for purification

Minyan/minyanim: prayer gathering of ten, the traditional requirement for communal prayer

Nachas: vicarious enjoyment

Rasha: the rebellious child described in the Passover *haggadah*

Seder: home celebration on the eve of Passover, consisting of a retelling through symbol and story of the events of the Exodus, with an accompanying festive meal

Sefer Torah: parchment scroll on which the Torah is written

Shabbas/Shabbat: the Sabbath day of rest (Saturday)

Shadchan: matchmaker

Shema: Biblical passages affirming the unity of God – the central statement of Jewish monotheism

Shikse: female gentile

Shiva: the seven-day mourning period following a death, during which the mourner receives visitors at home

Shoah: a Hebrew word found in the Book of Job, meaning 'emptiness, devastation, destruction', which has begun to supersede the Greek term 'holocaust' as an epithet denoting the destruction of European Jewry between 1939 and 1945

Shtetl: villages of eastern Europe where Jewish life flourished prior to the *shoah*

Shtibl/shtiblach: small, informal prayer communities

Shtum: silent

Shul: synagogue

Sukkah: the temporary booth erected for the festival of Sukkot

Tallis/tallit: prayer shawl

Talmud Torah: the study of traditional Jewish texts

Tephillin: phylacteries traditionally worn during weekday morning prayer

Ulpan: class for learning modern Hebrew

Yeshivah/yeshivot: traditional seminary for Jewish learning

Yiddishe kop: Jewish cleverness (lit. 'a Jewish head')

Yom Kippur: the Day of Atonement

Notes

INTRODUCTION

1. cf. chapter 1 of Lawrence Kushner's *The River Of Light: Spirituality, Judaism, and the Evolution of Consciousness* (Harper & Row, San Francisco, 1981)

2. C. G. Jung, *Memories, Dreams, Reflections* (Collins: Fontana library, 1967/1975), p. 166.

3. The words 'myth', 'mythical' and 'mythological' appear in this book in their original sense. Nowadays the word 'myth' is often used to signify that which is not true, that which is opposed to 'reality'. But a myth is a true revelation of reality in symbolic form: 'A great myth is the soul of the world speaking in terms that all human beings can understand' (Peter Brook). Or, as the rabbis of old said: 'The Torah speaks in the language of human beings.'

PART I: BEGINNING IN THE FAMILY
1: Jewish Families, Jewish History

1. Later on in the text (Genesis 17: 5) Abram's name changes to the more familiar 'Abraham', the meaning of which is connected to his destiny: 'father of a multitude'.

2. Paul Johnson, *A History of the Jews* (Weidenfeld & Nicolson, 1987), p. 2.

3. cf. M. Wicks and K. Kiernan, *Family Change* (Family Policy Studies Centre, 1990)

4. Jonathan Sacks, 'Women's role in our spiritual future', *Jewish Chronicle*, 23 February 1990

5. From the opening of Tolstoy's *Anna Karenina*.

6. Ezekiel 18: 1. The prophet quotes this old Israelite proverb in order to refute it: each individual is responsible before God for his or her own actions. Nevertheless, the reality that parental attitudes shape the contours of their children's emotional lives is incontrovertible.

7. In every extended Jewish family there is someone who is *broigus* with another member of the family. *Broigus* is an untranslatable Yiddish word signifying a

smouldering disgruntlement where one feels slighted and offended by somebody's words or actions, usually years ago. And what makes matters worse is that they don't even know about it.

2: 'All You Need Is Love'

1. Lynne Truss, *Independent On Sunday*, 11 February 1990
2. *ibid.*, 15 April 1990 (extract from R. Dinnage, *The Ruffian on the Stair: Reflections on Death*, Viking, 1990)
3. In medieval literature, including Jewish texts, one of the most popular images used to describe the community was that of the human body: 'Just as one would never think of deliberately injuring, or purposely neglecting, any limb of one's own body, so, too, every Jew must seek the well-being of all other members of the entity that is the Jewish people.' Quoted in A. Chill, *The Mitzvot: The Commandments and their Rationale* (Keter Books, Jerusalem, 1974), p. 234
4. Mary Levens, 'Psychological Conflicts in Jewish Families' (unpublished paper), p. 7
5. *Independent On Sunday*, 11 February 1990. The interviewee goes on to say: 'In the end, though, I realised it was a kind of loving and I didn't resent it. She came to terms with all of us before she died, and we came to terms with her. You are lucky if your mother lives long enough to give you the chance to do it.'
6. David Grossman, *See Under: Love* (Jonathan Cape, 1989)
7. Chaim Bermant, *Troubled Eden* (Vallentine, Mitchell, 1969), p. 258
8. *ibid.*, p. 259

3: Feeling the Pressure: Myth and Marriage

1. A. J. Heschel, *God in Search of Man* (Harper Torchbooks, Harper & Row, 1966), p. 283
2. *Jewish Chronicle*, 15 June 1990

4: 'Today I Am a Man'

1. The Torah is the recipient of a host of feelings projected onto it: feelings about Jewishness and God and religious authority and parental authority; guilty and hopeful and anxious feelings; a multitude of mixed feelings about the sacred and the profane; and so on.
2. 'Hebrew and Yiddish Legacies: A Symposium', *Times Literary Supplement*, 3 May 1985
3. Jacob's name is changed to 'Israel' after his night of wrestling with a mysterious stranger (Genesis 32: 29). The name 'Jacob' means 'heel' – the pun is in the original Hebrew text. The name 'Israel' contains a delightful ambiguity: it means 'the one who struggles *for* [on behalf of] God' and 'the one who struggles

with [against] God'. The text plays with these two names in a way that mirrors our own inner dividedness.

5: A New Consciousness

1. R. Friedman, 'The Jewish Mother in Modern Literature: a rotten press!', *Jewish Quarterly*, vol. 33, no. 2 (122), 1986, p. 34

2. cf. Dan Greenberg, *How to be a Jewish Mother*, (Price/Stern/Sloan, Los Angeles, 1980), p. 11

3. See, for example, lyrics by Jack Yellen quoted in L. Blue & J. Magonet, *The Guide to the Here and Hereafter* (Collins, 1988), p. 115

4. Baba Metzia 59a (Talmud)

5. Zohar, i, 50a

6. Jonathan Sacks, 'Women's role in our spiritual future', *Jewish Chronicle*, 23 February 1990

7. C. G. Montefiore and H. Loewe, *A Rabbinic Anthology* (Schocken Books, 1974), pp. 298–9

8. Berachot 24b (Talmud)

9. Adapted from H. Schauss, *The Lifetime of a Jew*, (UAHC, New York, 1950), pp. 71–2; and L. Ginsberg, *The Legends Of The Jews*, (JPSA, Philadelphia, 1937), pp. 65–6

10. Alix Pirani, 'The Healing Goddess', in *Manna*, 25, Autumn 1989, p. 31

11. *ibid.*, p. 31

12. This dream was first recorded, with a fuller discussion, in H. Cooper, 'Aspects of the Jewish Unconscious', in H. Cooper (ed.), *Soul Searching: Studies in Judaism and Psychotherapy* (SCM Press, 1988), p. 230

13. Sheila Shulman, 'A Radical Feminist Perspective on Judaism', *European Judaism*, vol. 21, no. 1, Summer 1987, p. 16

6: The Blessing of Abraham

1. Abraham Reisen (b. Russia 1876–d. USA 1953): Yiddish poet. 'I've Lost' is quoted from *The Golden Peacock: An Anthology of Yiddish Poetry*, compiled and edited by Joseph Leftwich (Robert Anscombe & Co, 1939)

2. M. Ostow, 'The Psychological Determinants of Jewish Identity' in M. Ostow, (ed.) *Judaism and Psychoanalysis* (Ktav, 1982), p. 159

3. 'Respecting one's father and mother; normative acts of generosity; coming early to the synagogue for morning and evening study; giving hospitality to strangers; visiting the sick; assisting the bride; attending to the dead; devotion in prayer; making peace between people. And the study of Torah,' says the tradition, 'leads to them all' (from Mishnah Peah 1: 1)

4. Naomi Dale, 'Jews, Ethnicity and Mental Health', in H. Cooper (ed.), *Soul Searching: Studies in Judaism and Psychotherapy* (SCM Press, 1988), p. 76

5. Genesis 31
6. Genesis 22
7. Quoted in Robert S. Wistrich, 'The German-Jewish Symbiosis in Central Europe', *European Judaism*, no. 44, Spring 1990, p. 27

PART 2: EXILE
7: Keeping the Flame Flickering

1. Gabriel Josipovici, address to Twenty-First Annual Jewish-Christian Bible Study Week, Bendorf, West Germany (*European Judaism*, no. 44, Spring 1990), p. 7
2. cf. N. N. Glatzer (ed.), *Franz Rosenzweig: His Life and Thought* (Schocken Books, 1970), pp. 214–34
3. Shabbat 21b (Talmud)
4. I am particularly indebted to Dr Tony Kushner for his help and comments on this section of the book. He is one of a 'new wave' of younger Jewish historians whose rereading of Anglo-Jewish history has helped inform my own perspective. While the approach of this group remains somewhat controversial, I follow it because it makes most sense of my experience. The errors and imbalances remain my own.
5. I am grateful to Richard Bolchover for this formulation.
6. Israel Finestein, 'East End, West End: Anglo-Jewry and the Great Immigration', *Jewish Quarterly*, no. 132, Winter 1988–9, p. 26
7. Bill Williams, 'East and West in Manchester Jewry', in David Cesarani (ed.), *The Making of Modern Anglo-Jewry* (Blackwell, 1990), p. 23
8. Rosalin Livshin, 'The Acculturation of Immigrant Jewish Children 1890–1930', in Cesarani (*ibid.*)
9. Louise London, 'Jewish Refugees, Anglo-Jewry and British Government Policy 1930–1940', in Cesarani (*ibid.*). These attitudes persisted even after the war when the full horror of the Holocaust had been revealed. It is extraordinary that in all the years of harassment of Jews, erosion of basic rights, confiscation of property, forced ghettoisation, mass shootings and gassings, only 50,000 Jews were admitted to Britain.
10. Unpublished thesis by Richard Bolshover
11. David Cesarani, 'The Transformation of Communal Authority in Anglo-Jewry, 1914–1940', in Cesarani (*op. cit.*), pp. 115–40
12. This furore arose when a play by Jim Allen asserted Zionist collusion with Nazi extermination policy. Protests by Jewish historians and others led to the Royal Court production being shelved.
13. See Tim Kelsey's report in the *Independent on Sunday*, 10 June 1990

PART 3: EXODUS
8: Exodus Past and Present

1. This echoes the statement in the Passover *haggadah* (based on Mishnah Pesachim 10: 4).

2. The Hebrew text of the book of Exodus reinforces this theme: the same verbal root (*'avad'*) is used of Israelite 'servitude' in Egypt and the 'service' of God for which they are liberated (see 1: 14/2: 23 and 3: 12/7: 16, etc.).

3. The centrality of the Bible in Western thought has led to the adoption of the exodus motifs for religious and secular revolutionary movements throughout the ages. Cf. Michael Waltzer, *Exodus and Revolution* (Basic Books, New York, 1985); Marc H. Ellis, *Toward a Jewish Theology of Liberation*, (Orbis Books, 1987)

4. Based on Norman Solomon, 'Liberation Theology: The Exodus Message in 1988', in *Manna*, no. 21, Autumn 1988 (p. 4 Theology Supplement)

9: Anglo-Jewry and Israel

1. In *Abraham Isaac Kook* (SPCK, 1979), p. 16

2. Based on Irving Greenberg, 'The Third Great Cycle in Jewish History', in *Perspectives* (National Jewish Resource Center, New York, 1981)

3. Elie Wiesel, *Night* (Fontana/Collins, 1972), p. 77

4. 'How delicious it was so suddenly to be transformed from a people of anaemic accountants and orthodontists to a people of muscular heroes . . .' (Leonard Fine), quoted in *Jewish Quarterly*, no. 132, Winter 1988–9, p. 4

5. Stephen Brook, *The Club* (Constable, 1989), p. 360

6. 'For pious Jews it was the hand of providence, for secular Jews a form of manifest destiny.' Paul Johnson, *A History of the Jews*, (Weidenfeld & Nicolson, 1987), p. 538

7. Emil Fackenheim, *God's Presence in History*, (New York University Press, 1970), p. 84

8. I. Greenberg, *op. cit.*, p. 10 (quoted in Marc H. Ellis, *Toward a Jewish Theology of Liberation*, Orbis Books, USA, 1987, p. 30)

9. cf. Stephen Brook, *op. cit.*, chapter 27: 'Opinion and Silence: Responding to Israel'

10. In outlining the grim options Israel faces in the absence of compromise, one assumes he is not advocating them as policy; but he gives voice to an ugly undercurrent of popular sentiment. Quoted in Marc H. Ellis, 'The Task Before Us: Contemporary Jewish Religious Thought and the Challenge of Solidarity' in *European Judaism*, no. 44, Spring 1990, p. 37

11. Dow Marmur, *Beyond Survival*, (DLT, 1982), p. 191

12. See Don Peretz, 'The Intifada', in *Jewish Quarterly*, no. 138, Summer 1990, pp. 12–18. Recognition of the potential problem goes back a long way: 'The terrible price which our enemies paid touched the hearts of many of our men . . . It may

well be that the Jewish people never learned and never accustomed itself to feel the triumph of conquest and victory, and we receive it with mixed feelings' – Yitzhak Rabin (!), June 1967. Quoted in A. J. Heschel, *Israel: An Echo Of Eternity*, (Farrar, Straus and Giroux, New York, 1974), p. 215

13. The phrase is quoted in *Jewish Quarterly*, no. 129, Spring 1988, p. 1

14. As we go to press, our first scenario has just begun to unfold ...

15. 'In 1977, ten years after Golda Meir called Sharon "a danger to democracy", Begin said that Sharon was capable of surrounding the Knesset with tanks.' See Avishai Margalit, 'High Noon at the Likud Corral', in *New York Review of Books*, 26 April 1990, p. 42

16. See Robert I. Friedman, 'Inside the West Bank Settlements', in *New York Review of Books*, 15 June 1989, p. 56

10: Anglo Jewry's Religious Revival

1. 'From this centre ... the spirit of Judaism will go forth to the great circumference, to all the communities of the Diaspora, and will breathe new life into them and preserve their unity.' Quoted in *Jewish Quarterly*, vol. 35, no. 1 (129), 1988, p. 2

2. Arthur Hertzberg, 'Israel: The Tragedy of Victory', in *New York Review of Books*, 28 May 1989, p. 12

3. 'Some 90 per cent of United Synagogue members do not come to *shul* even once a week.' We note the lingering expectation within that regret-filled (and finger-wagging?) 'even'. Jonathan Sacks, 'Building the Jewish Future', *L'Eylah*, no. 27, April 1989, p. 14

4. *ibid.*, p. 14

5. *Jewish Quarterly*, no. 133, Spring 1989, p. 34

6. David Cesarani, *ibid.*, p. 37

7. *Jewish Chronicle*, 6 April 1989

8. Gateshead *yeshivah* was founded in 1929 and since the war the town has become the largest centre of Orthodox *yeshivah*-based learning in Europe.

9. See Marc H. Ellis, *Toward a Jewish Theology of Liberation* (Orbis Books, 1987), pp. 34–5, which includes reference to I. Greenberg (*op. cit.*). A sign of the times however is Rabbi Jonathan Sacks: 'We must create contexts in which the Jewish experience is communicated in more intimate, informal and involving ways than in the *shul* itself.' (cf. note 3 *ibid.*, p. 14)

11: The Blossoming of Secularism

1. Jonathan Sacks, 'On Jewish Survival: Two Broadcast Talks', in *L'Eylah*, no. 27, April 1989, p. 6

2. *ibid.*, p. 6

3. Discussed by Jonathan Sacks in 'Towards 2000: The American Experience', in *L'Eylah*, no. 23, Spring 1987, pp. 23ff

4. *Jewish Quarterly*, no. 133, Spring 1989, p. 38

5. Stephen Brook, *The Club* (Constable, 1989), p. 362

6. David Cesarani, 'The Alternative Jewish Community', in *European Judaism*, no. 37/38, Winter 1985/Summer 1986, p. 52

7. *ibid.*, p. 53

8. *ibid.*, p. 53

9. Jonathan Sacks, (*op. cit.*, 'On Jewish Survival'), p. 5. For an amplification of this theme see also the same author's *Traditional Alternatives* (Jews' College Publications, 1989), p. 123

10. Julia Bard in *Jewish Quarterly*, no. 135, Autumn 1989, p. 71

11. *Jewish Quarterly*, no. 136, Winter 1989–90, pp. 70–1

12. '... fundamentally every [individual] and especially every Jew participates in the process of *tikkun* ... in Kabbalistic myth the Messiah becomes a mere symbol ... For it is not the act of the Messiah as executor of the *tikkun* ... that brings redemption, but your action and mine.' Gershom Scholem, *On the Kabbalah and its Symbolism* (Schocken Books, 1969), p. 117

13. Franz Kafka, *Parables and Paradoxes* (Schocken, 1946/1961), p. 81

12: The Renaissance of Jewish Learning

1. For the statistics see the editorial by Colin Schindler in *Jewish Quarterly*, no. 131, Autumn 1988, p. 4 and Stephen Brook, *The Club* (Constable, 1989), p. 228

2. *ibid.*, p. 3

3. *ibid.*, p. 4

4. See Dr Stephen Miller's observations quoted *ibid.*, p. 4

5. *L'Eylah*, no. 29, April 1990, p. 16

6. *Jewish Quarterly*, no. 131, p. 4

7. Jonathan Sacks, 'Towards 2000: The American Experience', in *L'Eylah*, no. 23, Spring, 1987, pp. 26–7

8. Louis Jacobs, *We Have Reason to Believe* (Vallentine, Mitchell, 1962), p. 59

9. George Steiner, 'Our Homeland, the Text', in *Salmagundi*, Winter/Spring 1985, p. 5

10. Jonathan Sacks, 'A Challenge to Jewish Secularism' in *Jewish Quarterly*, no. 134, Summer 1989, p. 33

11. *ibid.*, p. 32

12. Steiner, *op. cit.*, pp. 7–8

13. *ibid.*, p. 17

14. Sacks, *op. cit.*, p. 33

15. Steiner, *op. cit.*, p. 16

16. Jonathan Magonet, 'The Question of Identity' in H. Cooper (ed.), *Soul Searching: Studies in Judaism and Psychotherapy* (SCM Press, 1988), p. 190

17. 1 Samuel 2: 9

18. Quoted in *Forms of Prayer for Jewish Worship,* vol. 3 (Reform Synagogues of Great Britain, 1985), p. 517

19. All quotations taken from N. N. Glatzer, *Franz Rosenzweig: His Life and Thought* (Schocken, 1961), p. 231

PART 4: OUT OF THE WILDERNESS
13: Buried Treasure

1. T. S. Eliot, *Four Quartets* ('Little Gidding', lines 240–4), (Faber & Faber, 1969)

2. Martin Buber, *Hasidism and Modern Man* (Humanities Press International, 1955/1988), pp. 163–4

3. Alan Unterman, *The Wisdom of the Jewish Mystics* (Sheldon Press, 1976), pp. 72–3

4. As Clive Sinclair reminds us, the 'two mottos of Anglo-Jewry are "Don't give ammunition to the enemy" and "Don't wash our dirty linen in public."' *Jewish Quarterly,* no. 136, Winter 1989–90, p. 4

5. cf. C. G. Jung, *Collected Works* (Routledge & Kegan Paul, 1977), vol. 18, pp. 724–5

6. Adapted from *The Dybbuck* by S. An-ski (pseudonym of Solomon Rapaport, 1863–1920), Russian socialist, author and folklorist

7. G. Janouch, *Conversations with Kafka* (Village Press, 1971), pp. 35–6

14: The Gift from Within

1. From the Passover *haggadah.* As the late Rabbi Dr Eli Munk taught, the text emphasises the pronouns 'me' and 'us', 'so that we should consider the liberation not only as historical fact but as a personal experience. It happened to me – and to you' (personal notes, Yeshivat D'var Yerushalayim, Jerusalem, 1975).

2. Martin Buber, *Ten Rungs: Hasidic Sayings* (Schocken, 1970), pp. 59–60

3. T. S. Eliot, *Four Quartets* ('Burnt Norton', lines 44–6 & 149), (Faber & Faber, 1969)

4. cf. Gershom Scholem, *On the Kabbalah and its Symbolism,* (Schocken, 1969), p. 50

5. *Pirke Avot* 1: 17

6. Bernice Rubens, *Kingdom Come* (Hamish Hamilton, 1990), p. 255

7. Franz Kafka, *Shorter Works: Volume 1* (Secker & Warburg, 1973), p. 102

8. The imagery used for God's guiding presence during Israel's desert wanderings, cf. Exodus 40: 36–38

15: Wandering in the Wilderness

1. Gabriel Josipovici, *The Book Of God* (Yale University Press, 1988), p. 87

2. The Hebrew word appears in the first sentence of the book and it became the practice to adopt one of the distinctive opening words of each of the Five Books of Moses for their 'titles'.

3. Echoing the homiletical *midrash* which states: 'The Torah was given in public, openly in no-man's-land. For had it been given in the land of Israel, the Israelites could have said to the nations of the world: You have no share in it. But since it was given in the wilderness, publicly and openly, in no-man's-land, everyone who wished to accept it could come and accept it' (*Mechilta* to Exodus 19: 2).

4. George Steiner has described the Jews as 'a pilgrim tribe housed not in place but in time, not rooted but millennially equipped with legs' (in 'Our Homeland, the Text', *Salmagundi*, Winter/Spring 1985, p. 19). This is in accord with the traditional Jewish emphasis on the preeminence of time over space: 'The Bible is more concerned with time than with space. It sees the world in the dimension of time. It pays more attention to generations, to events, than to countries, things; it is more concerned with history than with geography ... Judaism is a religion of time aiming at the sanctification of time' – Abraham Joshua Heschel, *The Sabbath* (Harper Torchbooks, Harper & Row, New York, 1966), pp. 6–8

5. Quoted from *The Star of Redemption* in N. N. Glatzer, *Franz Rosenzweig: His Life and Thought* (Schocken, 1961), p. 323. Rosenzweig (1886–1929) was one of this century's most creative Jewish thinkers and the inspired architect of the conceptual framework of creation, revelation and redemption utilised in these chapters.

6. *ibid.*, p. 325

7. Seamus Heaney on the poems of Miroslav Holub

8. Rosenzweig (Glatzer, *op. cit.*), p. 325

9. T. S. Eliot, *Four Quartets* ('East Coker', line 209), (Faber & Faber, 1969)

10. 'Jews been acrobats since the beginning of the world', says Solomon, Miller's only specifically Jewish character in any of his plays, cf. *The Price*, in *Collected Plays: Two* (Methuen, 1988), p. 319

11. cf. Franz Kafka, *Parables and Paradoxes* (Schocken, 1946/1961), p. 189

12. Elie Wiesel, *Souls On Fire* (Weidenfeld & Nicolson, 1972), pp. 167–8

16: Creating Our Selves

1. Interview in *The Observer*, 6 September 1987

2. Vaclav Havel, 'Letters from Prison', in *Granta 21* (Penguin, 1987), pp. 227–8

3. Robert Alter, *The Art of Biblical Narrative* (Basic Books, New York, 1981), p. 12

4. Gabriel Josipovici, *The Book Of God* (Yale University Press, 1988), p. 88
5. Interview on BBC television, 30 January 1987

17: Living with the Questions

1. *Sifre,* 'Ekev'
2. See Andrew Samuels, 'Gender and Psyche: Developments in Analytical Psychology' in *British Journal of Psychotherapy,* 1: 1, Autumn, 1984, pp. 31–49; also chapter 7 of the same author's *Jung and the Post-Jungians* (Routledge & Kegan Paul, 1985)
3. Quoted in Nehama Leibowitz, *Studies in Shemot,* vol. 1 (World Zionist Organisation, Jerusalem, 1976), p. 321
4. Arthur Miller, *Timebends* (Methuen, 1987), p. 259
5. Quoted in *Forms of Prayer for Jewish Worship,* vol. 1 (Reform Synagogues of Great Britain, 1977), p. 387
6. Joseph Brodsky, *Less Than One: Selected Essays* (Penguin, 1987), p. 61
7. John Keats, *Letters* 32, 21 December 1817.
8. Vaclav Havel, 'Letters from Prison', in *Granta 21* (Penguin, 1987), p. 227
9. Salman Rushdie, *Is Nothing Sacred?,* (Granta, 1990), p. 9
10. *London Review of Books,* 27 July 1989, p. 12
11. Brodsky, *op. cit.,* p. 41